PROBLEMS IN
ENGINEERING SOILS

PROBLEMS IN
ENGINEERING SOILS

P. LEONARD CAPPER
T.D., M.Sc., F.I.Struct.E., M.I.C.E.
Formerly Senior Lecturer, University College, London

W. FISHER CASSIE, C.B.E.
LL.D., D.Tech., Ph.D., F.R.S.E., F.I.C.E., F.I.Struct.E., PP.I.H.E.
Emeritus Professor of Civil Engineering, University of Newcastle upon Tyne

JAMES D. GEDDES
Ph.D., F.I.C.E., F.ASCE., M.I.H.E., F.G.S.
*Professor of Civil Engineering, University of Wales Institute of Science
and Technology*

THIRD EDITION

LONDON AND NEW YORK
E. & F.N. SPON LTD

First published 1966 by E. and F. N. Spon Ltd.,
11 New Fetter Lane, London EC4P 4EE,
Second edition, 1971
Third edition, 1980

Published in the U.S.A. by
E. & F. N. Spon
in association with Methuen, Inc.
733 Third Avenue, New York, NY 10017
Printed in Great Britain by Richard Clay (The Chaucer Press) Ltd,
Bungay

ISBN 0 419 11840 3

British Library Cataloguing in Publication Data

Capper, Percival Leonard
  Problems in engineering soils.-3rd ed.
  1. Soil mechanics—Problems, exercises, etc.
  I. Title II. Cassie, William Fisher
  III. Geddes, James Douglas
  624'. 1513'076   TA710   79-41407

  ISBN 0-419-11840-3

Contents

Preface

Since this book first appeared in 1966 it has been translated into several languages and has served to introduce many thousands of young engineers to calculations in soil mechanics. In this third edition the original objectives have been maintained but the range and number of problems have been extended to mirror the increasing coverage of the subject of soil mechanics in civil engineering curricula. In keeping with present times, all the earlier problems have been reworked using hand calculators rather than sliderules and the layout of the edition has been modified. The book is intended to serve as a companion volume and supplement to *The Mechanics of Engineering Soils*, but it can be used without reference to that volume if the reader has some basic knowledge of Soil Mechanics.

The working out of practical problems is essential for the study of engineering subjects. Whether you work through the book from beginning to end, or merely investigate the solution of particular types of problem, it is very important that you should solve each problem for yourself.

The range of problems covered is that likely to be encountered in University and Polytechnic courses. In some chapters, where the topics are of greater difficulty, guiding explanations are given; where the subject of study is simpler, less detailed treatment is provided. Each problem has been carefully selected to illustrate a specific calculation method and, equally important, some aspect of soil behaviour. Thus by repeated practice in solving the problems, you will not only be able to attempt successfully a wide range of problems but will also gain a considerable insight into the behaviour of soils as structural materials.

The Authors express their gratitude to those writers, researchers and practitioners whose findings are quoted directly or whose methods of solution have been used in the problems, and to friends, colleagues, teachers and students whose comments have assisted in the production of this third edition.

1980   W. F. CASSIE
                                                          J. D. GEDDES

Reader's guide

An engineering textbook is a tool to be used for a specific purpose. This book and its companion *The Mechanics of Engineering Soils* are written to provide you (we visualize you as an undergraduate student or a young practising engineer) with an adequate understanding of the application of the principles of soil mechanics to civil and structural engineering problems and designs. The range of discussion in both volumes equates with that required for a first degree, but the books are also planned to have their use on construction sites. It is just possible that you may, ultimately, be in that minority of our profession which carries out the research necessary for advances in knowledge, but it is more likely that you will find soil mechanics to be directly concerned with construction. It is to this use of soil mechanics that the books are directed.

There is a wide disparity between soils as structural materials and such mainstays of the construction industry as steel and reinforced concrete. The latter are manufactured to produce desired properties. They can also be formed into units specifically designed to carry the loads imposed on the structure of which they form a part. Soils on a site, on the other hand, have properties determined by their geological origin and history and their current environment. Variability from point to point is frequently their most significant property. They must be accepted and used as they occur in nature. The design and construction of the structure with which they are to be associated must be adapted to their properties, although attempts may be made to modify their *in situ* properties locally by a variety of techniques such as drainage, compaction or consolidation. Sometimes, as in the construction of earth dams, road embankments and road bases, soils may be imported and placed with attempted control over their properties. However, even in the construction of these earth structures, uniformity represents an ideal which is seldom achieved.

Such variations and uncertainty have an important bearing on the precision of your calculations. When the properties of materials are controllable and can be specified with confidence, there is justification in placing more reliance on calculations than is generally possible with soils. The wide variation of soil properties over a site, and the varying and uncertain responses to loading make unqualified reliance on numerical calculation unwise. Engineering decisions, unsupported by experienced judgement, should seldom emerge solely from numerical data, especially when soils are the principal materials.

You must look on the problems in this book as the exercises which a pianist practices assiduously before progressing to concert performance. Such exercises are unreal in relation to the complexities of a concerto, and the problems in the following chapters are also unreal when compared with the complexities of problems on a construction site. The data in the problems for example, are given with a certitude impossible in normal construction. Typically each problem deals only with one site condition. In practice, within distances of a few metres, conditions may be widely different and this variation must be taken into account in the total design.

There has always been a tendency for students of civil and structural engineering to become slaves to the processes of calculations. This slavery has been intensified since the introduction of electronic calculators with their long array of apparently significant figures. Unless you, as a young engineer, have had some experience in practice, you will find it difficult to avoid the impression that accuracy and correctness are synonymous with figures after the decimal point! We understand this feeling and have prepared the problems so that the results given are those you will obtain from your calculator. There should be little discrepancy. In this way you will be able to check your calculations more easily. But in such exercises unreality may creep in. Giving pressures in kN/m^2 to two places of decimals, for example, is unreal in the context of construction in soils. A stress of one kN/m^2 is of the same order as that exerted by a household bag of sugar applied over the area of a paperback novel. In relation to the forces involved in full-scale soil structures, the variations likely to be encountered on a site will more than swamp results of this exactitude.

Keep in mind the fact that the reliability of results when dealing with soil structures, as opposed to the accuracy of a mathematical calculation, depends closely on the validity of the soils and site data. On large and important sites such data may be obtained for many locations over the site and over a range of depths below the surface. For small, relatively lightly loaded sites the cost of a full site exploration is normally considered to be uneconomic, and statistically less valid data may be used. The cost saved in this way has often been much less than that required for subsequent remedial measures.

According to the nature of the problem and whether the data have been obtained relatively accurately on a fine grid covering the site or, approximately, from one or two boreholes, time and effort spent on analysis can range from computer-assisted calculations to simple hand calculator approaches. Look to the validity of the data before utilizing sophisticated methods of analysis and developing the number of significant places in the final results.

The problems in this book may be assumed to start with accurate data. Work each problem again and again until you achieve the accuracy and speed applied by the pianist to a range of arpeggios, but always remember the variations encountered on site and the degree of validity of the facts with which you start. Develop a feeling for data and for the physical meaning of your calculated results. As soon as possible get out on a construction site where site exploration is being carried out and be inquisitive about the samples and data being collected. You will then be able to handle soils calculations with skill and with a sense of proportion related to the conditions encountered.

Notation

A Pore pressure coefficient; area; distance; volume of air; percentage air voids

A_b Area of base

A_f Area at failure; pore pressure coefficient at failure

A_s Area of pile shaft

a Spacing of sand drains; area

a_v Coefficient of compressibility

B Breadth of foundation, dam

$B, \bar{B}$ Pore pressure coefficients

b Breadth; width of slice

C Cohesion force

C' Cohesion force (in effective stress terms)

C_c Compression index; coefficient of curvature

C_u Uniformity coefficient

C_w Cohesion force on wall

c Cohesion (cohesive stress) referred to total stress

c' Cohesive strength (referred to effective stress)

c_a Adhesion stress

c_{cu} Cohesive strength (consolidated, undrained conditions)

c_d Cohesive strength (drained conditions)

c_h Coefficient of consolidation (horizontal, radial drainage)

c_u Cohesive strength (undrained conditions)

c_v Coefficient of consolidation (vertical drainage)

D Diameter of foundation; distance; depth; depth factor

D_{10} Effective size of soil particles

D_{30} Maximum size of smallest 30% of sample (by weight)

D_{60} Maximum size of smallest 60% of sample (by weight)

d Diameter; distance; drainage path length

E Soil modulus (Young's)

E_n, E_{n+1} Earth pressure forces

E_w, E_c Passive earth forces

e Void ratio

F Factor of safety

F' Frictional resistance force (in terms of

	effective stress)	L	Length (of foundation,
F_c	Factor of safety in		arc, chord)
	respect to cohesion	LL	Liquid limit
F_0, F_1, F_2	Residual in	l	Length; distance
	relaxation calculation	l, m, n	Direction cosines
F_ϕ	Factor of safety in		
	respect to friction	M, N	Critical state parameters
		m	Coefficient in seepage
G_s	Specific gravity of soil		problem
	particles	m, n	Dimensional ratios
g	Gravitational constant		$(B/z, L/z)$
	$(= 9.81)$	m_v	Coefficient of
			compressibility
H, h	Height; depth; thickness;		
	head of water; head loss	N	Normal thrust (total
h_w	Head of water		force terms)
		N'	Normal force (thrust)
I_f	Stress influence factor		(in effective force terms)
I_L	Liquidity index	N	Stability number
I_s	Influence factor for		(Taylor); penetration
	settlements		test value
i	Hydraulic gradient;	N'	Penetration test value—
	slope angle (Taylor's		corrected
	stability number)	N_c, N_q, N_ϕ	Bearing capacity
			factors
K	Stress influence factor	$N_{cq}, N_{\gamma q}$	Combined bearing
K_a	Active earth pressure		capacity factors
	coefficient		(Meyerhof)
K_D	Coefficient in immediate	n	Porosity;
	settlement calculations		normal direction to curve;
K_p	Passive earth pressure		effective drainage ratio—
	coefficient		sand drains
K_s	Earth pressure coefficient		
	for vertical surface of	P	Applied force; normal
	pile or foundation		force (total force terms)
K_ϕ	Earth pressure coefficient	P_a	Active thrust (force)
	due to ϕ	P'	Normal effective force
k	Coefficient of	PI	Plasticity index
	permeability (Darcy's	PL	Plastic limit
	coefficient)	P_p	Passive thrust (force)

p_a	Active earth pressure		to consolidation
p_o	Overburden pressure; pressure in failure zone	s_{oed}	Settlement in oedometer test
p_p	Passive earth pressure	s_t	Consolidation settlement
p_r	Resultant pressure		at time t
p_o'	Isotropic consolidation pressure	T	Thrust between soil
p'	Mean effective principal stress (p_f'—at failure)		masses
		T_R	Time factor, radial drainage
Q	Discharge quantity (of pore water)	T_V	Time factor, vertical drainage
Q_f, Q	Ultimate load capacity	t	Time; time interval;
q	Rate of flow (discharge) (of pore water); foundation contact pressure; ultimate bearing capacity (pressure)		tangential direction to curve
		U	Pore water force; degree of consolidation
q_{nett}	Nett ultimate bearing capacity (pressure)	U_R	Degree of consolidation, radial drainage
q'	Maximum effective principal stress difference (q_f'—at failure)	U_V	Degree of consolidation, vertical drainage
		u	Pore water pressure (or neutral pressure)
q_n	Nett bearing pressure	u_s	Excess pore water pressure
R	Radius; effective radius of sand drains; resultant force		
		V	Volume
		v	Velocity of flow (of pore water)
R_1	Radius of foundation		
RD	Relative density	v_o, v_f	Specific volume of soil (initial, at failure)
r	Radius of sand drain		
		v_s	Seepage velocity
S	Shearing force; shape coefficient	W	Mass of water; weight of soil block
S_g	Mass of soil solids (particles)	W_{sub}	Submerged (buoyant) weight of soil
S_r	Degree of saturation		
s	Shear stress; shear strength; settlement due	w	Water content (moisture content).

Notation

X_n, X_{n+1} Interslice forces (shearing)

$\left.\begin{array}{l}X, Y, Z \\ x, y, z\end{array}\right\}$ Cartesian co-ordinates; distances

z Depth in deposit

z_c Critical depth of crack

$\widehat{zz}$ Vertical stress component on horizontal planes

α Angle of inclination

β Slope angle to horizontal; coefficient in consolidation calculation

γ Unit weight

γ_{sat} Saturated unit weight

γ_w Unit weight of water

γ_{moist} Moist unit weight

γ_{sub} Submerged (buoyant) unit weight

δ, δ' Angle of skin friction, wall friction (total and effective pressures)

θ Slope angle; angle subtended by slip circle

ε Axial strain (in triaxial test)

ψ Conjugate function in seepage problems

ν Poisson's ratio

ϕ Angle of friction; angle of shearing resistance

$\left.\begin{array}{l}\phi' \\ \phi_d\end{array}\right\}$ Angle of shearing resistance (with reference to effective stress)

ϕ_{cu} Angle of shearing resistance (consolidated-undrained)

ϕ_u Angle of shearing resistance (undrained)

ϕ_f Angle of shearing resistance (at failure)

ϕ Potential function in seepage problems

ρ (Bulk) density

ρ_d Dry density

ρ_f Foundation settlement

ρ_i Immediate (elastic) settlement of foundation

ρ_m Mean immediate settlement of foundation

ρ_{ms} Mean immediate settlement of surface foundation

ρ_p Test plate settlement

ρ_w Density of water

σ Normal stress (total)

σ' Effective normal stress (pressure)

$\sigma_1, \sigma_2, \sigma_3$ Maximum, intermediate and minor total principal stresses

σ_3 Cell pressure (in triaxial test)

$\sigma'_1, \sigma'_2, \sigma'_3$ Maximum, intermediate and minor effective principal stresses

σ_{oct} Octahedral normal total stress

σ'_{oct}	Octahedral normal effective stress	μ_0, μ_1	Immediate settlement coefficients
σ_h, σ_v	Horizontal, vertical normal stresses (pressures)	μ	Coefficient
		∇	Laplace operator
σ'_h, σ'_v	Horizontal, vertical effective normal stresses (pressures)	τ_{oct}	Octahedral shear stress
		λ, Γ	Critical state parameters
$(\sigma_1 - \sigma_3)_f$	Maximum principal stress difference at failure	ψ	Angle for determining critical circles

Conversion table for S.I. units used in soil mechanics

Quantity	Imperial unit	SI unit	Abbreviation	Conversion factor
Density	pound per cu foot	megagram per cu metre gram per millilitre	Mg/m^3 g/ml	$1\ lb/ft^3 = 0{\cdot}016\ Mg/m^3$ $= 0{\cdot}016\ g/ml$
Unit weight	pound force per cu foot	kilonewton per cu metre	kN/m^3	$1\ lbf/ft^3 = 0{\cdot}016 \times 9{\cdot}81$ $= 0{\cdot}157\ kN/m^3$
Force	ton force, pound force	newton	N	$1\ tonf = 9{\cdot}964\ kN$ $1\ lbf = 4{\cdot}448\ N$
Pressure, stress	ton force per sq foot pound force per sq foot pound force per sq inch	kilonewton per sq metre	kN/m^2	$1\ tonf/ft^2 = 107{\cdot}25\ kN/m^2$ $1\ lbf/ft^2 = 0{\cdot}047\ 9\ kN/m^2$ $1\ lbf/in^2 = 6{\cdot}895\ kN/m^2$
Velocity, Coefficient of permeability	foot per second foot per year	metre per second	m/s	$1\ ft/s = 0{\cdot}304\ 8\ m/s$ $1\ ft/year = 9{\cdot}66 \times 10^{-9}\ m/s$
Rate of flow	cu foot per second cu foot per day	cubic metre per second	m^3/s	$1\ ft^3/s = 0{\cdot}028\ 32\ m^3/s$ $1\ ft^3/day = 0{\cdot}328 \times 10^{-6}\ m^3/s$
Coefficient of compressibility	sq foot per ton force	sq metre per kilonewton	m^2/kN	$1\ ft^2/tonf = 9{\cdot}324 \times 10^{-3}\ m^2/kN$
Coefficient of consolidation	sq foot per year sq inch per minute	sq millimetre per second	mm^2/s	$1\ ft^2/year = 2{\cdot}946 \times 10^{-3}\ mm^2/s$ $1\ in^2/min = 10{\cdot}75\ mm^2/s$

Fundamental Studies

CHAPTER ONE

Physical state and classification

The first group of problems in this chapter deals with the interpretation of the structure of soil in terms of solid particles, air
and water. Such interpretation can help the experienced engineer
to predict the probable behaviour of soil under stress. An intuitive
appreciation of the interaction of the various quantities studied
in this chapter is essential if the problems of later chapters are to be
understood. Such a grasp of the nature of a soil from a list of its
properties can be obtained only by repeated practice on problems
such as those presented here. The later problems deal with aspects
of classification into major soil groupings.

1.1 *Sketch a model soil sample and indicate the significance of this
device.*
*A sample of soil was found to have a mass of 67·5 g and a volume
of 39·2 ml. The sample lost no weight on drying. Determine the
volume of the voids if the specific gravity of the solid matter is 2·7.
What is the density of the whole sample in g/ml?*

Engineering soil usually consists of a mixture of air, water and
solids. The constituents are best represented by the *model soil
sample*, a sketch of which is given in Fig. 1.1. The solid particles are
brought together in one mass without void spaces while the voids
in the original soil, containing air and water, appear as layers
above the solid mass. A sketch of this soil sample should be used
in most of the problems of this chapter.

For convenience, the solid part is considered to be of unit
volume. The relationships existing between the various parts of the
model are then easily calculated, especially if the units are grams
and millilitres.

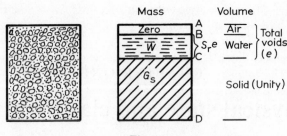

Fig. 1.1

The model soil and the extracted sample may be compared in tabular form

Model soil: Table 1.1A shows how each fact may be filled in by inspection of Fig. 1.1.

Table 1.1A *Model Soil*

	Portion of soil	Mass (g)	Volume (ml)	Mass density (g/ml)
1	AB(Air)	0	$e - W$	0
2	BC (Water)	W	W	1
3	AC (Void)	W	e	W/e
4	CD (Solid)	G_s	1	$G_s/1$
5	AD (Whole)	$G_s + W$	$1 + e$	$(G_s + W)/(1 + e)$

To obtain the final column, the quantities of mass are divided by the appropriate volume.

Extracted sample of soil: Turning now to the real soil, a similar table may be completed, with the known values entered in the appropriate spaces, and the unknown values given the symbol x.

Table 1.1B *Extracted Sample*

	Portion of sample	Mass (g)	Volume (ml)	Mass density (g/ml)
1	Air	0	x_3	0
2	Water	0	0	1
3	Void	0	x_3	0
4	Solid	x_1	x_2	$G_s = 2 \cdot 7$
5	Whole	67·5	39·2	x_4

In line 2 the mass of water is zero because the sample lost no weight on drying, and thus lost no water — it was dry already.

x_1 : There is no value of mass in this column except in line 5. Thus mass of the solid part of the sample must be 67·5 g.

x_2 : The volume of the solids is found by dividing the mass by the specific gravity. $x_2 = 67·5/2·7 = 25·0$ ml.

x_3 : In the volume column the whole volume is made up of $x_2 + x_3 = 39·2$. Thus x_3, the volume of voids = 14·2 ml.

x_4 : The mass density of the whole sample is mass/volume = $67·5/39·2 = 1·72$ g/ml.

1.2 *From a model soil sample determine the void ratio of a dry soil whose bulk density is 1·67 Mg/m^3. The specific gravity of the soil particles is 2·70.*

The value of 2·7 is worth remembering, since most soil particles have a specific gravity in the range 2·6 to 2·7. The significant word in this problem, however, is 'dry'. The voids contain air only, and the air has no weight of any importance in this problem. The soil sample and tables should be drawn out for this problem and for others until the various quantities can be assessed without their aid. At the start tables aid clear thinking.

The *bulk density* is the mass per unit volume of the whole sample. The *void ratio* is the ratio of the volume of voids to the volume of solids. In the model soil sample this quantity has the same numerical value as the volume of the voids, but is in fact a ratio of that volume to unity.

Table 1.2

Portion of soil model	Mass (g)	Volume (ml)	Bulk density (g/ml) (Mg/m^3)
Voids	0	e	0
Solids	2·70	1	2·70
Total	2·70	$1 + e$	1·67

Thus mass divided by volume of the total sample shows:

$$\frac{2·70}{1 + e} = 1·67$$

Thus, $e = void\ ratio = 0.62$

The void space is represented by 62% of the solid space, i.e. $0.62/(1 + e)$ or 38% of the total volume. This latter figure is the *porosity*, and is given the symbol n.

1.3 *A fully-saturated clay sample has a volume of 185 ml and a mass of 331 g. The specific gravity of the particles is 2·67. Determine the void ratio, porosity, water content and bulk density.*

The significant term in this problem is 'fully-saturated'. This indicates that the voids are completely filled with water, and that the air portion of the soil model vanishes. Sketch a model sample for mass and volume, and the following table results:

Table 1.3

Portion of soil sample or model	Mass (g)	Volume (ml)	Comment
Voids (model)	$e = W$	e	voids filled with water
Solids (model)	2·67	1	
Total (model)	$2·67 + e$	$1 + e$	
Total (sample as tested)	331	185	

Bulk density (mass per unit volume of the whole sample) is either $331/185$ or $(2·67 + e)/(1 + e)$, in g/ml (or Mg/m^3).
This equation gives

$$\frac{2·67 + e}{1 + e} = \frac{331}{185}$$

$$e = 1·12$$

or more than half of the sample is filled with water—a proportion common in clays.
Porosity is the ratio of the volume of voids to the total volume, and can be obtained either from the model or from the laboratory sample.

$$\text{Porosity} (n) = \frac{e}{1+e} = \frac{1\cdot 12}{2\cdot 12} = 0\cdot 53$$

or, the voids represent 53% of the total volume.

Water content (w) is the ratio of the weight or mass of water in the sample to the weight or mass of the solid matter. In practice this is obtained by weighing the sample, drying under standard conditions, and weighing again.

From the model soil sample, for the saturated soil

$$w = \frac{e}{2\cdot 67}$$

This gives a useful relation linking void ratio, water content and specific gravity of soil particles *for saturated soil only*:

$$e = wG_s$$

The water content, in this instance is

$$w = 1\cdot 12/2\cdot 67 = 0\cdot 42 \text{ or } 42\%$$

Bulk density is the ratio of the total mass to the total volume, or the mass per unit of volume, and equals

$$\frac{331}{185} = 1\cdot 79 \text{ g/ml (or Mg/m}^3)$$

1.4 *A soil sample has a bulk density of* 1·73 *Mg/m³ and a void ratio of* 0·84. *The specific gravity of the soil particles is* 2·70. *Determine the water content, dry density and degree of saturation of the sample.*

Table 1.4

Portion of soil sample or model	Mass (g)	Volume (ml)	Density (g/ml)
Air; model	0	$e - S_r e$	0
Water; model	$S_r e$	$S_r e$	1
Solids; model	2·70	1	2·70
Total; model	$2\cdot 70 + S_r e$	$1 + e$	bulk
Total; sample	–	–	1·73

The degree of saturation is the ratio of the volume of water in the sample to the volume of the total voids. It is given the symbol S_r and the model sample is as shown in Fig. 1.1, the total voids being e, and the volume of water being $S_r e$.

Degree of saturation is obtained by comparing the bulk densities of model and sample:

$$\frac{2 \cdot 70 + S_r e}{1 + e} = 1 \cdot 73$$

For $e = 0 \cdot 84$, $S_r = 0 \cdot 58$.

From this stage, the model clearly offers the best route to the other solutions.

Dry density is the mass of dried solids divided by the total volume:

$$\frac{2 \cdot 70}{1 + e} = 1 \cdot 47 \text{ g/ml (or Mg/m}^3)$$

Water content is the ratio of the mass of water to the mass of solids

$$w = \frac{S_r e}{2 \cdot 70} = \frac{0 \cdot 58 \times 0 \cdot 84}{2 \cdot 70} = 0 \cdot 18$$

Since bulk density (total mass per unit volume) and dry density (dried mass per unit of original volume) are in terms of Mg/m^3 or g/ml, they are indicated by the Greek letter rho (ρ and ρ_d, respectively) as shown in the next problem.

1.5 *By using sketches of model soil samples, and by drawing up tables of volumes and masses, fill in the missing quantities in place of the question marks in Table 1.5. Densities are in Mg/m^3. If for soil 2 the maximum and minimum possible void ratios are 1·00 and 0·40 respectively, what is the relative density?*

It is vital to remember that saturation cannot be assumed complete, nor can any soil be assumed to be dry. It is best to expect some value of S_r of less than unity. A reminder of two expressions which can be worked out from masses and volumes of the model sample, may help:

$$\rho = \frac{(1 + w)G_S}{1 + e} \text{ or } \frac{G_S + S_r e}{1 + e}$$

Table 1.5

Soil No.	ρ	ρ_d	e	n	S_r	w	G_s	Total volume (ml)	Mass (g) Wet	Mass (g) Dried
1	1·76	?	0·57	?	?	zero	?	—	—	—
2	?	?	?	0.48	?	0·34	2·65	—	—	—
3	1·73	?	0·73	?	?	?	2·71	—	—	—
4	1·90	1·45	?	?	?	?	2·71	?	19·1	14.4
5	?	?	?	0·46	0·90	?	2·60	—	—	—
6	?	?	?	?	1·00	?	2·65	86·2	162·0	?
7	1·79	?	?	?	?	?	2·68	31·0	56·4	48·5

e = void ratio; n = porosity; S_r = degree of saturation; ρ_d = dry density; ρ = bulk density.

From which $S_r e = w G_s$. In Problem 1.3 the special case of $e = w G_s$ for saturated soil ($S_r = 1·00$) was encountered.

The correct values of the quantities indicated by question marks in Table 1.5, in order, are:
Soil
1   1·76, 0·36, zero, 2·76
2   1·85, 1·38, 0·92, 0·98
3   1·57, 0·42, 0·39, 0·10
4   0·89, 0·47, 0·99, 0·33, 10·1
5   1·82, 1·41, 0·85, 0·30
6   1·88, 1·41, 0·87, 0.47, 0.33, 121.8
7   1·56, 0·72, 0·42, 0·61, 0·16

The *relative density* is a measure of the denseness of packing of the soil particles. It is given by the equation

$$\text{Relative density (RD)} = \frac{e_{max} - e}{e_{max} - e_{min}}$$

in which e is the existing density (often an *in situ* one).
For soil 2: $e = 0·92$, hence

$$RD = \frac{1·00 - 0·92}{1·00 - 0·40} = 0·13 \text{ or } 13\%$$

This indicates a very loose density.

9

1.6 *A sample of saturated clay was tested in the laboratory and found to weigh 175 g. When oven dried it weighed 105 g. Find the volume, bulk density, unit weight, void ratio and porosity of the sample. What changes in the latter figures would occur if the degree of saturation were 81%?*

Although the determination of a solution using the model soil sample with a solid volume of unity is useful, once skill has been obtained, the table can be completed as easily for a site sample. By placing the column displaying density or specific gravity between those for mass and volume, the progress of the calculation is more readily developed for samples from the site. In the table, data which are given in the statement of the problem, or which might be otherwise known, can be emphasized by italics or bold letters. The completion of the other spaces leads to the answers to the questions set.

For saturated sample:

Table 1.6A

Phase	Mass (g)	Density (g/ml) or specific gravity	Volume (ml)
Water	70 $\longrightarrow$	1·00 $\longrightarrow$	70·0 (also volume of voids)
Solids	105 $\longrightarrow$	2·70 $\longrightarrow$	38·9
Whole sample	175 $\longrightarrow$	1·61 $\longleftarrow$	108·9

Since the sample is saturated, it contains no air. Table 1.6A thus reduces to three lines:

(i)   Total volume $= 70 + 38·9 = 108·9$ ml;
(ii) Bulk density $=$ mass/volume $= 175/108·9 = 1·61$ g/ml (or Mg/m^3);
(iii) Unit weight $(\gamma) =$ weight/volume $= 1·61 \times 9·81 = 16·1$ kN/m^3 ;
(iv) Void ratio $=$ volume of voids/volume of solids $= 70·0/38·9 = 1·80$;
(v)   Porosity $= n = e/(1 + e) = 1·80/2·80 = 0·64$.

For unsaturated sample:
When there is a degree of saturation less than 1·0 (or 100%) the

volume of air must be taken into account. Assume the unknown volume of air is A ml.

Table 1.6B

Phase	Mass (g)	Density (g/ml) or specific gravity	Volume (ml)
Air	0	0	A
Water	70	1·00	70·0
Solids	105	2·70	38·9
Whole sample	175	1·40	$A + 108·9$

If $S_r = 81\%$, then volume of water/volume of voids, i.e.

$$70/(70 + A) = 0·81 \text{ and } A = 16·4 \text{ ml}$$

   (i) Total volume $= A + 108·9 = 16·4 + 108·9 = 125·3$ ml;
   (ii) Bulk density $=$ mass/volume $= 175/125·3 = 1·40$ g/ml;.
   (iii) Unit weight $= 1·40 \times 9·81 = 13·7$ kN/m^3;
   (iv) Void ratio $=$ volume of voids/volume of solids $= (70 + 16·4)/38·9 = 2·22$;
   (v) Porosity $= 2·22/3·22 = 0·69$.

Thus, with the other quantities remaining constant, the inclusion of air, as would be expected, reduces the bulk density, increases the volume, increases the void ratio and increases the porosity. This highlights the fact that full saturation should never be assumed when samples are being processed, otherwise large errors may occur.

1.7 *Dry soil and water are to be used to re-constitute a soil in the compacted state. A cylinder, 300 mm long and 100 mm in diameter is to be used to enclose the finally compacted sample, which will occupy the whole volume. The water content is to be 17% and the air content, 10%. Complete the usual table, and also give the void ratio and the degree of saturation. Assume that $G_S = 2·70$.*

The volume of the sample is the volume of the cylinder (2356 ml). Much of the basic calculation can be based on the mass of dry soil incorporated, and the table may be constructed with the symbol

11

S_g for the mass of solids in the final soil. From this, the mass of water is $0.17S_g$ (also the numerical value of the volume of water). The mass of the sample is obtained by adding the masses of solids and water, and the density of the whole sample can then be obtained. Similarly, on adding the volumes, the volume of air may be used to determine the numerical value of S_g.

Table 1.7A

Phase	Mass (g)	Density (g/ml) and specific gravity	Volume (ml)
A	0	0	$0.1 \times 2356 = 236$
W	$0.17 S_g$	1.00	$0.17 S_g$
S	S_g	2.70	$S_g/2.70$
Whole	$1.17 S_g$		2356

Total volume:

$$2356 = 236 + 0.17 S_g + (S_g/2.70) \quad \text{or } S_g = 3923 \text{ g}$$

Substituting this, Table 1.7A becomes Table 1.7B

Table 1.7B

Phase	Mass (g)	Density (g/ml) and specific gravity	Volume (ml)
A	0	0	236
W	667	1.00	667
S	3923	2.70	1453
Whole	4590	$4590/2356 = 1.95$	2356 which checks 2356 ml measured volume

Unit weight = $1.95 \times 9.81 = 19.1$ kN/m^3
Void ratio = $(236 + 667)/1453 = 0.62$ or 62%
Degree of saturation = $667/(236 + 667) = 0.74$ or 74%

1.8 *A sample of soil has a volume of 150 ml and loses 33 g when oven-dried from a bulk unit weight of 20.6 kN/m^3. What is the void ratio? What type of soil is this likely to be?*

A unit weight of 20·6 kN/m³ represents $20·6/9·81 = 2·10$ g/ml bulk density. From this and the volume find the mass of the sample as 315 g. The loss of 33 g represents a loss of water. Solid content = 282 g.

Using the specific gravity of solids as 2·70, complete Table 1.8.

Table 1.8

Phase	Mass (g)	Density (g/ml) and specific gravity	Volume (ml)
A	0	0	12·6
W	33	1·00	33·0
S	282	2·70	104·4
Whole	315	2·10	150·0

Unit weight = *20·6 kN/m³*
Void ratio = volume of voids/volume of solids = $45·6/104·4 = 0·44$

With the measured density and the calculated void ratio, this is likely to be a dense sand or gravel. A clay would have had a higher void ratio, and a loose sand would have had a lower density.

1.9 *On the application of the British Standard compaction test to a soil, the results shown in Table 1.9A were obtained. Obtain an estimate of the optimum moisture content, and draw the lines of zero and 10% air voids, relating dry density and moisture content. What is the air content at optimum conditions if the specific gravity of the particles is 2·65?*

Table 1.9A

Moisture content (per cent)	Bulk density (Mg/m³)
17·2	2·06
15·2	2·10
12·2	2·16
10·0	2·13
8·8	2·04
7·4	1·89

The curve relating moisture content to density is always referred to dry density. Table 1.9B shows the calculation for dry density:

$$\text{Dry density} = \text{Bulk density}/(1 + w)$$
$$\rho_d = \rho/(1 + w)$$

Table 1.9B

Moisture content (w)	$1 + w$	Dry density ρ_d (Mg/m^3)	ρ_d for zero air voids	ρ_d for 10% air voids
0·172	1·172	1·76	1·81	1·64
0·152	1·152	1·83	1·88	1·70
0·122	1·122	1·92	2·00	1·80
0·100	1·100	1·94	2·08	1·88
0·088	1·088	1·88	2·15	1·94
0·074	1·074	1·76	2·21	2·00

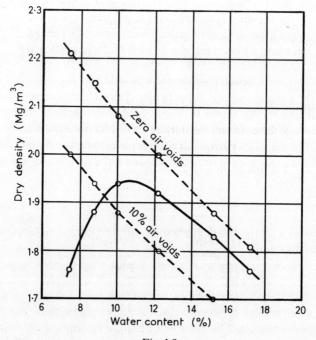

Fig. 1.9

The penultimate column for ρ_d is obtained from the equation

$$\rho_d = \frac{G_s \rho_w}{1+e} = \frac{G_s \rho_w}{1+wG_s}$$

for a soil without air voids.

The optimum moisture content can be read off from Fig. 1.9 as about 11%. At this moisture content, the soil is most easily compacted and forms the densest material for a given amount of work. This relates to the laboratory test. For field plant other relationships will apply.

For 10% air voids, use is made of the expression

$$\% \text{ air voids} = \left(1 - \frac{\rho_d(1 + wG_S)}{\rho_w G_S}\right) \times 100$$

$$\text{For } A = 10\% \text{ and } \rho_w = 1 \text{ g/ml}, G_S = 2\cdot65$$

$$\rho_d = 0\cdot9\, G_S/(1 + w\, G_S)$$

The value of ρ_d corresponding to the set of values of w are also given in Table 1.9B and these are plotted on Fig. 1.9.
Calculation of optimum air content.

$$\text{Maximum dry density} = 1\cdot94 \text{ Mg/m}^3$$

$$\text{Optimum water content} = 11\%$$

In *unit total volume* of the soil (i.e. 1 ml)

$$\text{Volume of soil particles} = 1\cdot94/2\cdot65 = 0\cdot732 \text{ ml}$$

$$\text{Volume of water} = 1\cdot94 \times 0\cdot11 = 0\cdot213 \text{ ml}$$

$$\text{Volume of air} = 1\cdot000 - 0\cdot732 - 0\cdot213 = 0\cdot055 \text{ ml}$$

Hence

$$\text{Air content} = 5\cdot5\%$$

This is a fairly usual percentage for the common laboratory compaction tests.

1.10 *In a British Standard compaction test a maximum dry density of 1·83 g/ml was produced. After compaction by field plant an undistorted sample of the same soil, obtained by core cutter, weighed 2072 g. The core cutter was 127 mm long with a diameter of 102 mm.*

Laboratory tests for water content and specific gravity yielded a dry mass of 1806 g and 2·67 respectively.

Determine for the field compacted soil sample:

  (i) *water content,*
  (ii) *bulk density,*
  (iii) *void ratio,*
  (iv) *air content,*
  (v) *degree of saturation,*
  (vi) *relative compaction,*
  (vii) *whether it is on the dry or wet side of optimum water content if the optimum air content is 6·0%.*

(i) Water content
 Loss of water on drying = 2072 − 1806 = 266 g
 Mass of dry soil = 1806 g

$$\text{Water content} = \frac{\text{mass of water}}{\text{mass of dry soil}} = \frac{266}{1806} = 0\cdot147$$

$$= 14\cdot7\%$$

(ii) Bulk density

$$\text{Volume of core cutter} = \pi \times \left(\frac{102}{2}\right)^2 \times \frac{127}{10^3}$$

$$= 1037\cdot8 \text{ cm}^3$$

 Bulk density = total mass per unit volume
$$= 2072/1037\cdot8 = 2\cdot00 \text{ g/ml}$$

(iii) Void ratio
 Volume of soil particles = 1806/2·67 = 676·4 cm^3

 Volume of voids = total volume − volume of soil particles
$$= 1037\cdot8 - 676\cdot4 = 361\cdot4 \text{ cm}^3$$

 Void ratio = 361·4/676·4 = 0·53

(iv) Air content

$$\text{Volume of water} = \frac{\text{mass of water}}{\text{density of water}}$$

$$= 266/1\cdot00 = 266 \text{ cm}^3$$

$$\text{Air content} = \frac{\text{volume of air}}{\text{total volume of sample}}$$

$$= \frac{1037 \cdot 8 - 676 \cdot 4 - 266}{1037 \cdot 8} = 0 \cdot 092$$

$$= 9 \cdot 2\%$$

(v) Degree of saturation

$$\text{Degree of saturation} = \frac{\text{volume of water}}{\text{total volume of voids}}$$

$$= \frac{266}{1037 \cdot 8 - 676 \cdot 4} = 0 \cdot 736$$

$$= 73 \cdot 6\%$$

(vi) Relative compaction

This is the ratio between the dry density achieved in the field and the maximum dry density obtained in a laboratory test. Since there are several forms of the latter in use there is no unique value of relative compaction. The laboratory test used should always be referred to in making a statement on relative compaction.

For this example in which the British Standard test was used:

$$\text{Relative compaction} = \frac{2 \cdot 00/(1 + 0 \cdot 147)}{1 \cdot 83}$$

$$= 0 \cdot 953 = 95 \cdot 3\%$$

(vii) In the laboratory compaction test

Working on the basis of unit *total* volume (i.e. 1 ml)

$$\text{Volume of air } = 0 \cdot 06 \text{ ml}$$

$$\text{Volume of soil} = 1 \cdot 83/2 \cdot 67 = 0 \cdot 69 \text{ ml}$$

Hence

$$\text{Volume of water} = 1 \cdot 00 - 0 \cdot 06 - 0 \cdot 69 = 0 \cdot 25 \text{ ml}$$

and

$$\text{Optimum water content} = \frac{0 \cdot 25 \times 1}{1 \cdot 83} = 0 \cdot 137 = 13 \cdot 7\%$$

Comparing the above with answer (i) the field sample is seen to be on the 'wet side' of optimum.

17

1.11 *Samples of three soils were passed through a nest of B.S. sieves. Table 1.11A shows the results obtained. Classify these soils, describe their appearance in the hand, and indicate any other tests necessary for a complete classification. What are the effective size and uniformity coefficient for soil G?*

The nature of a soil can be deduced from a particle size analysis, the coarser sizes being separated out by sieving and the finer sizes by sedimentation. If the soil is cohesive, a further set of tests to determine the action of the soil with varying amounts of water (liquid and plastic limits) allows of a more accurate prediction of the behaviour of the material in engineering structures.

In drawing up a grading chart, the same format should always be used. By this means, the shape of the grading curve for a soil soon begins to have a meaning in relation to possible physical properties. The standard proportions of the chart extending from 0·0001 mm to 40 mm, are about 2 to 1, length to height. The use of charts of other proportions militates against the possibility of consistent decisions on matters affecting grading and classification.

The grading curve describes the proportion of particles in the sample which are less than a given particle size. The masses

Table 1.11A

Sieve mesh or particle size (or close approximation) (mm)		Mass of soil found retained on each sieve (g)		
		E	F	G
6	Gravel	0	0	0
2		0	0	70
0·6		0	0	18
0·2	Sand	0	62	12
0·06		38	4	0
0·02		12	0	0
0·006	Silt	4	1	0
0·002		6	18	0
less than 0·002	Clay	40	15	0

mentioned in Table 1.11A, however, are those found in each sieve, having passed through from the sieve above, but being unable to pass to the one below.

To obtain the 'percentage passing' for a given sieve it is merely necessary to add together the amounts retained on sieves above a given size, and to subtract this from the total mass of the sample, finally expressing the figures as percentages of the sample mass. In this example, the total mass of each sample was 100 g, for convenience.

In soil E, for example, we subtract from 100 g the figures 0, 38, 38 + 12, 38 + 12 + 4 and so on. The result is shown in Fig. 1.11. The interpretation of these curves depends on the position of the curve on the chart and on the degree of steepness of its various parts. G, for example, is well to the right and is steep. F covers a wider range, and is further to the left. E is high and at the left-hand end of the chart. These positions and slopes indicate that G is a steeply graded (sometimes called uniformly-graded) fine gravel with some coarse sand. The number of different sizes of particles is small and in the hand the material would show about a third of its volume as sand.

The curve for Soil F shows a flat length – a gap grading – which shows that some of the particles of the natural soil have been removed. The material is a medium sand with nearly 40% of silt and

Table 1.11B

Sieve mesh or particle size (or close approximation) (mm)		Percentage of soil passing each sieve		
		E	F	G
6	Gravel	100	100	100
2		100	100	30
0·6		100	100	12
0·2	Sand	100	38	0
0·06		62	34	0
0·02		50	34	0
0·006	Silt	46	33	0
0·002	Clay	40	15	0

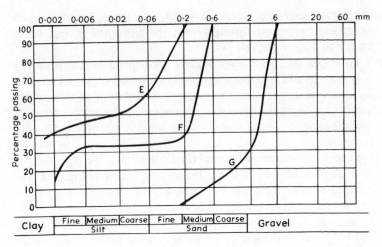

Fig. 1.11

clay intermixed with it. It is poorly graded. The high placing of curve E to the left of the chart indicates fine material. Plasticity tests would normally be carried out on a soil of this kind.

The effective size (D_{10}) is the maximum particle size of the smallest 10% (by weight) of the sample. Hence for soil G, reading off the size corresponding to 10% on the graph,

$$D_{10} = 0.45 \text{ mm}$$

The uniformity coefficient (D_{60}/D_{10}) is the ratio of the maximum size of the smallest 60% to the effective size. From the graph $D_{60} = 3.5$ mm (allowing for the semi-logarithmic plot), therefore

$$C_u = D_{60}/D_{10} = 3.5/0.45 = 7.8$$

A further measure of the shape of the grading curve can be obtained by evaluating the coefficient of curvature

$$C_c = \frac{D_{30}^2}{D_{10}D_{60}}$$

For soil G this equals

$$C_c = \frac{(2.0)^2}{3.5 \times 0.45} = 2.5$$

20

1.12 *Two materials, showing cohesion and plasticity, were tested for liquid and plastic limits by the standard methods. Table 1.12 shows the results obtained from the liquid limit apparatus. The plastic limit of soil H was 23% and of soil K was 33%. Describe these soils and indicate their probable classification. If a sample of soil K had a natural in situ water content of 60% and a clay content of 25%, what are its liquidity index and activity? What may be concluded from the latter value?*

Table 1.12

Number of blows to close standard gap	Water content	
	Soil H	Soil K
7	0·53	
9	0·50	
13	0·46	
15		0·77
18		0·74
20		0·72
27	0·36	
29	0·34	
30		0·65
33	0·33	
37		0·61
45		0·59

Plot water contents as ordinates on a natural scale, and number of blows horizontally on a logarithmic scale. Fig. 1.12A shows the plot for the two materials. Keeping in mind the plastic limits, and accepting the liquid limits as the water contents shown at 25 blows, consult the plasticity chart (Fig. 1.12B), which was developed by Casagrande from a study of many soils. The plasticity index is the difference between the liquid and plastic limits. Soil H is a clay (CL), and K is a heavy clay (CH). The more granular the material becomes, the less is its plasticity index (difference of LL and PL). For silts, verging on the fine-sand region, plasticity is very low indeed (Fig. 1.12B).

21

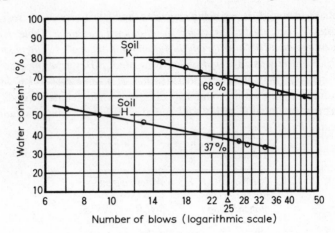

Fig. 1.12A

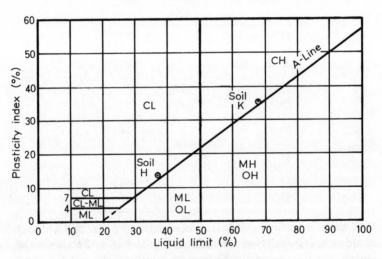

Fig. 1.12B Plasticity chart

The liquidity index is defined by the expression

$$I_L = \frac{w - PL}{PI}$$

and it is therefore a measure of the 'wetness' in relation to the plasticity indices. It can thus be used as a measure of the strength of

22

the soil although it must be remembered that the plasticity properties are determined on remoulded material.

For soil K

$$I_L = \frac{60 - 33}{68 - 33} = 0.77$$

The activity is defined by the ratio $\frac{PI(\%)}{\% \, Clay}$. For soil K the
activity is $35/25 = 1.4$.

This value indicates a preponderance of montmorillonite clay
mineral in the sample.

1.13 *Describe the engineering characteristics of the soils whose
places in the Unified Classification System are given as:*

Soil	LL	PI	Class
X	0	0	GW
Y	40%	40%	CL

Soil X is clearly a gravel, well-graded, as shown by the W in the
class symbol. The material will provide good drainage and,
because of its high angle of shearing resistance, will form an
excellent foundation for engineering structures if it is not underlain
by compressible strata.

Soil Y is a clay (C) but with a liquid limit below 50% (which is
the significance of the 'L' in the classification). A clay, to attain
such a low plasticity must be adulterated with fine sand, or silt
or a mixture of these. Careful testing will be required to establish its
suitability as a foundation material or as a constituent of an earth
bank. If, in the finished construction, this clay lies near ground
surface, the possibility of frost heave must be remembered. An
assessment of the amount of silt in the material is relevant.

1.14 *What range of liquid limit would you expect to find in soils C
and D? If natural drainage is important in the engineering construction proposed, which of these soils is the more suitable?*

Soil	LL	PI	Class
C	?	20%	SP
D	?	40%	CH

Soil C is poorly graded sand, shown by the letters P and S in the classification. There is, apparently, a preponderance of a narrow band of particle sizes within the sand range. This, in turn, would indicate a poor performance as a supporting stratum immediately under a foundation, but more acceptable at greater depths. Drainage through such a sand, despite the poor grading, would be good. The liquid limit would be zero and the 20% value for the plasticity index must be a mistake. Alternatively, there must be more clay in the material than is indicated by SP. A further check should be made to determine whether the soil should be classified as SC or as CL.

Soil D has a plasticity index which agrees with the classification. The liquid limit will be about 60%. This soil is impervious, so under the conditions given in the problem, Soil C is the more appropriate.

1.15 *What further tests are necessary to give a complete classification for soil L described below?*

Sieve aperture (mm)	63	20	6·3	2·0	0·6	0·212	0·063
% passing by weight	100	66	50	32	20	11	0

A plot of this grading on a chart such as is shown in Problem 1.11 (for soils E, F, G), shows that this is a well-graded material lying entirely in the gravel/sand range. The particles all show frictional characteristics: the soil falls into the classification GW. If there had been particles of silt or clay sizes, further tests would have been required, but for this, no further tests are needed. This material will not show plasticity properties and charts such as Fig. 1.12B in this chapter need not be consulted.

1.16 *Sieve analysis carried out on two soils A and B gave the results*

Table 1.16

Sieve mesh size (mm) (to a close approximation)		2	0·6	0·2	0·06	0·02	0·006	0·002
Percentage by weight passing sieve	A	100	33	23	19	14	13	0
	B	94	70	61	42	35	24	18

A field determination of the physical state of soil A revealed a bulk density of 1·72 g/ml, associated with a water content of 20·2%. Soil B was found by undisturbed sampling to have corresponding values of 2·01 g/ml and 23·2%. Soils A and B had grain specific gravities of 2·65 and 2·68 respectively. Classify the soils. Which of them is likely to have the highest strength and resistance to deformation under loading?

By plotting the grain size distribution curves it is possible, as in earlier problems, to give a classification on the basis of their shapes and positions relative to the size axis. As an alternative we will proceed to calculate size ranges.

Soil A

Sand size particles: $(100 - 19) = 81\%$

Silt size particles: $(19 - 0)\ \ = 19\%$

Total $= 100\%$

The soil is therefore a silty sand SM because the proportion of sand predominates.

Soil B

Gravel size particles: $(100 - 94) = \ \ 6\%$

Sand size particles: $(94 - 42) = 52\%$

Silt size particles: $(42 - 18) = 24\%$

Clay size particles: $(18 - \ \ 0) = 18\%$

Total $= 100\%$

This soil covers a wide range of particle sizes with a substantial proportion of fines. Plasticity tests on the finer material would yield further information of value. It can be described as a sandy-silty-clay and could be given the symbol SC, because 18% of clay size particles is capable of giving a significant cohesion.

For soil A
$$\text{Dry density} = 1\cdot72/1\cdot202 = 1\cdot43 \text{ g/ml}$$

In 1 ml of soil, volume of voids $= 1 - (1\cdot43/2\cdot65) = 0\cdot46$ ml. Thus

$$\text{Void ratio} = \frac{0\cdot46}{1 - 0\cdot46} = 0\cdot85 = e$$

and

$$\text{Porosity} = \frac{e}{1 + e} = \frac{0\cdot85}{1\cdot85} = 0\cdot46$$

The latter values denote a very loose condition for soil A and the strength and resistance to deformation under loading will therefore be low.

For soil B
$$\text{Dry density} = 2\cdot01/1\cdot232 = 1\cdot63 \text{ g/ml}$$
$$\text{Void ratio} = \frac{1 - 0\cdot61}{0\cdot61} = 0\cdot64$$
$$\text{Porosity} = 0\cdot64/1\cdot64 = 0\cdot39$$

Because of its plasticity (due to clay content) it is of importance to examine the moisture content of this soil. Hence

Mass of water $= 2\cdot01 - 1\cdot63 = 0\cdot38$ g in 1 ml of total volume
Volume of water $= 0\cdot38$ ml in 1 ml of total volume
Water content $= 0\cdot38/1\cdot63 = 23\cdot3\%$
Volume of voids in 1 ml of total volume $= 0\cdot39$ ml
Degree of saturation $= 0\cdot38/0\cdot39 = 0\cdot97$
Air content $= \dfrac{1\cdot00 - 0\cdot38 - (1\cdot63/2\cdot68)}{1} = 0\cdot01$, i.e. 1%

This soil is almost completely saturated. It cannot therefore suffer significant loss of strength on wetting to full saturation. Its water content is relatively low in relation to its possible plasticity properties and it is thus likely to have a relatively high strength and good resistance to deformation.

Soil B is hence the preferable soil for construction under the given conditions.

CHAPTER TWO

Influence of pore water

As one of the constituents of a soil, the pore water plays an important role in determining the physical and chemical behaviour of a soil mass. In this chapter consideration is given to problems which deal with its effects in producing gravitational stresses and stresses within the pore system when the water is not in motion. The concept of effective stress is introduced and problems show how changes in stress may be brought about by alterations to the ground water conditions and external loading. A final problem shows how moisture content profiles with depth may be obtained from a knowledge of stress conditions.

2.1 *Borings on a site showed a horizontal water table at a depth of 3 m and a horizontal rock stratum at a depth of 12 m. The boring log and laboratory tests gave conditions shown in Fig. 2.1. The problem is to determine the vertical pressure conditions in the soil at all depths.*

The bulk densities, as determined from samples by the methods of the previous problems, are important quantities which can be used to evaluate the pressure conditions within the soil mass. The vertical pressures (stresses) on horizontal surfaces may be considered as consisting of two separate pressures. One of these is exerted by the water in the soil pore space and the other by the soil particles.

The latter, which is not a true pressure *between particles* but rather an abstract pressure obtained by dividing a load by the cross-sectional area of the soil (including the intersected voids) which carries it, is known as the *effective pressure*. The load in the latter calculation *is the total load* reduced by the load carried by

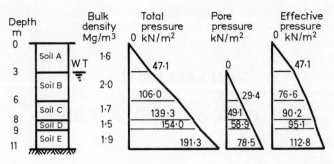

Fig. 2.1

the pore water. The pressure exerted by the water is called the *pore-water pressure* or simply *pore pressure*. If σ_v denotes the *total vertical pressure*, σ_v' the *effective* (vertical) *pressure* and u the *pore pressure*, then

$$\sigma_v = \sigma_v' + u \quad \text{or} \quad \sigma_v' = \sigma_v - u$$

Inherent in this equation is the assumption that all three pressures act over the same area (soil contact area plus pore area). In performing calculations using this equation it is usual to determine the total pressure and the pore pressure by calculation; the effective pressure is then obtained as their difference.

In the problem it is assumed that there is no movement of the water. The pressure distribution within it thus relates to a static condition. Movement of ground water through the pores of a soil under the influence of an hydraulic gradient induces other pressures. These are discussed in Chapter 3.

A mass of 1 kg acted on by gravity gives a weight (force) of 9·81 N, and similarly a mass of 1 Mg exerts a gravitational force of $9·81 \times 10^3$ N, or 9·81 kN. Consider a vertical column of soil A m^2 in cross-sectional area and height h m. The volume is Ah m^3 and if the unit weight of the soil is γ kN/m^3 the total weight of the column is γAh kN. *If there are no shearing stresses on the vertical faces of the column* (and this is so in this problem because of the horizontal ground surface existing over a wide area) the vertical pressure at the base of the column is $\gamma Ah/A = \gamma h$ kN/m^2. In terms of the density ρ (in Mg/m^3 or g/ml) the pressure at depth h is $9·81 \rho h$ kN/m^2.

Referring to Fig. 2.1, by adding the effects produced by the various *bulk* densities of soils A, B, C, D and E (i.e. the forces caused by gravity, or weight) a curve can be obtained which shows the *total pressure* at each depth. The *pore pressure* in the water is that due to the static head above the level considered. The pore pressure is zero at the water table and increases linearly with depth below it. It does so at the rate of $1 \cdot 0 \times 9 \cdot 81$ kN/m^2 for every metre of depth.

Hence

At base of soil

A: Total pressure $= 9 \cdot 81 \times 1 \cdot 6 \times 3 = 47 \cdot 09$ kN/m^2

B: Total pressure $= 47 \cdot 09 + (9 \cdot 81 \times 2 \cdot 0 \times 3) = 105 \cdot 95$ kN/m^2

C: Total pressure $= 105 \cdot 95 + (9 \cdot 81 \times 1 \cdot 7 \times 2) = 139 \cdot 30$ kN/m^2

D: Total pressure $= 139 \cdot 30 + (9 \cdot 81 \times 1 \cdot 5 \times 1) = 154 \cdot 02$ kN/m^2

E: Total pressure $= 154 \cdot 02 + (9 \cdot 81 \times 1 \cdot 9 \times 2) = 191 \cdot 30$ kN/m^2

The calculated values should be rounded to the first decimal place or to the nearest 1 kN/m^2. They are shown plotted in Fig. 2.1. The variation is linear over the depth of each stratum.

The pore pressure varies from 0 to $9 \cdot 81 \times (11 - 3) = 78 \cdot 5$ kN/m^2. The subtraction of the pore pressure at each depth from the corresponding total pressure gives the effective pressure (see Fig. 2.1). The same results for the effective pressure are obtained by use of *submerged* or *buoyant* densities for the soil layers below the water table, where submerged density $= (\rho_{\text{saturated}} - \rho_{\text{water}})$.

For example at the base of soil B

$$\text{Effective pressure} = (9 \cdot 81 \times 1 \cdot 6 \times 3) + [9 \cdot 81 \times (2 \cdot 0 - 1 \cdot 0) \times 3]$$
$$= 47 \cdot 09 + 29 \cdot 43 = 76 \cdot 52 \text{ kN/m}^2 = 76 \cdot 5 \text{ kN/m}^2$$

and at the base of soil C

$$\text{Effective pressure} = (9 \cdot 81 \times 1 \cdot 6 \times 3) + [9 \cdot 81 \times (2 \cdot 0 - 1 \cdot 0) \times 3]$$
$$+ [9 \cdot 81 \times (1 \cdot 7 - 1 \cdot 0) \times 2] = 76 \cdot 52 + 13 \cdot 73$$
$$= 90 \cdot 25 \text{ kN/m}^2 = 90 \cdot 3 \text{ kN/m}^2$$

The slight difference in the latter is due to rounding errors.

The foregoing kind of calculation which is often required in an examination of site conditions produces values of what are sometimes referred to as *geostatic stresses*.

Table 2.2

Stratum	Unit weight of soil (kN/m^3) (see Table 1.3)	Pressure from 1 m thickness of soil (kN/m^2)	Pressure at base of stratum (kN/m^2) Total	Pore	Effective
1 Sand (moist) $G_s = 2.65$ $e = 0.45$ $w = 0.05$	$\dfrac{9.81 \times G_s}{1 + 0.45} \times 1.05$ $= 18.83$	18.83	$2 \times 18.83 = 37.7$	0	37.7
2 Sand (sat.) $G_s = 2.65$ $e = 0.45$	$\dfrac{9.81(2.65 + 0.45)}{1.45}$ $= 20.97$	20.97	$37.66 + 20.97 = 58.6$	9.8	48.8
3 Clay (sat.) $G_s = 2.70$ $e = 0.90$	$\dfrac{9.81(2.70 + 0.90)}{1.90}$ $= 18.59$	18.59	$58.63 + (4 \times 18.59)$ $= 133.0$	$5 \times 9.81 = 49.1$	83.9

Unit weight of water = 9.81 kN/m³

2.2 *A layer of sand 3 m thick, overlies a stratum of saturated clay of unknown depth. The phreatic surface is at 2 m below ground level, and both the ground surface and the water table are horizontal. The upper surface of the clay below the sand is also horizontal. On the basis of the explanation given in Problem 2.1, draw graphs of the total, pore and effective pressures to a depth of 7 m. Assume no capillary rise in the sand and thus no negative pressure. Use estimated values of void ratio and specific gravity of particles.*

In this problem the sand will be assumed damp with a moisture content of 5% above the water table, and saturated below it. The clay is entirely saturated. The void ratio for the sand will be taken as 0·45 and for the clay 0·90. The specific gravity of sand particles can be assumed as about 2·65 and that of the clay particles greater at 2·70. The water table, synonymous with the term phreatic surface, is at 2 m below the surface.

The strata to be considered are: moist sand, saturated sand and saturated clay. A tabular presentation is the best way of ensuring that mistakes are rendered less likely.

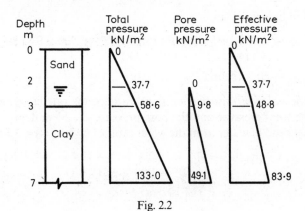

Fig. 2.2

2.3 *A site investigation shows that to a depth of at least 6 m the following stratification applies*

From the surface to 1·3 m, coarse sand, dry and not carrying any capillary fringe from the underlying water table ($\rho = 1·80$ Mg/m³). From 1·3 m down, there is a stratum of fine sand, 1·4 m thick ($\rho = 2·00$ Mg/m³). The water table lies at 1·4 m from the surface, but the fine sand is saturated above the water table by capillary action. From 2·7 m to the bottom of the borehole at 6 m there is a stratum of saturated clay ($\rho = 1·90\ Mg/m^3$). The void ratio (e) for coarse sand is 0·50, for fine sand is 0·60 and for clay is 0·90. Find (i) the total pressure at 2·1 m and 4·3 m below the surface, (ii) the effective pressure at 2·7 m, and (iii) the pore pressure at 3·7 m. Density of water = 1·00 Mg/m^3.

If this were an examination question, all the data presented would probably be relevant to the question. In practice a wide range of information is often collected from a site investigation, and a selection must be made for specific aspects of the design. In this instance, the void ratio has no direct bearing on the calculation of pressures.

(i) *The value of total vertical pressure* (σ_v) depends on the bulk densities. At 2·1 m below the surface:

$$\sigma_v = (1·3 \times 1·80 \times 9·81) + (0·8 \times 2·00 \times 9·81)$$
$$= 38·7\ kN/m^2$$

At 4·3 m below the surface:

$$\sigma_v = (1·3 \times 1·80 \times 9·81) + [(2·7 - 1·3) \times 2·00 \times 9·81]$$
$$+ [(4·3 - 2·7) \times 1·90 \times 9·81]$$
$$= 80·3\ kN/m^2$$

(ii) *The value of the effective pressure* depends on the values of the total pressure and the pore pressure. At 2·7 m depth there is a head of water from the water table of (2·7 − 1·4) = 1·3 m.

$$\text{Effective pressure} = (1·3 \times 1·80 \times 9·81) + (1·4 \times 2·00 \times 9·81)$$
$$- (1·3 \times 1·00 \times 9·81)$$
$$= 37·7\ kN/m^2$$

(iii) For a geostatic condition *the value of pore pressure* depends only on the depth below the water table. At 3·7 m below the surface there is a head of water, caused by the level of the water table, of 2·3 m.

$$\text{Pore pressure at 3·7 m below the surface} = 2·3 \times 1·00 \times 9·81$$
$$= 22·6\ kN/m^2$$

The solution of this problem is made easier by sketching the boring log, and marking on it the strata and the water table, with dimensions.

Note also that zero pore pressure is experienced at a depth of 1·4 m and pore pressures are calculated with this as datum. Above this horizon, capillary action in the fine sand produces saturation associated with negative pore pressures determined by height above the water table.

2.4 *A horizontal layer of gravel overlies a stratum of saturated clay, whose upper surface is also level. Below the clay lies impermeable base rock. The gravel is 10 m thick and the clay, 6 m thick. The water table lies, originally, at 3 m below the surface. Water is then removed from the gravel by pumping until the water table stabilizes at 9 m below the surface.*

Describe the change in the pattern of effective stress with depth throughout the clay, caused by the pumping operations.

The bulk densities of the materials are: dry gravel, 1·70 Mg/m³; saturated gravel, 2·06 Mg/m³; saturated clay, 1·90 Mg/m³.

Since pressures are measured in terms of newtons, the first step in the solution is to change the bulk densities to unit weights by multiplying by 9·81 (or by 10 if only an approximate figure is needed):

Dry gravel: 1·70 Mg/m³ corresponds to 16·7 kN/m³

Saturated gravel: 2·06 Mg/m³ corresponds to 20·2 kN/m³

Saturated clay: 1·90 Mg/m³ corresponds to 18·6 kN/m³

The problem is concerned only with pressures in the clay, so the conditions at its upper and lower surfaces will give the results required, since for this type of problem the results vary linearly.

Before pumping
If it is assumed that conditions prior to pumping have been established for a long time, then the strata will be in a state of static equilibrium and the method of calculation already used in the previous problems will be valid. Hence we obtain Table 2.4 A.

After pumping
After pumping it is important to distinguish long-term equilibrium conditions from the immediate and intermediate conditions. It

Table 2.4A

	Total pressure (kN/m^2)	Pore pressure (or neutral pressure) (kN/m^2)	Effective pressure (kN/m^2)
At upper surface of clay	$(3 \times 16\cdot7) +$ $(7 \times 20\cdot2)$ $= 191\cdot5$	$7 \times 9\cdot81 = 68\cdot6$	$191\cdot5 - 68\cdot6$ $= 122\cdot9$
At lower surface of clay	$(191.5) +$ $(6 \times 18\cdot6)$ $= 303\cdot1$	$13 \times 9\cdot81 = 127\cdot4$	$303\cdot1 - 127\cdot4$ $= 175\cdot7$

may be assumed that the extraction of the water from the gravel will be relatively rapid, *vis a vis* the clay, because of its high permeability. The pore water pressures in the gravel will also rapidly adjust to the changed phreatic level. It is safe to assume an immediate response.

For the clay however, its relatively low permeability substantially slows down its response to the changed conditions and the pore pressures and effective stresses within it thus vary with time. Up to a stage immediately after the water table is lowered it can be assumed that no drainage of the clay under the changed conditions will have taken place. The clay will thus not have deformed and this means that the effective stresses in it will not have changed either, since effective stresses alone (and not total stresses) are responsible for deformation. The pore pressures will, at this stage, no longer be in keeping with the new position of the water table. Hence flow of water will take place under the unbalanced pore pressures until equilibrium is re-established. For this problem we will look only at the immediate and long-term situations.

These values are shown in Table 2.4B. For the clay *immediately following water table lowering*

    (a) the total pressure decreases,
    (b) the pore pressure decreases,
    (c) the effective pressure remains the same,
        whereas in the *long term*
    (d) the total pressure decreases (same value as in (a) above),
    (e) the pore pressure decreases further,
    (f) the effective pressure increases beyond the initial value,

Table 2.4B

	Total pressure (kN/m^2)	Pore pressure (or neutral pressure) (kN/m^2)	Effective pressure (kN/m^2)
Immediate situation			
At upper surface of clay	$(9 \times 16 \cdot 7) +$ $(1 \times 20 \cdot 2)$ $= 170 \cdot 5$	$170 \cdot 5 - 122 \cdot 9$ $= 47 \cdot 6$	$122 \cdot 8$ (as before)
At lower surface of clay	$(170 \cdot 5) +$ $(6 \times 18 \cdot 6)$ $= 282 \cdot 1$	$282 \cdot 1 - 175 \cdot 7$ $= 106 \cdot 4$	$175 \cdot 7$ (as before)
Long-term situation			
At upper surface of clay	$170 \cdot 5$ (as above)	$1 \times 9 \cdot 8 = 9 \cdot 8$	$170 \cdot 5 - 9 \cdot 8$ $= 160 \cdot 7$
At lower surface of clay	$282 \cdot 1$ (as above)	$7 \times 9 \cdot 8 = 68 \cdot 6$	$282 \cdot 1 - 68 \cdot 6$ $= 213 \cdot 5$

(g) the increase in effective pressure is constant throughout the depth of the strata below the water table. In this problem

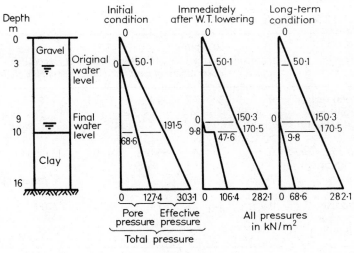

Fig. 2.4

it equals 37·8 kN/m². The long-term increase in effective pressure produces consolidation of the clay stratum and if this stratum were carrying foundation, settlement and structural damage could ensue.

2.5 *A horizontal stratum of fissured sandstone underlies 20 m of impervious clay which, in turn, supports 7 m of sand. The water table lies at 2 m below ground surface. There is an artesian pressure in the sandstone equivalent to a head of 30 m. Draw diagrams showing the total, neutral and effective pressures in the sand and clay. Draw further diagrams showing the equivalent pressures if the artesian pressure in the sandstone at its interface with the clay is decreased by 50 kN/m² and the water table is simultaneously lowered by 3 m. Assume that the latter changes in ground water conditions take place rapidly. The soil properties are: moist sand above the water table, $\gamma = 17·2$ kN/m³; saturated sand, $\gamma = 20·0$ kN/m³; saturated clay, $\gamma = 19·0$ kN/m³.*

As in the previous example there are two post-change conditions to be examined, i.e. immediate and long term. The sand can be assumed to exhibit an instantaneous response, whilst the condition of the clay will be time dependent. Proceeding as before, and noting

Table 2.5A   *Initial conditions*

	At ground surface	At depth of 2 m (i.e. at water table)	At bottom of sand	At top of clay	At bottom of clay
Total vertical pressure (kN/m²)	0	$2 \times 17·2$ $= 34·4$	$34·4 +$ $5 \times 20·0$ $= 134·4$	134·4	$134·4 +$ $20 \times 19·0$ $= 514·4$
Pore pressure (kN/m²)	0	0	$5 \times 9·8$ $= 49·0$	49·0	$30 \times 9·81$ $= 294·3$ (artesian)
Effective pressure (kN/m²)	0	34·4	85·4	85·4	220·1

Table 2.5B *Conditions immediately after change*

	At ground surface	At depth of 5 m (i.e. at new water table)	At bottom of sand	At top of clay	At bottom of clay
Total vertical pressure (kN/m²)	0	5×17.2 $= 86.0$	$86.0 +$ 2×20.0 $= 126.0$	126.0	$126.0 +$ 20×19.0 $= 506.0$
Pore pressure (kN/m²)	0	0	2×9.8 $= 19.6$	$126.0 -$ 85.4 $= 40.6$	$506.0 -$ 220.1 $= 285.9$
Effective pressure (kN/m²)	0	86.0	106.4	85.4 (as in Table 2.5A)	220.1 (as in Table 2.5A)

Table 2.5C *Long-term conditions*

	At ground surface	At depth of 5m	At bottom of sand	At top of clay	At bottom of clay
Total vertical pressure (kN/m²)	0	86.0	126.0	126.0	506.0
Pore pressure (kN/m²)	0	0	2×9.8 $= 19.6$	19.6	$294.3 -$ 50.0 $= 244.3$
Effective pressure (kN/m²)	0	86.0	106.4	106.4	261.7

that the presence of an artesian pressure at the sandstone/clay interface will establish a uniform pressure gradient from the top to the bottom surface of the clay when sustained for a sufficiently long period, we obtain Tables 2.5A, B, C.

In Table 2.5B, it is assumed that the ground water lowering leads to the same moist density being established in the former saturated sand.

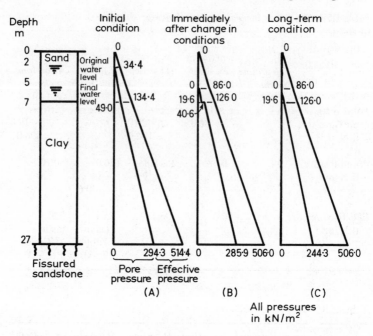

Fig. 2.5

It should be noted that for the *initial* conditions:

(a) the respective total, pore and effective pressures in the sand and clay at their interface are the same;

(b) the artesian pressure produces a uniform pore pressure gradient in the clay. The pore pressures at the two surfaces equal the respective 'water table' pressures.

Immediately after the change in ground water conditions:

(c) the total pressures in the sand and clay at their interface are the same, but the pore pressures and hence effective stresses are not;

(d) there is a similar imbalance in the pore pressures at the clay/sandstone interface;

(e) the effective stresses in the clay are the same as those formerly existing;

(f) the discontinuity in the pore pressures referred to in (c) and (d) will be eliminated almost immediately, but very high pressure gradients will remain in the vicinity of the interface. In the long term:

(g) equality of the respective pore and effective stresses at the strata interfaces is re-established, at values in accord with the new ground water conditions;

(h) there is a resultant increase in the effective pressures in the clay stratum, and hence this will be associated with settlement.

Although in strict terms consolidation will produce changes in the unit weight of the clay, differing from horizon to horizon, this effect has been ignored in calculating the pressures. For very thick deposits this densification may be of significance.

2.6 *A 4 m thick layer of uniform sand* ($G_S = 2.65$) *overlies an intact clay 8 m in thickness, which in turn rests on a gravel/sand deposit of great depth. A permanent water table is located at a depth of 3.5 m below the horizontal ground surface and an artesian pressure in the gravel/sand deposit produces a piezometric level 0.5 m below the top of the sand. The sand is believed to have a relative density of 70%, its moisture content above the water table is 8%, and its limiting void ratios are 0.38 and 0.97. The clay has a bulk density of 2.15 Mg/m³.*

As part of a construction project a 2 m thickness of the sand layer is removed over a very large area. Are any problems likely to arise as a result of the ground water conditions?

Commence by calculating the unit weights.
For the clay
$$\gamma_{sat} = 2.15 \times 9.81 = 21.1 \text{ kN/m}^3$$
For the sand
$$\text{RD} = 0.70 = \frac{0.97 - e}{0.97 - 0.38} \quad \text{(see Problem 1.5)}$$
and
$$e = 0.56$$

Hence below the water table

$$\gamma_{sat} = \frac{G_S + e}{1 + e} \times 9.81$$

$$= \frac{(2.65 + 0.56)}{1.56} \times 9.81 = 20.2 \text{ kN/m}^3$$

Table 2.6

	At top of clay			At bottom of clay		
	Before construction	*Immediate post-stripping*	*Long term*	*Before construction*	*Immediate post-stripping*	*Long term*
Total vertical pressure (kN/m²)	$(3{\cdot}5 \times 18{\cdot}0)$ $+ (0{\cdot}5 \times 20{\cdot}2) = 73{\cdot}1$	$(1{\cdot}5 \times 18{\cdot}0)$ $+ (0{\cdot}5 \times 20{\cdot}2) = 37{\cdot}1$	37·1	$73{\cdot}1 + (8 \times 21{\cdot}1)$ $= 241{\cdot}9$	$37{\cdot}1 + (8 \times 21{\cdot}1)$ $= 205{\cdot}9$	205·9
Pore pressure (kN/m²)	$0{\cdot}5 \times 9{\cdot}81 = 4{\cdot}9$	−31·1	4·9	$11{\cdot}5 \times 9{\cdot}81 = 112{\cdot}8$	76·8	112·8
Effective vertical pressure (kN/m²)	68·2	68·2	32·2	129·1	129·1	93·1

and above the water table

$$\gamma = \frac{G_s \times 9\cdot81}{1+e} = \frac{2\cdot65 \times 9\cdot81}{1\cdot56} = 16\cdot7\,\text{kN/m}^3$$

and

$$\gamma_{\text{moist}} = 16\cdot7 \times 1\cdot08 = 18\cdot0\ \text{kN/m}^3$$

These calculations are based on the fact that, in general, wetting or drying of a sand deposit does not affect its dry density or dry unit weight. The same void ratio may therefore be used above and below the water table. On the other hand a change in the moisture content of a clay alters its void ratio and dry density due to the property of shrinkage (and swelling).

The calculation of the various pressures follows the lines established earlier. The results are given in Table 2.6.

From the table it is seen that stripping the sand leads to an immediate short-term reduction in the pore pressures in the clay (negative pore pressures or suctions being developed in the top horizons). These gradually return to their former values. The long-term effect is to reduce the effective vertical pressure and this will result in a swelling of the clay and its weakening. Lightly loaded structures, and features such as pipelines and sewers, placed above it could be damaged by upward movements. The final effective pressure at the base of the clay remains sufficiently large to guard against bodily uplift of the clay layer, although the factor of safety against this happening has been reduced.

2.7 *A homogeneous clay stratum exists at the bottom of a lake under 10 m of water. Its unit weight averages 22·3 kN/m³ over a substantial depth. If the level of the lake is lowered permanently by 2 m, what long-term effect could this have on a structure based upon the clay?*

In answering this question it is necessary to remember that the water above the surface of the clay contributes to the total pressure as well as to the pore pressure.

Before lowering
The total vertical stress $= (10 \times 9\cdot81 + 22\cdot3z)\ \text{kN/m}^2$, where z(m) is the depth below the clay surface.

Pore pressure $= 9\cdot81(10 + z)\ \text{kN/m}^2$

Effective pressure $= 98\cdot1 + 22\cdot3z - 9\cdot81(10 + z)\,\text{kN/m}^2$
$$= 12\cdot5z\,\text{kN/m}^2$$

After lowering

Total vertical stress $= (8 \times 9\cdot81 + 22\cdot3z)\,\text{kN/m}^2$

Pore pressure $= 9\cdot81(8 + z)\,\text{kN/m}^2$

Effective pressure $= (22\cdot3 - 9\cdot81)z = 12\cdot5z\,\text{kN/m}^2$

In this instance the effective pressure is the same before and after the lowering of the water level. Hence no long-term effects would be produced on any structure. The calculation demonstrates that the decrease in total pressure equates with the decrease in pore pressure.

2.8 *An element of soil in situ is subjected to a vertical total stress of 120 kN/m². The horizontal effective stress is 0·4 times the vertical effective stress. The pore water pressure is 49 kN/m². What is the total horizontal stress? If the vertical total stress is increased by 15 kN/m² and the horizontal total stress by 8 kN/m², what additional pore pressure is immediately generated? The soil is saturated and the pore pressure coefficient A for the stress range involved is 0·69. What are the final total stresses, pore pressure and effective stresses if no drainage takes place?*

The initial vertical effective stress is

$$\sigma_v - u = 120 - 49 = 71\,\text{kN/m}^2$$

The initial horizontal effective stress is

$$0\cdot4 \times 71 = 28\cdot4\,\text{kN/m}^2$$

and hence the total initial horizontal stress is

$$28\cdot4 + 49 = 77\cdot4\,\text{kN/m}^2$$

In the earlier problems, pore pressure changes were brought about by alterations to the water table level, artesian pressure fluctuations and uniform changes of vertical loading over large areas. In this problem variations of loading in two orthogonal directions are involved. These variations produce distortion under conditions of no drainage and hence induce changes in effective stresses. For this situation, on the assumption that the vertical and horizontal stresses are principal stresses, use may be made of the concept of pore pressure coefficients. By this means the pore pressure change (Δu) produced *under conditions of no drainage* (i.e. rapid loading) is given in terms of the changes in total principal stresses σ_1 and σ_3 by the expression

$$\Delta u = B[\Delta\sigma_3 + A(\Delta\sigma_1 - \Delta\sigma_3)]$$

For a saturated soil, $B = 1$. In this problem, $A = 0.69$. Hence

$$\Delta u = 1[8 + 0.69(15 - 8)] = 12.8 \text{ kN/m}^2$$

The final total stresses are

$$\sigma_1 = \sigma_v = 120 + 15 = 135 \text{ kN/m}^2$$
$$\sigma_3 = \sigma_h = 77.4 + 8 = 85.4 \text{ kN/m}^2$$

The final pore pressure is

$$u = 49 + 12.8 = 61.8 \text{ kN/m}^2$$

The final effective stresses are

$$\sigma'_v = 135 - 61.8 = 73.2 \text{ kN/m}^2$$
$$\sigma'_h = 85.4 - 61.8 = 23.6 \text{ kN/m}^2$$

2.9 *The water table on a site is lowered by a wellpoint system to permit construction of a building. After the building is completed drainage of the site is stopped and the water level rises, eventually stabilizing at a depth of 1·5 m below ground surface. The building is provided with a watertight basement to a depth of 6 m below ground. The basement is 15 m wide and 40 m long. Determine the distribution of the uplift pressure on the underside of the basement floor and the total uplift force.*

The underside of the floor is 4·5 m below the final level of the water table. Since no water flow is taking place due to the watertight nature of the basement and the static water level, the pore pressure acting on the floor (the uplift pressure) will be the hydrostatic one related to the water level.
Thus

Uplift pressure = $(6.0 - 1.5) \times 1.00 \times 9.81 = 44.15 \text{ kN/m}^2$

and this is uniform over the entire basement.

Total uplift force = $44 \cdot 15 \times 15 \times 40 = 26487$ kN = $26 \cdot 5$ MN

In a practical design the dead loading of the completed structure must exceed this uplift force or otherwise the structure will float. Additionally the basement slab must be capable of sustaining this pore pressure in bending and against leakage. If pressures are excessive, they may be relieved by the installation of relief wells or other forms of drainage. As earlier problems have shown, such remedial measures can lead to additional settlement due to increases in effective pressures in the supporting soil(s).

2.10 *A natural, undisturbed clay stratum is unloaded except for its own weight. The water table is 0·6 m below the horizontal surface, and is also horizontal. The specific gravity of the soil particles is 2·75. A consolidation test shows a variation of void ratio with effective pressure as defined in Fig. 2.10 A. Determine the probable variation in water content throughout a depth of 5 m – the equilibrium water content.*

The effective pressure at various selected depths is first found by assuming an average bulk density for the soil over a depth of 6 m. If there were several layers, this operation would be conducted for each stratum separately, and the results added as in Problem 2.1. Suppose the soil can be assumed to have a bulk density of 2·1 Mg/m^3. One metre depth of this soil exerts a pressure of $2 \cdot 1 \times 9 \cdot 81 = 20 \cdot 6$ kN/m^2. Water has a density of 1·0 Mg/m^3 and thus exerts a pressure of 9·81 kN/m^2 per metre of depth.

Table 2.10

$h(m)$ (a)	$\sigma'(kN/m^2)$ (b)	e (c)	$w = e/G_s$ (d)
0	5·9	0·702	0·255
2	26·5	0·674	0·245
3	36·8	0·665	0·242
5	57·4	0·655	0·238
7	78·0	0·649	0·236

Average 0·669

Effective pressure = total pressure due to density – pore pressure

$$\sigma' = \gamma h - \gamma_w(h - H)$$

where h is the depth from the surface to the section under consideration and H is the depth to the water table.

$$\sigma' = 20{\cdot}60\,h - 9{\cdot}81(h - 0{\cdot}6)$$
$$= (10{\cdot}8h + 5{\cdot}9)\,\text{kN/m}^2$$

Column (b) of Table 2.10 shows how the effective pressure varies with depth. These figures are obtained by substitution for h in the equation above. From column (b) and the results of the consolidation test (Fig. 2.10 A) the void ratio can be determined at each level and recorded in column (c). The soil is considered saturated – even above the water table by capillary action – and thus $e = wG_s$. The water content for the particular values of pressure and void ratio can be obtained by dividing the values of column (c) by the specific gravity given as 2·75.

$$\text{Bulk density} = \frac{G_s + e}{1 + e}\,\rho_w = \frac{2{\cdot}75 + 0{\cdot}669}{1{\cdot}669}$$
$$= 2{\cdot}05\ \text{Mg/m}^3$$

This figure agrees closely with the assumed value, and the distribution of water content represented by column (d) can be

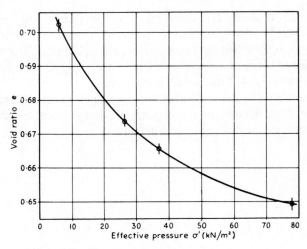

Fig. 2.10 A

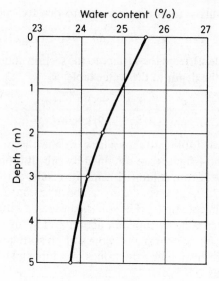

Fig. 2.10 B

accepted as that likely to be encountered in the uniform conditions postulated. If the calculated density is not found to be in agreement with the value first selected, the whole derivation should be repeated with a new and more probable assumption of the value of the bulk density.

Fig. 2.10B shows the variation of water content with depth. This is the *equilibrium moisture content* or the moisture content likely to be reached at each level when equilibrium has been established between the position of the water table and the pressure due to the weight of the soil (column (d)).

In practice, the distribution of water content with depth depends on the stress history of the deposit. What has been calculated represents the probable initial distribution.

CHAPTER THREE

Effects of flowing water

A study of the flow of water through soils may be important for different reasons. In the first instance the amount of water in motion may be of primary importance. This, for example, is the case when excavation in water-bearing strata is involved, when the yield of wells has to be determined or when loss of water from underneath water-retaining structures is concerned. Secondly the flow establishes a pattern of pore water pressures which, because of their influence on the shearing strength, may be responsible for the development of critical stability conditions. In a third type of problem considered in Chapter 8 changing flow conditions may give rise to volume changes in the soils involved which in turn produces settlement or heaving at the ground surface.

Flow may be steady or unsteady. For example the flow of water underneath a massive dam or through an earth dam will be unsteady at first but will then stabilise after a time lag. In addition flow may be saturated or non-saturated. In this chapter we are concerned only with steady-flow conditions in saturated soils.

The ease with which flow takes place depends upon the permeability of the soils being traversed, and the early problems are concerned with an estimation of this property. In the later problems various practical situations are investigated.

3.1 *A falling-head permeability test was performed on a sample of clean uniform sand. The initial hydraulic head was 900 mm, the final head was 400 mm and 60 s was required for the water level in the standpipe to fall. The cross-sectional area of the standpipe was 100 mm². The sample was of 40 mm diameter and had a length of 180 mm. Determine the coefficient of permeability in Darcy's law.*

Darcy's law states that

$$q = Aki \text{ or } v = ki$$

where q = flow in unit time through a cross-sectional area A of soil,
  k = coefficient of permeability,
  i = hydraulic gradient,
  v = velocity of flow.

It will be appreciated that in the falling-head permeability test the hydraulic gradient changes with time and an integration procedure is involved in solving for k. It can be shown that the solution is given by

$$t = \frac{a}{A}\frac{l}{k}\log_e \frac{H_1}{H_2}$$

in which t = time of fall,
  H_1 and H_2 = initial and final heights of water in the standpipe above the level in the container,
  A = cross-sectional area of the sample,
  a = cross-sectional area of the standpipe, and
  l = length of sample.

Thus in the problem

$$a = 100 \text{ mm}^2$$

$$A = \frac{\pi}{4} \times 40^2$$

$$= 400\,\pi \text{ mm}^2$$

$$l = 180 \text{ mm}$$

$$t = 60 \text{ s}$$

$$H_1 = 900 \text{ mm}$$

$$H_2 = 400 \text{ mm}$$

Substituting in the equation and solving for k

$$k = \frac{100}{400\pi} \times \frac{180}{60} \log_e \frac{900}{400} = \frac{0\cdot75}{\pi}\log_e 2\cdot25$$

$$= \frac{0\cdot75}{\pi} \times 0\cdot81093 = 0\cdot193 \text{ mm/s}$$

3.2 *During a constant-head permeability test on a sand sample 260 ml of water were collected in 2 min. If the sample had a length of 100 mm, a diameter of 40 mm and a maintained head of 200 mm, what is its coefficient of permeability?*

In this case the discharge Q during the time interval t is given by

$$Q = Akit$$

in which A = area of the sample,

      i = constant hydraulic gradient during the test.

In the problem

$$Q = 260 \text{ ml} = 260 \times 10^3 \text{ mm}^3$$

$$t = 2 \text{ min} = 120 \text{ s}$$

$$A = \frac{\pi}{4} \times 40^2 = 400 \, \pi \text{ mm}^2$$

$$i = 200/100 = 2$$

Thus

$$k = \frac{260 \times 10^3}{400\pi \times 2 \times 120} = 0{\cdot}862 \text{ mm/s}$$

3.3 *A pumping test was made in sands extending to a depth of 15 m where an impermeable stratum was encountered (Fig. 3.3). The initial ground-water level was at the ground surface. Observation wells were sited at distances of 3 and 7·5 m from the pumping well. A steady state was established at about 20 hours when the discharge*

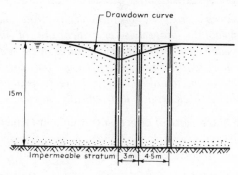

Fig. 3.3

was 3·80 l/s. The drawdowns at the two observation wells were 1·5 m and 0·35 m. Calculate the coefficient of permeability.

The solution to this problem is given by the equation

$$k = \frac{q \log_e r_2/r_1}{\pi(h_2^2 - h_1^2)}$$

in which k = coefficient of permeability,
    q = rate of flow,
    h_1 = height of water table above bottom of well at radial distance r_1,
    h_2 = height of water table above bottom of well at radial distance r_2.

In this example

$$q = 3\cdot80 \text{ l/s} = 3\cdot80 \times 10^6 \text{ mm}^3/\text{s}$$

$$r_1 = 3\text{m}$$

$$r_2 = 7\cdot5 \text{ m}$$

$$h_1 = (15 - 1\cdot5) = 13\cdot5 \text{ m}$$

$$h_2 = (15 - 0\cdot35) = 14\cdot65 \text{ m}$$

Hence

$$k = \frac{3\cdot80 \times 10^6 \times \log_e 2\cdot5}{\pi \times 28\cdot15 \times 1\cdot15 \times 10^6}$$

$$= \frac{3\cdot80 \times 0\cdot91629}{\pi \times 28\cdot15 \times 1\cdot15} = 0\cdot034 \text{ mm/s}$$

3.4 *Fig. 3.4 shows a cross section through the strata underlying a site the permeability properties of which are of importance. Calculate the equivalent permeability of the layered system in the vertical and horizontal directions. Assume the coefficients of permeability in the horizontal and vertical directions to be the same in each stratum (i.e. each layer is hydraulically isotropic).*

Consider flow in the vertical direction through an element 1 m² in plan area.

$$q = Aki \quad \text{(Darcy's law)}$$

$$= Ak\frac{h}{l}$$

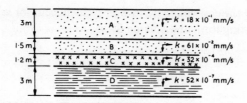

Fig. 3.4

Thus

$$q_A = 1 \times k_A \times \frac{h_A}{l_A}$$

$$q_B = 1 \times k_B \times \frac{h_B}{l_B} \text{, etc.}$$

If there are no volume changes in the different layers, then continuity of flow requires

$$q_A = q_B = q_C = q_D$$

Thus

$$h_A = \frac{l_A q_A}{k_A} = \frac{3q_A}{18 \times 10^{-4}} \text{ m}$$

$$h_B = \frac{1 \cdot 5 q_B}{61 \times 10^{-5}} \text{ m}$$

$$h_C = \frac{1 \cdot 2 q_C}{32 \times 10^{-7}} \text{ m}$$

and

$$h_D = \frac{3q_D}{52 \times 10^{-10}} \text{ m}$$

The total head loss is

$$h_A + h_B + h_C + h_D = h$$

The total flow path length is

$$l = (3 + 1 \cdot 5 + 1 \cdot 2 + 3) = 8 \cdot 7 \text{ m}$$

Therefore

$$q = q_A = q_B = q_C = q_D = 1 \times k_v \times \frac{h}{8 \cdot 7}$$

51

where k_v = the equivalent permeability coefficient for vertical flow.
   Substituting for h and solving for k_v gives

$$k_v = \frac{8\cdot7}{h} q$$

$$= 8\cdot7 \left[\frac{1}{\dfrac{3}{18 \times 10^{-4}} + \dfrac{1\cdot5}{61 \times 10^{-5}} + \dfrac{1\cdot2}{32 \times 10^{-7}} + \dfrac{3}{52 \times 10^{-10}}} \right]$$

$$= 1\cdot51 \times 10^{-8}\,\text{m/s} = 1\cdot51 \times 10^{-5}\,\text{mm/s}$$

In this case the equivalent permeability is related to the permeabilities of the individual layers by an equation similar to that giving the equivalent electrical conductivity for a number of conductors in series, i.e.,

$$\frac{l}{k_v} = \frac{l_A}{k_A} + \frac{l_B}{k_B} + \frac{l_C}{k_C} + \frac{l_D}{k_D}$$

Now consider the flow in a horizontal direction through a section 1 m deep in the direction perpendicular to the plane of Fig. 3.4.
   Apply Darcy's law to each layer in turn. Since the flow is considered to be horizontal, the boundaries between A and B, B and C, etc., are flow lines and the equipotential lines will therefore be perpendicular to these boundaries. Consider two adjacent equipotential lines separated by a horizontal distance x. The head loss will be equal to h, say.
   For each layer therefore

$$i = \frac{h}{x} = \text{constant}$$

Thus, considering flows through elements 1 m deep normal to the plane of the section:

$$q_A = 3 \times 18 \times 10^{-4}\, i\,\text{m}^3/\text{s}$$

$$q_B = 1\cdot5 \times 61 \times 10^{-5}\, i\,\text{m}^3/\text{s}$$

$$q_C = 1\cdot2 \times 32 \times 10^{-7}\, i\,\text{m}^3/\text{s}$$

$$q_D = 3 \times 52 \times 10^{-10}\, i\,\text{m}^3/\text{s}$$

The total flow is

$$q = q_A + q_B + q_C + q_D = (3 + 1\cdot5 + 1\cdot2 + 3) \times k_h i\,\text{m}^3/\text{s}$$

where k_h = the equivalent permeability coefficient in the horizontal direction.

Hence

$$k_h = \frac{(54 \times 10^{-4} + 91 \cdot 5 \times 10^{-5} + 38 \cdot 4 \times 10^{-7} + 156 \times 10^{-10})}{8 \cdot 7}$$

$$= 7 \cdot 26 \times 10^{-4} \, \text{m/s} = 0 \cdot 726 \, \text{mm/s}$$

It should be noted that in this case the equivalent permeability can be determined by an application of a formula similar to that giving the equivalent electrical conductivity of a parallel array of electrical conductors, i.e.,

$$lk_h = (l_A k_A + l_B k_B + l_C k_C + l_D k_D)$$

If there is a significant difference in the permeability of the various layers and they are of a similar order of thickness, the least permeability plays a large part in determining the equivalent vertical permeability and the greatest permeability the major part in determining the equivalent horizontal permeability. In the example

$$k_v \text{ is nearer in value to } k_C \text{ and } k_D \text{ than to } k_A$$
$$k_h \text{ is nearer in value to } k_A \text{ than to } k_C \text{ and } k_D$$

The ratio of the permeabilities in the horizontal and vertical directions is

$$\frac{7 \cdot 26 \times 10^{-1}}{1 \cdot 51 \times 10^{-5}} = 48000 : 1$$

3.5 *A glacial lake clay deposit is found to have a series of silt partings in it at an average vertical spacing of 2 m. The silt layers are about 3 mm in thickness and have a permeability 100 times that of the clay. Assume both materials to be hydraulically isotropic. Determine the ratio of the horizontal and vertical permeabilities.*

Because of the alternating nature of the layers it will suffice to study two adjacent layers.

Thus in the horizontal direction

$$2 \cdot 003 \, k_h = 2 \, k_c + 0 \cdot 003 \, k_s$$

where k_c and k_s are the coefficients of permeability of the clay and silt layers respectively.

But $k_s = 100\, k_c$.

Therefore

$$k_h = k_c \frac{2 + 0.3}{2.003} = 1.148\, k_c$$

In the vertical direction

$$\frac{2.003}{k_v} = \frac{2}{k_c} + \frac{0.003}{100\, k_c} = \frac{2.00003}{k_c}$$

therefore

$$k_v = 1.001\, k_c$$

The ratio

$$\frac{k_h}{k_v} = \frac{1.148}{1.001} = 1.147$$

Note that the horizontal permeability is affected by 14·8% although the silt partings represent a thickness of only 0·15% of the total thickness. This shows the sensitivity of permeability to apparently minor features of the ground conditions. The practical effect in problems in which flow is predominantly horizontal, such as in sand drain installations, can obviously be profound.

3.6 *In the experiment set up as shown in Fig. 3.6 flow is taking place under a constant head through the soils* A *and* B *of different hydraulic properties.*

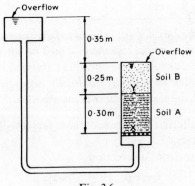

Fig. 3.6

(a) *Determine the hydraulic head and piezometric head at point* X.

(b) *If 35% of the excess hydrostatic pressure is lost in flowing through soil* A, *what are the hydraulic and piezometric heads at point* Y?

(c) *If the permeability of soil* A *is 0·40 mm/s, what quantity of water is flowing through unit plan area of the soil per second?*

(d) *What is the coefficient of permeability of soil* B?

(a) The hydraulic head is the head causing flow between point X and the surface of the soil B. It is therefore equal to 0·35 m.

The piezometric head is the height to which water would rise above a point if a standpipe were to be erected at that point.

Therefore for point X it is 0·90 m.

(b) The excess hydrostatic pressure is the pressure responsible for flow between two points. In this problem it is therefore equal to $0·35\ \gamma_w$ or, as a head, it is equal to the hydraulic head 0·35 m.

35% of this is lost in flowing to point Y from point X, namely 0·1225 m.

The hydraulic head at Y is therefore

$$0·35 - 0·1225 = 0·2275 \text{ m}$$

The piezometric head at Y is equal to 0·25 m plus the head which would be lost by the water in flowing from Y to the surface, that is, 0·2275 m.

The piezometric head at $Y = 0·4775$ m.

(c) $q = Ak_A\, i$ in which

$$A = 1 \text{ m}^2$$

$$k_A = 0·40 \text{ mm/s}$$

$$i = \frac{\text{head lost}}{\text{distance traversed}} = \frac{0·35 \times 0·35}{0·30} = 0·408$$

Therefore

$$q = 1 \times 0·4 \times 10^{-3} \times 0·408 = 1·632 \times 10^{-4} \text{ m}^3/\text{s}$$

(d) The same flow must take place through the upper layer. For soil B the hydraulic gradient

$$i = 0·65 \times \frac{0·35}{0·25} = 0·910$$

Hence

$$k_B = \frac{1 \cdot 632 \times 10^{-4}}{1 \times 0 \cdot 910} = 1 \cdot 79 \times 10^{-4} \, \text{m/s} = 0 \cdot 179 \, \text{mm/s}$$

Alternatively, working on the basis of equivalent permeabilities (see Problem 3.4),

$$\frac{0 \cdot 55}{k_v} = \frac{0 \cdot 30}{k_A} + \frac{0 \cdot 25}{k_B}$$

and

$$1 \cdot 632 \times 10^{-4} = 1 \times k_v \times \frac{0 \cdot 35}{0 \cdot 55}$$

$$k_v = 2 \cdot 56 \times 10^{-4} \, \text{m/s}$$

Hence

$$\frac{0 \cdot 55 \times 10^4}{2 \cdot 56} = \frac{0 \cdot 30 \times 10^4}{4 \cdot 00} + \frac{0 \cdot 25}{k_B}$$

$$k_B = 1 \cdot 79 \times 10^{-4} \, \text{m/s}$$

3.7 *If in Problem 3.6 the void ratios and specific gravities of the soils are*

	e	G_s
Soil B	0·65	2·70
Soil A	0·55	2·65

determine the discharge velocity and seepage velocity through each soil and the hydraulic head at which instability occurs.

$$\text{The discharge velocity} = \frac{q}{A} = \frac{1 \cdot 632 \times 10^{-4}}{1}$$

$$= 1 \cdot 632 \times 10^{-4} \, \text{m/s}$$

$$\text{The seepage velocity} = v_s = v \frac{1 + e}{e}$$

Thus for soil B

$$v_s = 1 \cdot 632 \times 10^{-4} \times \frac{1 \cdot 65}{0 \cdot 65} = 4 \cdot 143 \times 10^{-4} \, \text{m/s}$$

for soil A

$$v_s = 1 \cdot 632 \times 10^{-4} \times \frac{1 \cdot 55}{0 \cdot 55} = 4 \cdot 599 \times 10^{-4} \, \text{m/s}$$

For a given head the greatest hydraulic gradients occur in soil B, therefore instability will occur in this material before it occurs in soil A. The gradients in B are 0·910/0·408 or 2·23 times those in A, whereas the critical gradients are sensibly the same.

The critical hydraulic gradient for B is

$$\frac{G_s - 1}{1 + e} = \frac{1·70}{1 + 0·65} = 1·03$$

Therefore when instability occurs

$$\text{head loss through B} = 1·03 \times 0·25$$
$$= 0·26 \text{ m}$$

This is 65% of the total head loss.

Therefore head required above surface of B to cause instability is

$$0·26 \times \frac{100}{65} = 0·40 \text{ m}$$

3.8 *Define and illustrate the different kinds of boundary conditions that are involved in problems concerning the two-dimensional flow of water through soils.*

There are four types of boundaries involved. These are considered in turn.

(a) Impervious boundary
At such a boundary the water cannot penetrate, thus the velocity normal to the boundary must equal zero.

Hence

$$\frac{\partial \phi}{\partial n} = 0 = -v_n$$

where ϕ is the potential and n denotes the normal direction, and

$$\frac{\partial \psi}{\partial t} = 0$$

where ψ is the conjugate function and t is the tangential direction. For a horizontal boundary

$$v_z = 0 = -\frac{\partial \phi}{\partial z} \quad (z \text{ is the vertical coordinate})$$

For a vertical boundary

$$v_x = 0 = -\frac{\partial \phi}{\partial z} \quad (x \text{ is the horizontal coordinate})$$

An impervious boundary defines the locus of a flow line. Similarly any flow line satisfies the conditions for an impervious boundary and can be taken as such. In Fig. 3.8A, 1–2–3–4–5 and 7–8 represent flow lines.

(b) Permeable boundaries of structures
Along the boundaries of structures retaining water the pressure

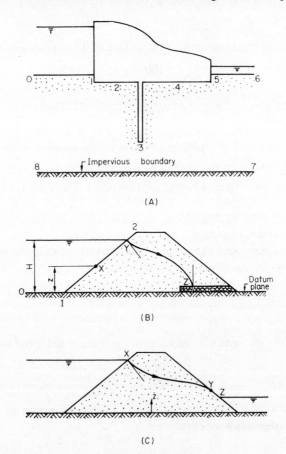

(A)

(B)

(C)

Fig. 3.8 A, B, C

distributions can be taken as hydrostatic. Thus in Fig. 3.8 B, point X will have a water pressure applied to it of

$$u = \gamma_w(H - z)$$

also $$h = H$$

and therefore $$\phi = \text{constant}$$

Thus lines 0–1, 5–6 of Fig. 3.8A and 1–2 of Fig. 3.8B are equipotential lines.

(c) Surface of seepage

The surface of seepage YZ of Fig. 3.8C represents a boundary where

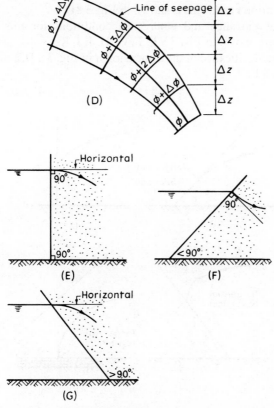

Fig. 3.8 D, E, F, G

the seepage flow enters an area free of soil and water. The pressure on this surface is atmospheric, assumed zero, and this requires that

$$\phi - kz = \text{constant}$$

(d) Free surface or seepage line
This is represented by XY in Fig. 3.8C and YZ in Fig. 3.8B and is the upper flow line in the flow domain. It separates the saturated region of flow from that part in which flow does not occur. Everywhere along its length the pressure is zero, or atmospheric. Thus along this line

$$\phi - kz = \text{constant}$$

The velocity potential and total head therefore vary linearly with elevation head. This is shown in Fig. 3.8D.

Various entrance and emergence conditions for this line of seepage are shown in Fig. 3.8 E, F, G, H, I, J, K.

For the significance of the dimension *a* in Fig. 3.8 H, I and J see Problem 3.10.

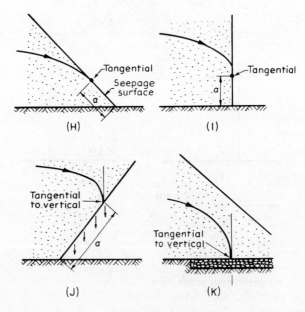

Fig. 3.8 H, I, J, K

3.9 *A homogeneous earth dam (Fig. 3.9) is provided with a filter drain to control the seepage. If the coefficient of permeability of the soil from which the dam is made is 0·347 mm/s calculate the seepage loss per day from a 100 m length of the dam.*

As a first stage in the determination of the flow quantity the flow net must be drawn. In this example the net will be obtained by sketching. First of all decide on the boundary conditions. These are

AB: Equipotential line. Therefore the flow lines will intersect at right angles.

AC: Impermeable. Therefore it is a flow line.

BD: The position of D is unknown at first. It corresponds to point Z of Fig. 3.8B. The line BD is the top flow line or seepage line, and the equipotential lines must cut it as shown in Fig. 3.8D.

CD: The flow lines must intersect at right angles as in Fig. 3.8K.

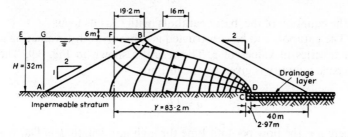

Fig. 3.9

To find the approximate position of BD we will use the construction proposed by A. Casagrande and Kozeny.

Along the water surface BE set off distance BF equal to 0·3BG, where G lies vertically above A. A parabola is then drawn through F with focus at C according to the relationship

$$x = \frac{z^2 - X^2}{2X}$$

in which

$$X = \sqrt{(Y^2 + H^2)} - Y$$

The parabola is joined to point B by a smooth curve which is tangential to it and which cuts AB at right angles. The total height *H*

61

is then subdivided into a number of convenient equal intervals which give the points of intersection of the equipotential lines with the seepage line BD. The remainder of the net can then be sketched in to produce a 'square' grid pattern which complies with the boundary requirements detailed above. Some adjustment of the top flow line can be made to obtain the final result.

Substituting the numerical values of the example,

$$BF = 0.30 \times 64 = 19.2 \text{ m}$$
$$X = \sqrt{(Y^2 + H^2)} - Y$$
$$= \sqrt{[(83.2)^2 + (32)^2]} - 83.2$$
$$= 5.94 \text{ m} = \text{distance CD} \times 2$$

Therefore $CD = 2.97$ m

$$x = \frac{z^2 - (5.94)^2}{11.88}$$

is the equation of the 'basic parabola' with C as its focus.

The parabola can be constructed graphically or by evaluating x for a series of values of z. The result is shown in Fig. 3.9. The seepage quantity is given by the formula

$$q = kh\frac{M}{N}$$

where q is the flow per unit time through unit length, k is Darcy's coefficient, M is the number of flow channels, and N is the number of potential drops in the 'square' diagram. Thus

$$q = 0.347 \times 10^{-3} \times 60^2 \times 24 \times 32 \times \frac{3}{16} \text{ m}^3/\text{day/m}$$

or $q = 180 \text{ m}^3/\text{day/m}$
$$= 18\,000 \text{ m}^3/\text{day}/100 \text{ m length}$$

3.10 *Draw the flow net and estimate the seepage quantity for the earth dam of Problem 3.9, if the filter drain is omitted.*

The procedure for solving this problem commences in the same way as that used for Problem 3.9, with the modification that point E becomes the focus of the 'basic parabola' instead of point C used in

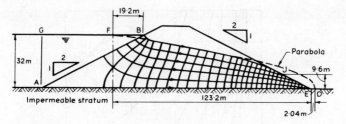

Fig. 3.10A

the previous case. The parabola thus formed outcrops on the downstream slope and its point of intersection with the slope is then modified according to the method detailed below.

Set off

$$BF = 0.30 \times 64 = 19.2 \text{ m}$$

$$X = \sqrt{[(123.2)^2 + (32)^2]} - 123.2$$
$$= 4.09 \text{ m}$$

therefore

$$ED = 2.04 \text{ m}$$

and

$$x = \frac{z^2 - (4.09)^2}{8.18} \text{ m}$$

The parabola can now be drawn in by determining the related coordinates x and z. This is shown in Fig. 3.10A. The seepage surface must intersect the slope normally at point B. This part of the curve is drawn in by inspection.

To determine the true point of intersection with the downstream slope we will use the modification due to Gilboy (see Fig. 3.10B).

$$\beta = \tan^{-1} 0.50 = 26° 33'$$

$$\frac{Y}{H} = \frac{123.2}{32} = 3.85$$

Hence

$$m = 0.3$$

The revised height at which the seepage surface intersects $= 0.3 \times 32 = 9.6$ m above the base. This is shown as point J on

63

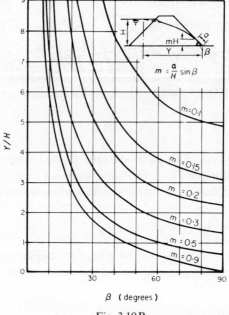

Fig. 3.10B

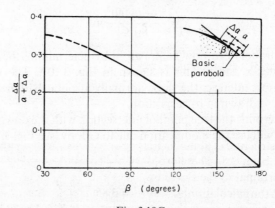

Fig. 3.10C

Fig. 3.10A. The curve is then modified locally to run in tangentially at point J as shown. The curve BJ is then divided into a convenient number of equal vertical intervals and the flow net completed, paying due attention to the required boundary conditions.

The seepage quantity is thus

$$q = 100 \times 0.347 \times 10^{-3} \times 60^2 \times 24 \times 32\,\frac{5}{32}$$

$$= 15000 \text{ m}^3/\text{day}/100 \text{ m length}$$

In problems where β is greater than 90° the discharge point can be determined by reference to Fig. 3.10C, the length $(a + \Delta a)$ at which the basic parabola cuts the slope surface being reduced to a as shown.

3.11 *A retaining wall 5 m high with a vertical back is provided with a drain as shown in Fig. 3.11 A and rests on an impermeable stratum. The backfill is saturated, with the water table established at its upper horizontal surface. The angle of shearing resistance of the backfill is 35°. Rain falls at a rate sufficient to maintain this water table. What effect will the seepage flow have on the total horizontal thrust on the wall compared with the case of the wall with no drainage provided?*

The boundary conditions are:

Surface AD: impermeable

$$v_z = 0 = -\frac{\partial \phi}{\partial z} = -\frac{\partial h}{\partial z} \quad \text{[case (a) Problem 3.8]}$$

Surface BC: equipotential line

$$\phi = \text{constant} \quad \text{[case (b) Problem 3.8]}$$

Surface AB: if the drain is well designed the flow will not be sufficient to saturate it and the water will move down through the drain structure at atmospheric pressure. This corresponds to case (c) of Problem 3.8. Therefore $\phi - kz = \text{constant}$ and the ϕ value is proportional to the elevation.

For the calculation we can therefore assume that $\phi = 100$ units on BC and that the flow lines must intersect BC at right angles. On AB, ϕ varies linearly from a maximum of 100 at B to a minimum of 0 at A. Note that it is not required that the flow lines intersect AB at right angles since this is not an equipotential line. On AD ϕ varies according to the gradient requirement which implies that the equipotential lines must cut this surface at 90 degrees.

65

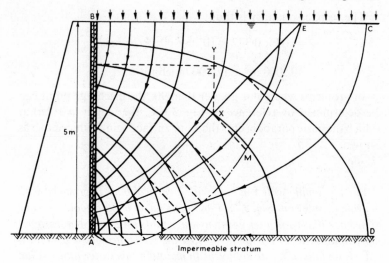

Fig 3.11 A

The flow net can now be sketched giving the results in Fig. 3.11 A.

The wall is subjected to a thrust due to the tendency of the backfill to slide on a plane such as AE. On this surface pore pressures vary from point to point, the distribution being found as follows:

At a typical point X where an equipotential line intersects the surface AE erect a vertical line XY. From the point of intersection of the *same equipotential line* with the back of the drain project a horizontal line. The intersection point of these two lines is Z. Height XZ then represents the piezometric head or pore-water pressure at point X divided by γ_w because the piezometric pressure at the drain is everywhere zero and the piezometric level is constant for any equipotential line. This height XZ can then be set off as XM normally to AE. Repetition of this procedure for each equipotential line intersection point enables the piezometric head diagram to be drawn. The total water thrust on the possible failure plane is U, and this is equal to the area of the piezometric head diagram multiplied by γ_w. In this example

$$U = 1000 \times 9{\cdot}81 \times 1 \times 6{\cdot}205$$
$$= 60871 \text{ N/m run of wall}$$
$$= 60{\cdot}87 \text{ kN/m run of wall}$$

If flow does not occur and the water table is maintained at the surface of the backfill, the piezometric head diagram is a hydrostatic one varying from 0 at the surface to a maximum of 5 m at the base of the wall. On the possible failure plane AE this would give a total water thrust of

$$U = \frac{5}{2} \times 7{\cdot}06 \times 9{\cdot}81 \times 1 \text{ kN/m run of wall}$$

$$= 173{\cdot}15 \text{ kN/m run of wall}$$

The thrust on the wall can be determined according to the methods of Chapter 6. For our purpose we are required to determine the effect of the pore-water pressure only.

Consider the equilibrium of the wedge of soil ABE. This is acted on by five forces shown in Fig. 3.11 B.

W is the saturated weight of the soil ABE.
P is the thrust on the wall (assumed to act normal to the back of the wall in this example).
N' is the normal effective thrust on the failure plane AE.

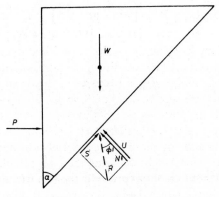

Fig. 3.11B

S is the shearing force on AE and equals $N' \tan \phi'$ (shearing strength being governed by effective normal stress).
U is the pore-water thrust (found as described earlier).

A polygon of forces can be drawn (Fig. 3.11 C):

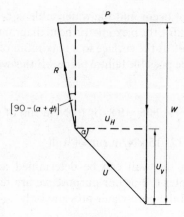

Fig. 3.11C

W is known (obtained from the saturated unit weight).
U is known.
N' and S can be combined to give resultant R inclined at angle ϕ' to the normal to the plane.

This diagram shows that:

$$P = U_H + R \sin\left[90° - (\alpha + \phi')\right]$$
$$= U_H + (W - U_V)\tan\left[90° - (\alpha + \phi')\right]$$

Now

$$U_H = U \cos \alpha$$

and

$$U_V = U \sin \alpha$$

Thus

$$P = U \cos \alpha - U \sin \alpha \cot(\alpha + \phi') + W \cot(\alpha + \phi')$$

In this problem the two values of U are 60·87 kN/m and 173·15 kN/m for seepage and no-seepage conditions respectively. For the possible failure surface drawn:

$$\alpha = 45° \quad \phi' = 35°$$

Thus the absence of the drain would produce an increase in total horizontal thrust of

68

$$P = (173 \cdot 15 - 60 \cdot 87) \cos 45° - (173 \cdot 15 - 60 \cdot 87) \sin 45° \cot 80°$$
$$= 65 \cdot 39 \text{ kN/m run of wall}$$

It is of interest to note that *for the case of hydrostatic pressure*

$$U = \gamma_w \frac{HL}{2}$$

where H is the height of the wall and L is the slope length AE. Therefore

$$U_H = \gamma_w \frac{HL}{2} \times \frac{H}{L} = \gamma_w \frac{H^2}{2}$$

(the normal hydrostatic thrust on the back of a wall of height H), and

$$U_V = \gamma_w \frac{HL}{2} \times \frac{BE}{L} = \gamma_w \frac{H \times BE}{2}$$

(the weight of water in an area ABE).

The total thrust P therefore is the sum of the hydrostatic thrust produced by water acting on the back of the wall and a force produced by an effective soil weight $(W - U_V)$ equal to the submerged weight of the soil in the zone ABE under consideration, i.e.,

$$P = \gamma_w \frac{H^2}{2} + W_{SUB} \cot (\alpha + \phi')$$

In practice a series of values of α would be chosen and that giving the maximum P would be used for design purposes.

3.12 *A dam of breadth B = 30 m rests on the horizontal upper surface of a uniform soil deposit of depth D = 30 m underlain by an impermeable stratum. It is provided with an impermeable cut-off at its mid-point which extends to a depth of 15 m below the dam base. The nett head of water effective in producing flow is H = 18 m and the coefficient of permeability of the soil is k = 0·00169 mm/s.*
Sketch the flow net and determine

(i) *the seepage quantity,*
(ii) *the maximum exit hydraulic gradient of the seepage water,*

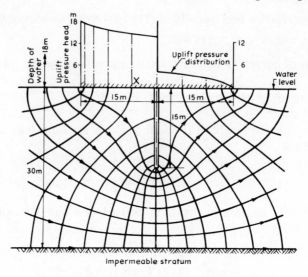

Fig. 3.12

(iii) *the distribution of uplift pressure on the base of the dam,*
(iv) *the pressure drop that the cut-off effects.*

The boundary conditions are determined according to the rules laid
down in Problem 3.8, and the flow net is then sketched in to
produce a square configuration of flow and equipotential lines.
The result appears in Fig. 3.12. For reasons of symmetry only
one-half of the diagram need be drawn.

(i) The number of flow channels is 8. The number of potential
drops is 20. The seepage quantity is, therefore

$$q = 0.00169 \times 10^{-3} \times 18 \times 1 \times \frac{8}{20}$$
$$= 0.0122 \times 10^{-3} \text{ m}^3/\text{s/m length of dam}$$
$$= 1.05 \text{ m}^3/\text{day/m length of dam}$$

(ii) The maximum hydraulic gradient (where the equipotential
lines are most closely spaced) is seen to occur near the edge of the
dam. The head loss of $18 \div 20 = 0.9$ m occurs over a length
(measured on the diagram) of about 0.75 m. The maximum
hydraulic gradient is therefore greater than unity, i.e. 1.2. The
sketched flow net is of doubtful accuracy in this region, however,

and an experimental or calculated determination would be more valid.

(*iii*) At point X, the potential line representing a head loss of $(4 \div 20) \times 18$ m intersects the base of the dam. If the level of the impounded water is 18 m above base level (with the tail-water level 0 m), then the pore-water pressure at X equals

$$18 - \left(\frac{4}{20} \times 18 \right) = 14.4 \, \text{m} = 141.3 \, \text{kN/m}^2$$

The values for other points along the base can be determined similarly giving the distribution shown in the figure. (Note the striking reduction in passing from one side of the cut-off to the other side.)

(*iv*) On the upstream side of the cut-off, the pressure head at base level is

$$18 - (4.5 \div 20)\, 18 = 13.95 \, \text{m}$$

On the downstream side, the pressure head at base level is

$$18 - (15.5 \div 20)\, 18 = 4.05 \, \text{m}$$

Thus,

$$\text{drop in pressure head} = 9.9 \, \text{m}$$

This represents 55% of the nett head producing flow, or $9.9/18 = 0.55$.

The uplift is thus dramatically reduced.

Flow nets are of value as a solution procedure only if they provide a rapid processing of the figures within the limits of tolerance dictated by the conditions on site. To obtain a perfectly accurate flow net of unimpeachable appearance is not necessary for most site problems. If that measure of accuracy is required, then numerical solutions, such as shown in Problem 3.14 would be appropriate. The *sketched* flow net of Problem 3.12, although it could be adjusted still further to improve its appearance, already gives an identical discharge to that obtained by a so-called 'exact' solution.

3.13 *A vertical sheet-pile wall penetrates 6 m into a sand deposit which is 12 m thick and overlies an impermeable soil. The water* *level on one side of the wall is 3 m and on the other 0·6 m above ground surface level. The sand stratum is anisotropic with a horizontal permeability 9 times that in the vertical direction. The latter has a k value of 0·0176 mm/s. Determine the seepage flow per day.*

The horizontal permeability coefficient therefore is

$$9 \times 0·0176 = 0·1584 \text{ mm/s} = k_x \text{ and } k_z = 0·0176 \text{ mm/s}$$

To obtain the flow net for the anisotropic soil the net is drawn according to the conventions used in former examples but with the horizontal dimensions multiplied by the factor

$$\sqrt{\left(\frac{k_z}{k_x}\right)} = \sqrt{\left(\frac{1}{9}\right)} = \frac{1}{3}$$

The resultant net is shown in Fig. 3.13A drawn to its distorted scale, and in Fig. 3.13 B part of it is drawn to true scale. The 'square' intersections are only obtained in the distorted diagram.

For the purpose of computing the seepage flow the equivalent permeability must be taken as

$$k = \sqrt{(k_x k_z)} = \sqrt{(0·1584 \times 0·0176)} = 0·0528 \text{ mm/s}$$

The number of flow channels = 10

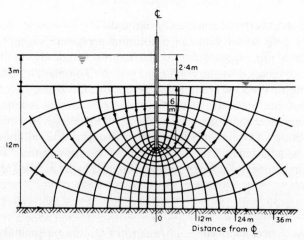

Fig. 3.13A

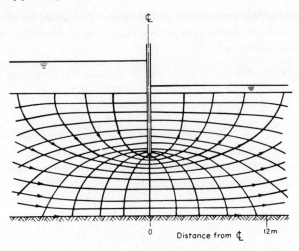

Fig. 3.13B

The number of potential drops $= 22$

The seepage quantity $= 0.0528 \times 10^{-3} \times 60^2 \times 24 \times (3 - 0.6) \times \dfrac{10}{22}$

$$= 4.977 \text{ m}^3/\text{day/m of wall}$$

$$= \text{say } 5 \text{ m}^3/\text{day/m}$$

An exact analytical solution, rather than this sketched solution, gives 11 flow channels instead of the 10 (for 22 drops in potential) as shown. The seepage for 11 channels instead of for 10, is $5.5 \text{ m}^3/\text{day/m}$. This, compared with the 5 m^3 given by the sketched solution is within the tolerances of site works of this type.

3.14 *An excavation 12 m wide by 12 m deep and of great length is made in a sand deposit of total thickness 36 m which rests on an impermeable rock. The upper surface of the sand is horizontal and the sides of the excavation are retained by sheet piling driven to a depth of 12 m below the bottom of the excavation. Water is standing on both sides of the sheet piling to a depth of 6 m above the respective ground levels. The coefficient of permeability is 1.22×10^{-4} m/s in all directions. Determine the flow net by means* *of a relaxation calculation and estimate the quantity of water flowing into the excavation per metre of length. Is the excavation safe against heaving?* (Fig. 3.14A)

To apply the relaxation procedure we replace the governing equation $\nabla^2 \phi = 0$ by its finite difference approximation i.e.

$$0 = \phi_1 + \phi_2 + \phi_3 + \phi_4 - 4\phi_0$$

in which ϕ_1, ϕ_2, etc., represent the values of the function ϕ at adjacent positions as indicated in Fig. 3.14B. The region of the problem is covered by a grid of the type shown and the values of ϕ at each nodal point determined by the application of some simple rules. It can be seen from the above equation that if the values of ϕ_0 to ϕ_4 are not correct the equation can be written

$$\phi_1 + \phi_2 + \phi_3 + \phi_4 - 4\phi_0 = F_0$$

and the object is to make F_0 near zero in value.

Now
$$\frac{\partial F_0}{\partial \phi_1} = \frac{\partial F_0}{\partial \phi_2} = \frac{\partial F_0}{\partial \phi_3} = \frac{\partial F_0}{\partial \phi_4} = +1$$

and
$$\frac{\partial F_0}{\partial \phi_0} = -4$$

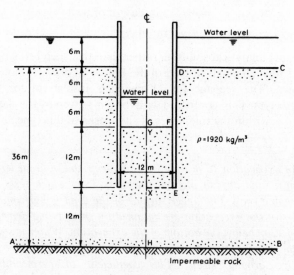

Fig. 3.14A

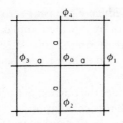

Fig. 3.14B

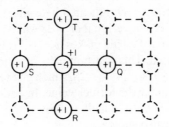

Fig. 3.14C

Thus a change of $+1$ in the value of ϕ_1, ϕ_2, ϕ_3 or ϕ_4 will change the value of the *residual* F_0 by $+1$ and a change of $+1$ in the value of ϕ_0 will change the value of F_0 by -4. This can be illustrated by means of the relaxation molecule (Fig. 3.14C) which shows the effect of a change of $+1$ in the value of the ϕ at any nodal point on the value of the *residual at that point and at the four surrounding points*. Thus in the molecule depicted, the ϕ value at P is altered by $+1$ (shown outside the circle); this represents a change of $+1$ in the value of ϕ_0 for point P, and F_0 at point P is changed by -4 (shown inside the circle). For nodal point Q, however, the ϕ value which has been changed by $+1$ at P represents its ϕ_3 value, and thus the value of F_0 at point Q is altered by $+1$ (shown in the circle). The same reasoning applies to points R, S, T, each being imagined as the central nodal point of Fig. 3.14B in turn.

In application therefore we assign values of ϕ at each of the nodal points, determine the residual at each point in turn by an application of the equation

$$F_0 = \phi_1 + \phi_2 + \phi_3 + \phi_4 - 4\phi_0$$

75

and then proceed to reduce F_0 to near zero values throughout the domain of the problem by repeated applications of the operation illustrated by the relaxation molecule. When this stage is reached the ϕ value at each nodal point represents the answer to the problem.

As an example consider the portion of a grid shown in Fig. 3.14D, representing any stage in a calculation.

The ϕ values written in the top right quadrant at each nodal point. The F_0 values are given underneath in the bottom right quadrants. The elimination of the residuals can take place in any order by the process being indicated herewith.

Consider point P. The residual of $+28$ will be reduced by adding $+7$ to the ϕ value at P. This makes $\phi = +71$, the old value being deleted and replaced. This addition of $+7$ to the ϕ value alters the F_0 value at P by $+7 \times -4 = -28$, which gives a new F_0 value of 0 which is written under the former value. In addition the F_0 values at Q, R, S and T must be altered by $+7 \times +1 = +7$. Their revised values are also shown.

The residual of $+47$ at point R can be reduced to -1 by adding $+12$ to the ϕ value at point R, and at the same time the F_0 values at the surrounding four points will be changed by $+12$.

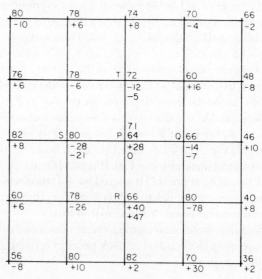

Fig. 3.14D

The procedure is repeated at all the necessary nodal points until F_0 is near zero throughout.

There are some additional requirements for points at the boundaries. The various boundary conditions have already been discussed in Problem 3.8. These have their relaxation equivalents as follows for the boundaries involved in this problem.

(a) *Impervious boundary* (AHB, DE, EF and BC of Fig. 3.14A)

$$\frac{\partial \phi}{\partial n} = 0$$

which gives

$$\frac{\partial \phi}{\partial z} = 0 \quad \text{and} \quad \frac{\partial \phi}{\partial x} = 0$$

for horizontal and vertical boundaries respectively.

For the former requirement this means that

$$\frac{\phi_2 - \phi_4}{2a} \doteq 0$$

when ϕ_0 is on the boundary or

$$\phi_2 = \phi_4$$

Eliminating ϕ_2 from the $\nabla^2 \phi = 0$ equation we obtain

$$F_0 = \phi_1 + \phi_3 + 2\phi_4 - 4\phi_0 \qquad .$$

which is applicable *for the points on* the impermeable horizontal boundary. Hence

$$\frac{\partial F_0}{\partial \phi_1} = \frac{\partial F_0}{\partial \phi_3} = +1; \qquad \frac{\partial F_0}{\partial \phi_4} = +2; \qquad \frac{\partial F_0}{\partial \phi_0} = -4$$

The relaxation molecule is thus (Fig. 3.14E):

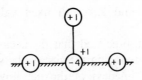

Fig. 3.14E

and for the *next row in* from the boundary (Fig. 3.14F):

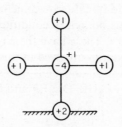

Fig. 3.14F

For vertical impermeable boundaries these diagrams can be rotated through 90 degrees.

At the junction of two perpendicular boundaries, both of which are impermeable, we have for the nodal point one row in from the boundaries (Fig. 3.14G):

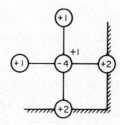

Fig. 3.14G

The axis of symmetry GH can be dealt with as an impermeable boundary, only one-half of the domain need then be considered.

(*b*) *Permeable boundaries of structures* (CD and FG of Fig. 3.14A) ϕ is constant and therefore values can be written in at the appropriate nodal points and left with fixed value throughout the calculation.

It will be readily appreciated that the accuracy of the solution will be enhanced by reducing the size of the squares forming the grid. Increasing the fineness of the net however increases the amount of work involved and in zones of small rates of change of ϕ

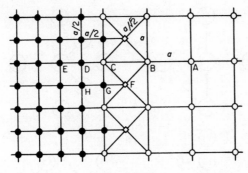

Fig. 3.14H

the differences achieved may be small. A compromise solution is therefore frequently adopted, a fine grid being used in zones where ϕ is expected to vary rapidly and a coarser grid elsewhere. The junctions of these two sizes of grid introduce modifications to the *standard* relaxation molecule. Fig. 3.14H illustrates an area in which this situation develops, the large grid of side length a being on the right and the fine grid of side length $a/2$ being on the left. In the figure those nodal points regarded as belonging to the large grid are shown by open circles, those belonging to the smaller grid by solid circles and special diagonal nodes by open squares. The latter form with some of the other points a grid of side length $a/\sqrt{2}$.

The operator ∇^2 is invariant with respect to a rotation of the axes of co-ordinates therefore the equation

$$F_0 = \phi_1 + \phi_2 + \phi_3 + \phi_4 - 4\phi_0$$

is applicable to the diagonal grid as well as to the large and small grids. Initial residual values are therefore easily calculable for all nodal points. The relaxation patterns in the junction zone are as shown in Fig. 3.14J.

We can now proceed as follows:

For calculation purposes we have to impose finite boundaries on the problem. Therefore BC is chosen at a distance of 54 m from the centre-line, this being deemed sufficiently far removed so as not to influence the results in the region of the excavation. A square grid of arm length $a = 3$ m is drawn over the region bounded by BCDEFGH. Because of the rectilinear nature of the boundaries

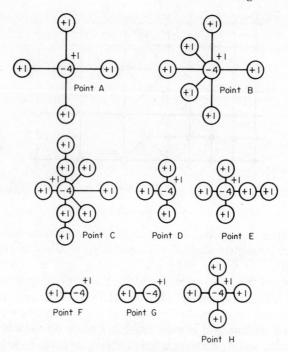

Fig. 3.14J

and the choice of *a*, all boundaries coincide with lines of the grid and therefore nodal points fall on the boundaries.

An arbitrary value of 100 can now be written in for all nodal points on CD, and a similar arbitrary value of 0 can be written in for the nodal points on FG. These 100 units represent the head of 12 m responsible for the production of flow. These are the only boundaries on which precise final values of ϕ can be calculated at the beginning. Other ϕ values are placed against all other nodal points of the grid. These can be guessed or estimated in various ways and they will in general be significantly far from the correct values.

The values of F_0 for each point are now evaluated by an application of the finite difference form of

$$\nabla^2 \phi = 0$$

for points within the boundaries and from the modified equations for points on the impermeable boundaries. Where ϕ is permanently fixed in value from the commencement of the calculation the residuals need not be computed.

The values of F_0 are then systematically reduced to near zero by applying the processes defined by the appropriate relaxation molecules. Periodically F_0 values should be checked using current ϕ values to ensure that errors have not occurred in calculation, the new values of F_0 being used from that stage onwards.

A word of warning is desirable concerning the distribution of F_0 values when the calculation is completed. These should be small in value throughout the region *and positive and negative values should be distributed at random.* Large areas of, say, positive small F_0 will give ϕ values which may be considerably in error.

Fig. 3.14K shows the result of the calculation with the equipotential lines interpolated from the calculated values and a number of flow lines drawn in at right angles to these contours and obeying the boundary requirements.

> The number of flow channels is   5
>
> The number of potential drops is   20

The discharge quantity per metre length of the excavation is therefore

$$q = k \times 12 \times \frac{5}{20} = 3k$$

$$= 1 \cdot 22 \times 10^{-4} \times 3 \times 60 \times 60 \times 24 \text{ m}^3/\text{day}$$

$$= 31 \cdot 62 \text{ m}^3/\text{day (half the total quantity)}$$

If failure occurs by heaving, it is most likely in the zone extending from the inside of the sheet piling for a distance of about half the depth of penetration. To determine the factor of safety against heaving we therefore examine the stability of the block of soil (and water) FEXY in which

$$EX = 0 \cdot 5 \; FE = 6 \text{ m}$$

The effective downward weight

$$= \text{submerged weight}$$

$$= 6 \times 12 \times (1920 - 1000) \times 9 \cdot 81 \text{ N/m}$$

$$= 649 \cdot 8 \text{ kN/m run}$$

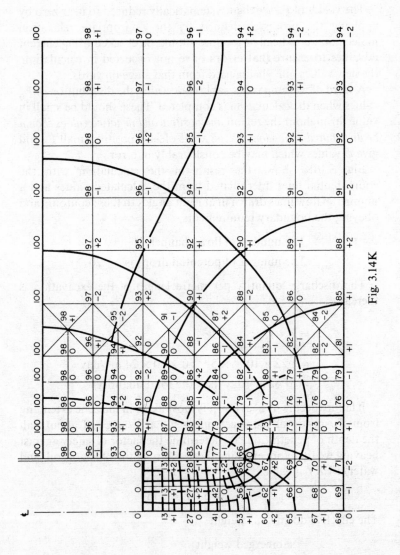

Fig. 3.14K

The average excess pressure at the level of the toe of the piling is

$$0.57 \times 12 = 6.84 \text{ m}$$

The upward force is therefore

$$6.84 \times 1000 \times 9.81 \times 6 = 402.6 \text{ kN/m run}$$

and the factor of safety is

$$\frac{649.8}{402.6} = 1.6$$

CHAPTER FOUR

Shearing resistance

The examples given in this chapter are concerned mainly with the determination of the shear strength of soils from the results of tests, and with the relationship between the shear stress parameters under different conditions of drainage. The application of shear strength to problems relating to stability of slopes, retaining walls and foundations will be found in their respective chapters.

Most problems on shear strength are best solved graphically. Sometimes, analytical methods, based on the trigonometry of the Mohr circle, are found to be effective. Examples of both these types of solution are given in this chapter.

4.1 *Samples of compacted, clean, dry sand were tested in a large shear box, 254 mm by 254 mm in plan, and the following results were obtained:*

Normal load (kg)	500	1000	1500
Peak shear load (kN)	4·92	9·80	14·62
Residual shear load (kN)	3·04	6·23	9·36

Determine the angle of shearing resistance of the sand in (a) the dense, and (b) the loose state.

With compacted sands the shearing resistance builds up until the *peak load* is reached, at which failure begins. The resistance then falls off as shearing continues, finally reaching a steady value known as the residual strength. The value of ϕ obtained from the peak stress represents the angle of shearing resistance of the sand in its initial compacted state; that obtained from the residual or ultimate shear corresponds to the sand when loosened by the shearing action.

84

If initially the sand had been loose it would have tended to compact during the process of shearing. The density at which the sand will neither expand nor compact during shearing is known as the *critical density*.

The area of this shear box is 0.0645 m^2.

Normal stress for 500 kg load

$$= \frac{500 \times 9.81}{0.0645} = 76000 \text{ N/m}^2 = 76.0 \text{ kN/m}^2$$

Similarly for the other normal loads.

The shear stresses (in kN/m^2) are the shearing loads in kN divided by 0.0645.

Table 4.1 (kN/m^2)

Normal stress σ	76.0	152·1	228·1
Peak shear stress, s_1	76·3	151·9	226·7
Residual shear stress, s_2	47·1	96·6	145·1

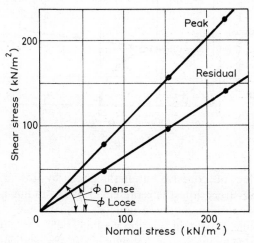

Fig. 4.1

From Fig. 4.1 the values of the angles of shearing resistance are found to be

(a) dense state: $\phi = 45°$
(b) loose state: $\phi = 32°$

4.2 *Three specimens of clay having a small air-void content were tested in the shear box. Shear loading was started immediately after the application of the normal load, and was completed in 10 min. The results were as follows:*

Normal stress (kN/m²)	*145*	*241*	*337*
Shear stress at failure (kN/m²)	*103*	*117*	*132*

Find the apparent cohesion and angle of shearing resistance of the clay. What value of c would be obtained from an unconfined compression test on the same soil?

By direct plotting of the results, the required values are found to be:

$$c_u = 87 \text{ kN/m}^2$$
$$\phi_u = 7°$$

From the data given about the duration of the test, these are obviously the *undrained values* referred to total stress.

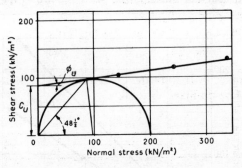

Fig. 4.2

The value of cohesive strength given by the unconfined compressive-strength test is represented by the radius of a Mohr circle passing through the origin ($\sigma_3 = 0$) and tangent to the Coulomb line. To obtain this, draw a line at $45° + \phi/2$ (or $48\frac{1}{2}°$ in this instance) to the horizontal axis and a perpendicular to the Coulomb Line fixes the centre of the circle on the horizontal axis. The value of c_u as obtained by the unconfined compression test is the radius of this circle, or 98 kN/m². Thus, if a soil shows an apparent angle of shearing resistance in the undrained test, the unconfined compression test will give a high value of apparent cohesion.

In this problem and in Problem 4.4 it has been assumed for simplicity that the various test procedures, i.e., triaxial, unconfined compression and shear box, give the same results when the drainage conditions are the same. In practice this is not always the case.

4.3 *The following results were obtained from undrained triaxial compression tests on three identical specimens of saturated soil:*

Lateral pressure (kN/m²)	70	140	210
Total axial stress (kN/m²)	217	294	357
Inclination of plane of rupture to cross section of specimen	51°	53°	52°

Determine c_u and ϕ_u for the soil, and its angle of internal friction. From what type of soil would results such as these be expected?

By plotting the Mohr circles, which have diameters of 217–70, 294–140 and 357–210, we determine Fig. 4.3. By scaling, $c_u = 75$ kN/m², and it is clear that the common tangent is substantially horizontal, so $\phi_u = 0°$.

Taking the mean angle of the plane of rupture as 52°,

$$45° + \phi_f/2 = 52° \text{ or } \phi_f = 14°$$

The value of $\phi_u = 0°$ indicates a saturated clay, tested under conditions of no drainage.

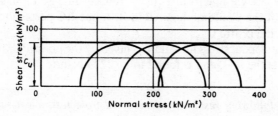

Fig. 4.3

4.4 *The following results were obtained from undrained shear-box tests on specimens of sandy clay. The cross section of the shear box was 60 mm × 60 mm.*

Normal load (N)	200	400	800
Shearing force at failure (N)	204	260	356

If a specimen of the same soil is tested in triaxial compression with a cell pressure of 100 kN/m², find the total axial stress at which failure will be expected to occur.

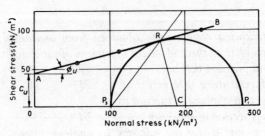

Fig. 4.4

The area of the shear box is 3600 mm², or 0·0036 m².

Stresses (kN/m²) are:

Normal	56	111	222
Shear	57	72	99

By plotting these stresses (Fig. 4.4) we find that

$$c_u = 44 \text{ kN/m}^2 \text{ and } \phi_u = 14°.$$

Having obtained this line, the Mohr circle for the triaxial test at 100 kN/m² cell pressure must be fitted to it. To find the centre of the circle draw a line from $P_3(\sigma_3 = 100 \text{ kN/m}^2)$ at $45° + \phi_u/2$, or 52°, to cut the Coulomb line AB in R. A line RC perpendicular to AB fixes the centre C.

The total axial stress for failure is given by the point P_1 where the circle cuts the axis, and is found to be 277 kN/m².

4.5 *The following results were obtained from tests on a saturated clay soil:*

   (a) *Undrained triaxial tests:*

Cell pressure σ_3 (kN/m²)	100	170	240
Principal stress difference at failure,			
$\sigma_1 - \sigma_3$ (kN/m²)	136	142	134

   (b) *Shear-box tests in which the soil was allowed to consolidate fully under the influence of both the normal and the shear loads:*

Normal stress (kN/m²)	62	123	185
Shear stress at failure (kN/m²)	73	99	128

Determine the shear strength properties of the soil which can be deduced from these results.

(*a*) From a plot of the three Mohr circles (Fig. 4.5) the best Coulomb line gives $c_u = 68$ kN/m^2 and $\phi_u = 0°$.

(*b*) Direct plotting of the shear-box tests gives the parameters for the drained condition:

$$c_d = 42 \text{ kN/m}^2 \text{ and } \phi_d = 24\tfrac{1}{2}°$$

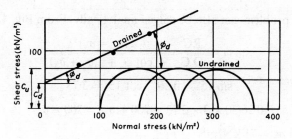

Fig. 4.5

4.6 *A cohesive soil has an angle of shearing resistance of $\phi_u = 15°$ and a cohesion of $c_u = 30$ kN/m^2. If a specimen of this soil is subjected to an undrained triaxial compression test, find the value of the lateral pressure in the cell for failure to occur at a total axial stress of 200 kN/m^2.*

Draw the Coulomb line AB representing $30 + \sigma \tan 15°$. Set out $OP_1 = \sigma_1 = 200$ kN/m^2 and draw a Mohr circle passing through P_1 tangent to AB. The circle defines OP_3, which is the required value of σ_3 and is 71 kN/m^2. This is the cell pressure necessary for a failure at 200 kN/m^2 total axial stress.

The method of drawing the circle is as follows: Draw from P_1 (defined by $OP_1 = 200$) a line $P_1 R$ at $45° - \phi_u/2$ or $37\tfrac{1}{2}°$ to the horizontal axis, to intersect the Coulomb line in R. A line from R at right angles to RP_1 is at the inclination of the plane of rupture ($45° + \phi_u/2$ or $52\tfrac{1}{2}°$) and a line RC at right angles to AB defines the centre of the circle, C.

89

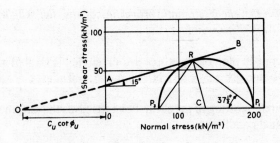

Fig. 4.6

This problem can also be solved analytically. From Fig. 4.6,

$$\sin \phi_u = \frac{RC}{O'C} = \frac{\frac{1}{2}(\sigma_1 - \sigma_3)}{c_u \cot \phi_u + \frac{1}{2}(\sigma_1 + \sigma_3)}$$

$$\sin 15° = 0·26, \quad \cot 15° = 3·73$$

$$0·26(30 \times 2 \times 3·73 + 200 + \sigma_3) = 200 - \sigma_3$$

whence $\sigma_3 = 71$ kN/m^2.

4.7 *The results of undrained triaxial tests (with pore pressure measurement) on compacted soil at failure are as follows:*

Lateral pressure σ_3 (kN/m^2)	70	350
Total axial pressure σ_1 (kN/m^2)	304	895
Pore-water pressure u (kN/m^2)	−30	+95

Determine the apparent cohesion and angle of shearing resistance (a) referred to total stress, and (b) referred to effective stress.

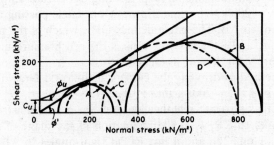

Fig. 4.7

For (*a*) the Mohr circles A and B are plotted in the usual way. From the common tangent, $c_u = 50$ kN/m^2, and $\phi_u = 21°$.

For (*b*) the effective stresses ($\sigma - u$) are.

$$\sigma'_1 \qquad 304 + 30 = 334 \qquad 895 - 95 = 800$$
$$\sigma'_3 \qquad 70 + 30 = 100 \qquad 350 - 95 = 255$$

From these figures the effective-stress circles C and D are plotted. Note that their radii are the same as those of the total-stress circles. The tangent gives $c' = 0$ and $\phi' = 31\frac{1}{2}°$ (Fig. 4.7).

4.8 *Drained and undrained triaxial compression tests on specimens of a saturated soil gave the results at failure shown in Table 4.8A. The drained tests were carried out without a back pressure. All specimens were of 38 mm diameter and 76 mm long. Obtain the shear strength parameters in relation to (i) total stresses, and (ii) effective stresses.*

Table 4.8A

Test		Cell pressure (kN/m^2) σ_3	Axial load applied through piston (N) P	Change in length (mm) δl	Change in volume (ml) δV
(*a*)		(*b*)	(*c*)	(*d*)	(*e*)
Drained	1	100	282	− 10·98	− 4·8
	2	200	449	− 13·50	− 6·0
	3	400	853	− 17·80	− 8·6
Undrained	4	100	199	− 10·32	0
	5	200	200	− 12·21	0
	6	400	216	− 16·17	0

For all specimens:

Original length = 76 mm = l
Original diameter = 38 mm = d
Original area = $\pi \times 38^2 = 1134$ mm^2 = A_0
Original volume = $A_0 \times l = 1134 \times 76 = 86193$ mm^3
= 86·2 ml = V

The calculations are best set out in tabular form (Table 4.8B).

Table 4.8B

Test	Volume at failure $V + \delta V$ (ml)	Length at failure $l + \delta l$ (mm)	(cm)	Mean area at failure $A_f = \dfrac{\text{Col.}(f)}{\text{Col.}(h)}$ (cm^2)	Minor principal stress at failure (kN/m^2) Total	Effective	Principal stress difference $(\sigma_1 - \sigma_3)_f$ $= (\sigma'_1 - \sigma'_3)_f$ $= (P/A_f)_f$ (kN/m^2)	Major principal stress at failure (kN/m^2) Total	Effective
(a)	(f)	(g)	(h)	(j)	(k)	(l)	(m)	(n)	(o)
1	81·4	65·02	6·502	12·52	100	100	225	325	325
2	80·2	62·50	6·250	12·83	200	200	350	550	550
3	77·6	58·20	5·820	13·33	400	400	640	1040	1040
4	86·2	65·68	6·568	13·12	100	?	152	252	?
5	86·2	63·79	6·379	13·51	200	?	148	348	?
6	86·2	59·83	5·983	14·41	400	?	150	550	?

It is first of all necessary to calculate the mean cross-sectional area at failure by allowing for volume change and axial shortening. Thus

$$\text{Mean area at failure} = \frac{V + \delta V}{l + \delta l} = A_f \qquad \text{(column (j))}$$

The axial load applied through the piston at failure, when divided by the mean area at failure, gives the principal stress difference $(\sigma_1 - \sigma_3)_f = (\sigma'_1 - \sigma'_3)_f$. When combined with the minor principal stress σ_3 (cell pressure) or σ'_3 (cell pressure – pore pressure), this determines σ_1 and σ'_1 respectively, at failure.

In the undrained test, the pore pressures being unknown, the results give the total stress parameters.

In the drained test, the pore pressure u is zero throughout (no back pressure), and hence $\sigma_1 = \sigma'_1$ and $\sigma_3 = \sigma'_3$. The results thus give effective stress parameters.

The Mohr circle plots of the data in columns (k), (l), (n) and (o) are shown in Fig. 4.8. From this

(i) $c_u = 75 \text{ kN/m}^2$; $\phi_u = 0°$
(ii) $c' = 25 \text{ kN/m}^2$; $\phi' = 24°$

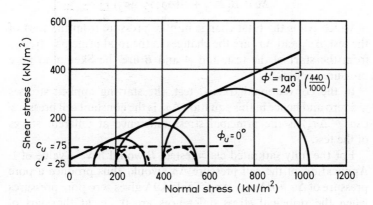

Fig. 4.8

4.9 *During application of the axial load in undrained triaxial tests on saturated clay soils, the pore pressures given in Table 4.9A were recorded. Plot the results and calculate the values of the pore pressure coefficient A during the progress of the tests. What conclusions can be drawn?*

Table 4.9A

Principal stress difference $(\sigma_1 - \sigma_3)$ (kN/m^2)		0	200	300	400	475	505	500	550	580	560
Pore pressure (kN/m^2)	Soil P	0	88	175	260	280	—	—	250	190	175
	Soil Q	0	132	205	286	370	430	425	—	—	—
Axial strain (%)	Soil P	0	0·7	1·3	2·1	3·0	—	—	4·5	6·7	8·5
	Soil Q	0	2·5	4·6	7·7	13·0	20·0	23·0	—	—	—

The pore pressures in an undrained test are often described by the equation:

$$\Delta u = B[\Delta\sigma_3 + A(\Delta\sigma_1 - \Delta\sigma_3)]$$

in which Δu is the total change in pore pressure from the start of the test, $\Delta\sigma_3$ and $\Delta\sigma_1$ are the changes in the total principal stresses from the start of the test, and A and B are the Skempton pore pressure coefficients.

In the conventional triaxial test, the starting applied stresses are zero and hence in this equation $\Delta\sigma_3$ is the constant cell pressure, $(\Delta\sigma_1 - \Delta\sigma_3)$ is the principal stress difference at different stages of the test.

For the fully saturated clays tested, B would have a value of 1. Application of the cell pressure $\Delta\sigma_3$ would thus produce a pore pressure of $\Delta u = B\Delta\sigma_3 = \Delta\sigma_3$. Table 4.9A gives zero pore pressures when the principal stress differences are 0, i.e. at the start of shearing, and hence the tabulated values exclude the pore pressure produced by application of the cell pressure.

Hence the tabulated pore pressures $= BA (\Delta\sigma_1 - \Delta\sigma_3)$ and taking $B = 1$,

A = tabulated pore pressure/principal stress difference.

Table 4.9B

Principal stress difference (kN/m^2)		0	200	300	400	475	505	500	550	580	560
Pore pressure coefficient, A	Soil P	0	0·44	0·58	0·65	0·59	—	—	0·45	0·33	0·31
	Soil Q	0	0·66	0·68	0·72	0·78	0·85	0·85	—	—	—

The calculated values of A are given in Table 4.9 B and are plotted in Fig. 4.9 B.

From the shapes of the curves of Figs 4.9A and B:

> Soil Q is a normally consolidated clay
>
> Soil P is an overconsolidated clay

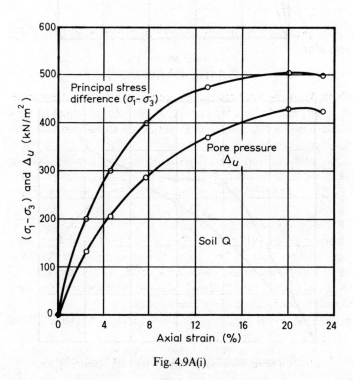

Fig. 4.9A(i)

95

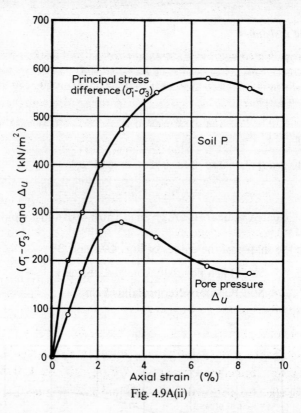

Fig. 4.9A(ii)

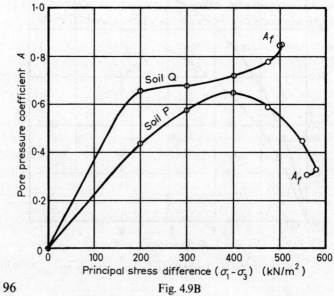

96   Fig. 4.9B

4.10 *Consolidated-undrained triaxial tests (with pore pressure measurement) on specimens of a saturated clay gave the failure conditions in Table 4.10A. Determine the apparent cohesion and angle of shearing resistance, referred to (a) total stress, and (b) effective stress, using (i) a Mohr circle construction, and (ii) a plot of stress points at failure.*

Table 4.10A

Cell pressure, σ_3 (kN/m^2)	200	400	600
Maximum principal stress difference, $(\sigma_1 - \sigma_3)_f$ (kN/m^2)	120	230	356
Pore pressure at failure, u (kN/m^2)	102	200	299

The required values of the principal stresses are given in Table 4.10B, using the relationships:

Major total principal stress at failure $\sigma_1 = (\sigma_1 - \sigma_3)_f + \sigma_3$

Major effective principal stress at failure $\sigma_1' = (\sigma_1 - \sigma_3)_f + \sigma_3 - u$

Minor total principal stress at failure $\sigma_3 = \sigma_3$ (Table 4.10A)

Minor effective principal stress at failure $\sigma_3' = \sigma_3 - u$

The stress points are defined by the uppermost point on the respective Mohr circles. At failure they have coordinates:

$$\frac{(\sigma_1 + \sigma_3)_f}{2} \quad \text{and} \quad \frac{(\sigma_1 - \sigma_3)_f}{2} \qquad \text{for total stresses}$$

and

$$\frac{(\sigma_1' + \sigma_3')_f}{2} \quad \text{and} \quad \frac{(\sigma_1' - \sigma_3')_f}{2} \qquad \text{for effective stresses}$$

These are also given in Table 4.10B.

The Mohr circles are plotted in Fig. 4.10A. The equations for the envelopes give:

(a) (i) For total stresses

$$c = 0 \text{ kN/m}^2; \quad \phi = 13°$$

(b) (i) For effective stresses

$$c' = 0 \text{ kN/m}^2; \quad \phi' = 22°$$

Table 4.10B

Major total principal stress at failure, σ_1 (kN/m^2)	320	630	956
Major effective principal stress at failure, $\sigma'_1 = \sigma_1 - u$ (kN/m^2)	218	430	657
Minor total principal stress at failure, σ_3 (kN/m^2)	200	400	600
Minor effective principal stress at failure, $\sigma'_3 = \sigma_3 - u$ (kN/m^2)	98	200	301
$\dfrac{(\sigma_1 + \sigma_3)_f}{2}$ (kN/m^2)	260	515	778
$\dfrac{(\sigma'_1 + \sigma'_3)_f}{2}$ (kN/m^2)	158	315	479
$\dfrac{(\sigma'_1 - \sigma'_3)_f}{2} = \dfrac{(\sigma_1 - \sigma_3)_f}{2}$ (kN/m^2)	60	115	178

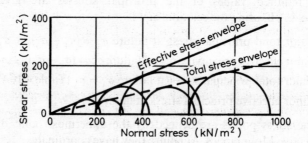

Fig. 4.10A

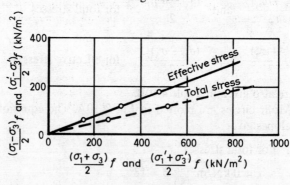

Fig. 4.10B

The stress point plots (Fig. 4.10B) give:

(a) (ii) For total stresses

$$a = 0 \qquad \text{the intercept on the } \frac{(\sigma_1 - \sigma_3)_f}{2} \text{ axis}$$

$$\alpha = 12° 41' \quad \text{the slope of the failure line}$$

Hence

$$\phi = \sin^{-1}(\tan \alpha) = 13° \quad \text{and} \quad c = \frac{a}{\cos \phi} = 0 \text{ kN/m}^2$$

(b) (ii) For effective stresses

$$a = 0 \quad \alpha = 20° 24'$$

Hence

$$\phi' = 22° \quad \text{and} \quad c' = 0 \text{ kN/m}^2$$

These values of the shear strength parameters are the same as those obtained from the Mohr circle construction.

4.11 *A specimen of saturated clay was subjected to a consolidated-undrained triaxial test in which pore pressure measurements were made during the undrained stage of the test. The results are given in Table 4.11A.*

(i) *Plot the effective stress path to failure.*
(ii) *By plotting a stress path on the same diagram, determine the maximum principal stress at which an identical specimen*

Table 4.11A

Minor principal stress (cell pressure), σ_3 (kN/m^2)	Principal stress difference, $\sigma_1 - \sigma_3$ $= (\sigma'_1 - \sigma'_3)$ (kN/m^2)	Pore pressure, u (kN/m^2)
(a)	(b)	(c)
600	0	0
	152	72
	256	136
	280	192
	328	256
	336 (failure)	296

would fail, if after isotropic consolidation at a cell pressure
of 600 kN/m² it is sheared under conditions of full drainage
with zero back pressure.

(iii) Similarly, find the effect on the maximum principal stress
at failure if the consolidation and shearing stages of (ii) are
each carried out against a back pressure of 200 kN/m².

(i) The coordinates of the effective stress points are

$$\frac{\sigma'_1 + \sigma'_3}{2} = \frac{\sigma_1 + \sigma_3}{2} - u \qquad \text{(abscissa)}$$

and

$$\frac{\sigma'_1 - \sigma'_3}{2} = \frac{\sigma_1 - \sigma_3}{2} \qquad \text{(ordinate)}$$

Table 4.11B

Minor effective principal stress $\sigma'_3 = \sigma_3 - u$ (kN/m^2)	Major effective principal stress, $(\sigma'_1 - \sigma'_3) + \sigma'_3$ $= \sigma'_1 (kN/m^2)$	$\dfrac{\sigma_1 + \sigma_3}{2} - u$ $= \dfrac{\sigma'_1 + \sigma'_3}{2}$ (kN/m^2)	$\dfrac{\sigma'_1 - \sigma'_3}{2}$ (kN/m^2)
(d)	(e)	(f)	(g)
600	600	600	0
528	680	604	76
464	720	592	128
408	688	548	140
344	672	508	164
304	640	472	168

These are evaluated in Table 4.11B and are plotted in Fig. 4.11.

(ii) For a normally consolidated saturated clay, the effective
stress point failure envelope will pass through the origin (i.e. $c = 0$)
and through the failure point of (i) above. This is drawn in Fig. 4.11.

The fully drained test, with zero back pressure, will have a
stress path moving along the horizontal axis to (600, 0 kN/m²) and
then inclined from this point at 45° to the horizontal axis. This is
also shown on Fig. 4.11. The line meets the failure envelope at
point (935, 335 kN/m²). Hence

$$\frac{(\sigma'_1 + \sigma'_3)_f}{2} = 935 \qquad \frac{(\sigma'_1 - \sigma'_3)_f}{2} = 335$$

100

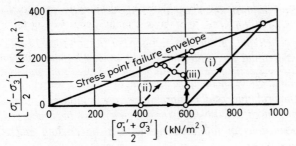

(i) Consolidated undrained test
(ii) Fully drained test - zero back pressure
(iii) Fully drained test - 200 kN/m² back pressure

Fig. 4.11

From which

$$(\sigma'_1 + \sigma'_3)_f = 1870 \qquad (\sigma'_1 - \sigma'_3)_f = 670$$
$$2\sigma'_{1f} = 2540$$

The maximum effective principal stress at failure is 1270 kN/m² and $\sigma'_{3f} = 600$ kN/m² (check = cell pressure).

(iii) For the specimen subjected to a back pressure of 200 kN/m², the stress path moves along the horizontal axis to (400, 0 kN/m²), and then is inclined at 45° to the horizontal axis. The point of intersection with the failure envelope has coordinates

$$\frac{(\sigma'_1 + \sigma'_3)_f}{2} = 625 \text{ kN/m}^2$$

and

$$\frac{(\sigma'_1 - \sigma'_3)_f}{2} = 225 \text{ kN/m}^2$$

From which

$$\sigma'_{1f} = 850 \text{ kN/m}^2 \quad \text{and} \quad \sigma'_{3f} = 400 \text{ kN/m}^2$$

(check = cell pressure − back pressure).

The maximum principal stress at failure is hence reduced by $1270 − 850 = 420$ kN/m².

4.12 *For the test described in Table 4.11A, the water content at failure was found to be 20%. Plot a σ_1' versus $\sigma_3'\sqrt{2}$ stress path for the specimen and, on the assumption that the soil tested behaved in a purely frictional way, determine:*

(i)   *the angle of shearing resistance;*
(ii)   *the probable axial compressive stress at failure if, after consolidation to 600 kN/m², the specimen had been sheared under conditions of full drainage with σ_1 increasing and σ_3 held constant;*
(iii) *the value of effective lateral stress at which failure would have occurred, if shearing had been effected, with full drainage, by reducing the cell pressure whilst maintaining the axial effective stress at 600 kN/m²;*
(iv) *the cell pressure at which consolidation would have to be carried out to produce failure at a water content of 20% by the application of an increasing axial stress under conditions of full drainage.*

From the previous problem:

Table 4.12

σ_1' (kN/m²)	600	680	720	688	672	640
σ_3' (kN/m²)	600	528	464	408	344	304
$\sigma_3'\sqrt{2}$(kN/m²)	849	747	656	577	486	430

In Fig. 4.12 the values of σ_1' are plotted against $\sigma_3'\sqrt{2}$ (line **PS**). The point S (430, 640) represents failure, and hence lies on a failure envelope passing through the origin of axes (purely frictional behaviour). The line OP connects points representing all-round stresses.

(i) From the Mohr circle construction:

$$\frac{\sigma_1'}{\sigma_3'} = \frac{1 + \sin\phi'}{1 - \sin\phi'} \quad \text{at failure}$$

Point S has

$$\sigma_1' = 640 \text{ kN/m}^2 \quad \text{and} \quad \sigma_3' = 304 \text{ kN/m}^2$$

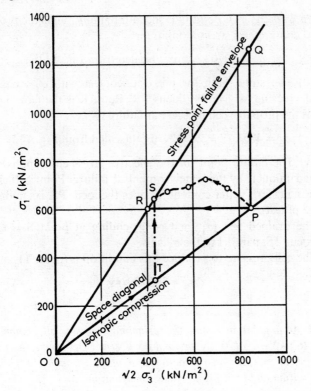

Fig. 4.12

Thus

$$\frac{640}{304} = \frac{1 + \sin \phi'}{1 - \sin \phi'} \quad \text{and} \quad \phi' = 20{\cdot}85° = 20° \, 51'$$

Alternatively, if θ is the slope of the failure envelope

$$\phi' = \sin^{-1}\left(\frac{\sqrt{2} \times \tan \theta - 1}{\sqrt{2} \times \tan \theta + 1}\right)$$

$$\tan \theta = 1190/800 \quad \text{(from Fig. 4.12)}$$

Hence

$$\phi' = 20{\cdot}83° = 20° \, 50'$$

(ii) The stress path for the drained test with $\sigma_3' = $ constant, is

103

given by locus PQ. Point Q is the failure point. Thus the probable axial compressive stress at failure is

$$\sigma_1' = 1270 \text{ kN/m}^2 \quad \text{(scaled from Fig. 4.12)}$$

(iii) The stress path for the drained test with $\sigma_1' = $ constant, σ_3' decreasing, is given by locus PR. Point R is the failure point. Thus the probable cell pressure at failure is

$$\sigma_3' = 405/\sqrt{2} = 286 \text{ kN/m}^2 \quad \text{(scaled from Fig. 4.12)}$$

(iv) The failure point on the effective stress envelope is determined uniquely by the water content at failure. Point S therefore represents 20% water content (as does the locus PS, i.e. undrained stage of test).

The drained test (σ_1' increasing) ending at point S is shown by locus TS, parallel to the σ_1' axis.

The cell pressure to produce this condition is (point T)

$$\sigma_3' = 300 \text{ kN/m}^2$$

4.13 *At a point in a soil the principal stresses, all compressive, are 160 kN/m², 120 kN/m² and 65 kN/m². Determine the normal and shear stresses on the octahedral plane through the point, by calculation and by a Mohr circle construction.*

Also obtain the octahedral shear stress by plotting deviatoric stress components in the octahedral plane.

By definition, the octahedral plane is inclined at equal angles to the three principal planes. Its direction cosines *l*, *m* and *n* are therefore equal and since

$$l^2 + m^2 + n^2 = 1$$
$$l = m = n = 1/\sqrt{3}$$

By calculation

For the octahedral plane, the normal stress σ_{oct} is given by

$$\sigma_{\text{oct}} = \tfrac{1}{3}(\sigma_1 + \sigma_2 + \sigma_3) = \tfrac{1}{3}(160 + 120 + 65) = 115 \text{ kN/m}^2$$

The octahedral shear stress τ_{oct} is given by

$$\tau_{\text{oct}} = \tfrac{1}{3}[(\sigma_1 - \sigma_2)^2 + (\sigma_2 - \sigma_3)^2 + (\sigma_3 - \sigma_1)^2]^{1/2}$$
$$= \tfrac{1}{3}[40^2 + 55^2 + (-95)^2]^{1/2} = 39 \text{ kN/m}^2$$

Alternatively

$$\tau_{oct} = [\tfrac{1}{3}(\sigma_1^2 + \sigma_2^2 + \sigma_3^2) - \sigma_{oct}^2]^{1/2}$$
$$= [\tfrac{1}{3}(160^2 + 120^2 + 65^2) - 115^2]^{1/2} = 39 \text{ kN/m}^2$$

By Mohr circle construction
Refer to Fig. 4.13A.

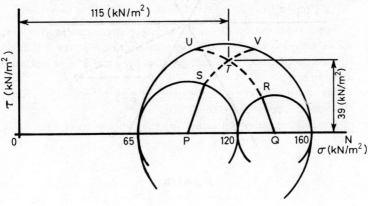

Fig. 4.13A

Draw the three circles shown, using pairs of the normal stresses in turn.

The octahedral plane is inclined at $\cos^{-1}(\sqrt{\tfrac{1}{3}})$ to the three principal planes, i.e. at $54° 44' 08''$.

At P set off angle $(2 \times 54° 44' 08'')$ clockwise from PO, giving point S.

At Q set off the same angle anti-clockwise from QN giving point R.

With centre P and radius PR draw arc RU.

With centre Q and radius QS draw arc SV.

The intersection T gives the values of the octahedral normal and shear stresses, i.e. 115 and 39 kN/m^2.

Deviatoric stress plot
The deviatoric stress components are $\sigma_1 - \sigma_{oct}$, $\sigma_2 - \sigma_{oct}$ and $\sigma_3 - \sigma_{oct}$. Hence their values are $160 - 115 = 45$, $120 - 115 = 5$, and $65 - 115 = -50$ kN/m^2 respectively.

105

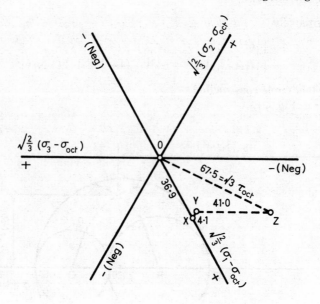

Fig. 4.13B

These values, each multiplied by the factor $(\frac{2}{3})^{1/2}$ ($= 0.82$), are plotted in Fig. 4.13B in their appropriate directions as shown such that

$$OX = 0.82 \times 45 = 36.9 \text{ kN/m}^2$$
$$XY = 0.82 \times 5 = 4.1 \text{ kN/m}^2$$
$$YZ = 0.82 \times -50 = -41.0 \text{ kN/m}^2$$

By scaling $OZ = 67.5 \text{ kN/m}^2$. It can be shown that $OZ = \tau_{oct}\sqrt{3}$, hence

$$\tau_{oct} = 67.5/\sqrt{3} = 39 \text{ kN/m}^2$$

4.14 *A cohesionless soil tested in triaxial compression failed under effective stresses $\sigma'_1 = 738$ kN/m² and $\sigma'_2 = \sigma'_3 = 200$ kN/m². Plot this stress condition on a σ'_1 versus $\sigma'_3\sqrt{2}$ coordinate system and from this derive the Mohr-Coulomb boundaries on the octahedral plane passing through the stressed point.*

106

Calculate the octahedral normal and shearing stresses and show
how a plot of the deviatoric components of stress on the octahedral
plane accords with the failure condition and the value of the octahedral
shear stress at failure.

Will failure occur under the stress systems of Table 4.14?

Table 4.14

Stress system	kN/m^2		
	σ'_1	σ'_2	σ'_3
(a)	748	240	150
(b)	238	500	400
(c)	338	200	600

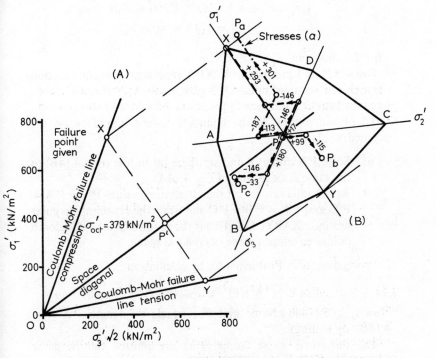

Fig. 4.14A, B

Refer to Fig. 4.14A.

On axes σ'_1 and $\sigma'_3\sqrt{2}$ plot the failure point $\sigma'_1 = 738$ kN/m², $\sigma'_3\sqrt{2} = 200\sqrt{2} = 283$ kN/m². This determines point X.

Since the soil is cohesionless, the stress point failure envelope will pass through the origin O. For envelope OX (see Problem 4.12)

$$\phi' = \sin^{-1}\left(\frac{\sqrt{2}\times\tan\theta - 1}{\sqrt{2}\times\tan\theta + 1}\right) = \sin^{-1}\left(\frac{\sqrt{2(738/283)} - 1}{\sqrt{2(738/283)} + 1}\right)$$

$$= 35°$$

For $\sigma'_3 > \sigma'_1$ failure occurs when

$$\sigma'_1 = \frac{1 - \sin\phi'}{1 + \sin\phi'}\sigma'_3 = 0\cdot271\,\sigma'_3$$

This is plotted as line OY, i.e. with a slope of $0\cdot271/\sqrt{2} = 0\cdot19{:}1$. Fix point P′ at the mean all round stress, i.e. at

$$\tfrac{1}{3}(\sigma'_1 + \sigma'_2 + \sigma'_3) = \tfrac{1}{3}(738 + 200 + 200)$$
$$= 379 \text{ kN/m}^2 = \sigma'_{\text{oct}}$$

Thus for this point $\sigma'_1 = 379$ kN/m² $= \sigma'_2 = \sigma'_3$.

Draw XP′ and produce to Y. XP′Y represents a normal section through the required octahedral plane, and X, Y denote Mohr–Coulomb stress conditions.

To obtain a view of the complete failure boundary on the octahedral plane:

(i)　Scale P′X and P′Y and set these off in line (Fig. 4.14B) to the same scale as that of Fig. 4.14A.

(ii)　At 60° intervals set off the alternating values P′Y = P′A = P′D and P′X = P′B = P′C and draw the resultant irregular hexagon XABYCDX. This is the required Mohr–Coulomb failure envelope on the octahedral plane.

Proceeding as in Problem 4.13, by calculation

$$\sigma'_{\text{oct}} = 379 \text{ kN/m}^2 \qquad \tau_{\text{oct}} = 254 \text{ kN/m}^2$$

Now $\tau_{\text{oct}}\sqrt{3} = 440$ kN/m² and this equals the length P′X (Fig. 4.14B – by scaling).

The deviatoric stress components are plotted on the same figure with a scale factor of $(\tfrac{2}{3})^{1/2}$, giving vector lengths of

108

$$(\tfrac{2}{3})^{1/2}(738 - 379) = 293 \text{ kN/m}^2$$
$$(\tfrac{2}{3})^{1/2}(200 - 379) = -146 \text{ kN/m}^2$$
$$(\tfrac{2}{3})^{1/2}(200 - 379) = -146 \text{ kN/m}^2$$

These produce a resultant coinciding with point X, thus proving the condition of failure.

Other stress condition (Table 4.14)

By calculation, each combination of principal effective stresses has $\sigma'_{oct} = 379 \text{ kN/m}^2$. The point P' of Fig. 4.14A therefore applies for each stress system and hence the same failure boundary (Fig. 4.14B) will be applicable.

Using the methods described earlier, the deviatoric stress component vectors are plotted for each stress system with the results shown in Fig. 4.14B.

Stress system (*a*) gives an octahedral shear stress P'P$_a$ lying beyond the failure boundary and hence denotes a failure condition, whereas (*b*) and (*c*) represent conditions of safety against shear failure (octahedral shear stresses P'P$_b$ and P'P$_c$ respectively).

4.15 *A sample of saturated clay is normally consolidated under isotropic conditions in a triaxial cell and is then sheared by applying an axial load increment. If the cell pressure is maintained at 300 kN/m² and the soil's critical state parameters are* $\Gamma = 2.41$, $\lambda = 0.13$, $M = 0.92$ *with* $N = 2.60$, *determine the values of the effective minor principal stress, the effective major principal stress and the void ratio at failure when shearing is carried out under (a) drained conditions, and (b) undrained conditions.*

For this soil, the normal consolidation curve is described by

$$v_0 = N - \lambda \log_e p'_0$$

in which v_0 is the specific volume under isotropic consolidation pressure p'_0; N and λ are soil constants. Hence

$$v_0 = 2.60 - 0.13 \log_e 300$$
$$= 1.86$$

But $v_0 = 1 + e_0$, so $e_0 = 0.86$, the void ratio prior to shearing.

(a) Drained second stage

The stress path can be defined by the quantities mean effective principal stress (abscissa) and maximum effective principal stress difference. For the triaxial test these are $p' = \frac{1}{3}(\sigma'_1 + 2\sigma'_3)$ and $q' = (\sigma'_1 - \sigma'_3)$ respectively.

In a drained test stage, σ'_3 remains constant, and the stress path therefore rises at a slope of 3:1 as shown in Fig. 4.15, to end

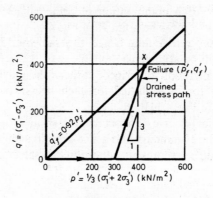

Fig. 4.15

on the failure envelope (critical state line) which follows the equation

$$q'_f = M\,p'_f \qquad \text{(1st critical state equation)}$$

Failure therefore takes place under stresses represented by point X. In the problem: $q'_f = 0.92p'_f$ but

$$p'_f = 300 + q'_f/3 \quad \text{or} \quad q'_f = 3p'_f - 900$$

Hence

$$0 = 2.08\,p'_f - 900 \text{ and } p'_f = 433 \text{ kN/m}^2$$

from which

$$q'_f = 0.92 \times 433 = 398 \text{ kN/m}^2$$

Therefore

$$p'_f = \tfrac{1}{3}(\sigma'_1 + 2\sigma'_3)_f = 433 \quad \text{and} \quad q'_f = (\sigma'_1 - \sigma'_3)_f = 398$$

Solving:

$$\sigma'_{1f} = 699 \text{ kN/m}^2$$
$$\sigma'_{3f} = 300 \text{ kN/m}^2 \qquad \text{(Check – cell pressure)}$$

Also

$$v_f = \Gamma - \lambda \log_e p'_f \qquad \text{(2nd critical state equation)}$$

in which v_f is the specific volume at failure under mean effective stress p'_f, and Γ and λ are soil constants.

Thus

$$v_f = 2 \cdot 41 - 0 \cdot 13 \log_e 433 = 1 \cdot 62$$

from which the void ratio at failure is 0·62.

With drainage the soil thus fails at a void ratio of 0·62, under major and minor principal effective stresses of 699 and 300 kN/m^2 respectively.

(b) Undrained second stage

For a saturated soil there is no volume change and therefore the final void ratio is equal to the initial void ratio. Hence

$$\text{final void ratio} = 0 \cdot 86$$

From the second critical state equation

$$v_f = 1 \cdot 86 = 2 \cdot 41 - 0 \cdot 13 \log_e p'_f$$

thus

$$\log_e p'_f = \frac{2 \cdot 41 - 1 \cdot 86}{0 \cdot 13} \quad \text{and} \quad p'_f = 68 \cdot 8 \text{ kN/m}^2$$

From the first critical state equation

$$q'_f = 0 \cdot 92 \times 68 \cdot 8 = 63 \cdot 3 \text{ kN/m}^2$$

Hence

$$(\sigma'_1 - \sigma'_3)_f = 63 \cdot 3 \quad \text{and} \quad \tfrac{1}{3}(\sigma'_1 + 2\sigma'_3)_f = 68 \cdot 8$$

from which

$$\sigma'_{1f} = 111 \text{ kN/m}^2 \qquad \sigma'_{3f} = 47 \cdot 7 \text{ kN/m}^2$$

Without drainage the soil thus fails at a void ratio of 0·86, under major and minor principal effective stresses of 111 and 48 kN/m² respectively. The pore water pressure at failure is hence $300 - 48 = 252$ kN/m², and the major total principal stress is $111 + 252 = 363$ kN/m².

4.16 *An embankment consists of clay fill for which $c' = 25$ kN/m² and $\phi' = 26°$ (from consolidated-undrained tests with pore-pressure measurement). The average bulk density of the fill is 1·9 Mg/m³. Estimate the shear strength of the material on a horizontal plane at a point 20 m below the surface of the embankment, if the pore pressure at this point is shown by a piezometer to be 180 kN/m².*

The unit weight of the fill is $1·90 \times 9·81$, or 18·64 kN/m³. At a depth of 20 m this causes a vertical pressure of $18·64 \times 20 = 373$ kN/m².

$$\text{Effective pressure } \sigma' = \sigma - u = 373 - 180$$
$$= 193 \text{ kN/m}^2$$
$$\text{Shear strength } s = 25 + 193 \tan 26°$$
$$= 25 + 193 \times 0·488$$
$$= 119 \text{ kN/m}^2$$

4.17 *A vane, $4\frac{1}{2}$ in. long, 3 in. in diameter, was pressed into soft clay at the bottom of a borehole. Torque was applied and gradually increased to 45 N m when failure took place. Find the shear strength of the clay on a horizontal plane.*

It is normally assumed that the shear stress is uniformly distributed over the surface of the cylinder sheared by the vane.

The torque resisted by the curved surface at failure is

$$\text{cohesion} \times \text{area} \times \text{moment arm} = c\pi dh \frac{d}{2} = \frac{c\pi d^2 h}{2}$$

Torque resisted by one end (uniform stress) is

$$\frac{c\pi d^3}{12}$$

Hence total resisting torque is

$$c\pi\left(\frac{d^2h}{2} + \frac{d^3}{6}\right)$$

The applied torque is equal to this at failure.
Here $h = 4\frac{1}{2}$ in. $= 114\cdot3$ mm; $d = 3$ in. $= 76\cdot2$ mm.
Using the metre as the unit of length,

$$T = c\pi\left(\frac{76\cdot2^2 \times 114\cdot3}{2} + \frac{76\cdot2^3}{6}\right) \times 10^{-9}$$
$$= 4\cdot06 \times 10^{-4}\, c\pi\ \text{Nm}$$

Equating this to 45 Nm we get

$$c = 35\,300\,\text{N/m}^2 \text{ or } 35\cdot3\,\text{kN/m}^2.$$

4.18 *An embankment is being constructed of soil whose properties are* $c' = 50\,kN/m^2$, $\phi' = 21°$ *(referred to effective stress) and* $\rho = 1\cdot6\,Mg/m^3$. *The pore-pressure parameters as found from triaxial tests are* $A = 0\cdot5$ *and* $B = 0\cdot9$. *Find the shear strength of the soil at the base of the embankment just after the height of fill has been raised from 3 m to 6 m. Assume that the dissipation of pore pressure during this stage of construction is negligible, and that the lateral pressure at any point is one-half of the vertical pressure.*

The relation between increase of pore pressure and increase of principal stresses is given by

$$\Delta u = B[\Delta\sigma_3 + A(\Delta\sigma_1 - \Delta\sigma_3)]$$
$\Delta\sigma_1$ = increase in vertical pressure due to 3 m of fill
$$= 3 \times 1\cdot6 \times 9\cdot81 = 47\ \text{kN/m}^2$$
$\Delta\sigma_3 = \dfrac{\Delta\sigma_1}{2}$ by assumption $= 23\cdot5\ \text{kN/m}^2$

Therefore

$$\Delta u = 0\cdot9(23\cdot5 + 0\cdot5 \times 23\cdot5) = 0\cdot9 \times 35\cdot3 = 32\ \text{kN/m}^2$$
Original pressure $= \sigma_1 = 3 \times 1\cdot6 \times 9\cdot81 = 47\ \text{kN/m}$

Therefore,

$$\text{Effective stress } \sigma' = \sigma_1 + \Delta\sigma_1 - \Delta u$$
$$= 47 + 47 - 32 = 62 \text{ kN/m}^2$$

$$\text{Shear strength} = c' + \sigma' \tan \phi'$$
$$= 50 + 62 \tan 21°$$
$$= 74 \text{ kN/m}^2$$

GROUP 2
Prevention of Instability

CHAPTER FIVE

Stability of slopes

The analysis of the stability of slopes in cohesive soil is generally based on the assumption of a cylindrical surface of rupture. The trace of such a surface on a cross-section is a circular arc. In order to find the most critical condition, that is, the surface which offers the least resistance to sliding, it is necessary to try several alternatives.

For any assumed slip surface the stability is usually analysed by the *method of slices*. When it can be assumed that $\phi = 0°$ (saturated clay under conditions of no drainage) a simpler analysis can be made. The *ϕ-circle method* is an alternative which can be used in certain simplified conditions.

For simple slopes in homogeneous soil *stability numbers* have been calculated from which the necessary results can be found without recourse to trial slip surfaces. Even in complicated problems stability numbers are often useful as a preliminary approximation. Stability numbers can be found from Table 5.2 and Fig. 5.9. The term γ in the expression for the stability number is the *unit weight*, that is the density $\times$ 9·81.

Not all potential or actual failures involve circular arcs. A few calculations towards the end of the chapter show how these other failures may be handled. Analyses may be performed in terms of total stresses or effective stresses, the latter requiring a knowledge of pore pressures whilst the former are based on the assumption that the site conditions produce pore pressures similar to those generated by the test methods used in measuring undrained stress parameters. For clays, these alternative forms of calculation may be used to estimate short- and long-term stability, respectively.

The methods used in this chapter are often applied to investigation of the stability of existing slopes or to the study of the causes of slips which have occurred in order that suitable remedial measures may be adopted. When applied to design, however, it is necessary to decide on a minimum factor of safety. This is often assumed to be 1·5 or even less, in order to keep down the cost of earthworks. Such a low factor of safety can be accepted only if the soil properties can be accurately predicted and the analysis very carefully carried out.

5.1 *Fig. 5.1 shows the original cross-section of a railway cutting in which a slip has occurred. The soil is clay of average density 1·73 Mg/m³. Borehole investigations show that the surface of the slip approximates closely to a circular arc AE of radius 20 m. Estimate the mean shear strength of the clay along the surface AE when the soil is about to slip. Take* $\phi = 0$ *and assume a tension crack DE, 2 m deep.*

The area of the disturbed soil ABCDE, measured by planimeter, is found to be 104·6 m² The centroid G of this area, located by the cardboard template method, is at $d = 4·25$ m horizontally from the vertical through O.

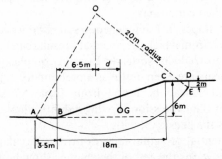

Fig. 5.1

The mass of a volume of cross-section ABCDE and unit thickness is 1·73 × 104·6 = 181 Mg and its weight 181 × 9·81 = 1776 kN.

For equilibrium, disturbing moment = resisting moment (moments about centre of rotation O).

Therefore 1776 × 4·25 = average cohesion c × length of arc AE × radius OE.

The angle AOE measures 81°, therefore the length of the arc AE is (81/180) (π × 20) = 28·28 m.

Therefore 1776 × 4·25 = c × 28·28 × 20, whence $c = 13·4$ kN/m².

5.2 *The slope of a cutting, 12 m deep, is 1·6 vertical to 1 horizontal. The soil is saturated clay of density 1·92 Mg/m³ and cohesion 50 kN/m². Find the factor of safety against circular slip, taking* $\phi_u = 0°$.

With the soil behaving in a purely cohesive way in the strength test, the calculation will reflect the immediate and intermediate-term stability. The analysis will be a total stress one.

To find the most dangerous circle, the factor of safety should be calculated for several trial slip surfaces and the least value taken.

In this case, with homogeneous soil, an approximate position for the centre of the most critical circle can be obtained by using the data in Table 5.2.

$$\text{Slope angle} = i = \tan^{-1}(1·6) = 58°$$

From the table, by interpolation between 45° and 60° the angles for setting out the centre of the critical circle are $\psi = 35°$ and $\theta = 71°$. The resulting slip surface, passing through the toe, is shown in Fig. 5.2. The radius R of the curve measures 18·0 m.

Allowance should be made for a tension crack DE of depth

$$\frac{2c}{\gamma} = \frac{2 \times 50}{1·92 \times 9·81} = 5·31 \text{ m}$$

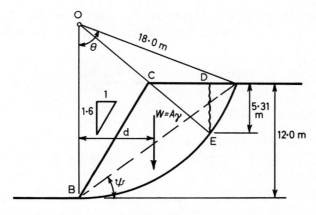

Fig. 5.2

The presence of this crack invalidates the direct use of the table in solving the problem.

The resulting mass of disturbed soil is BCDE and its area A measures 98 m². The distance d of the centroid from the vertical through 0 is 8·1 m.

The angle BOE measures 47°, therefore the length L of the arc BE is $(47/180)(\pi \times 18·0) = 14·8$ m.

The factor of safety F for this circle is

$$\frac{\text{maximum resisting moment}}{\text{disturbing moment}} = \frac{cLR}{A\gamma d}$$

$$= \frac{50 \times 14·8 \times 18·0}{98 \times 1·92 \times 9·81 \times 8·1} = 0·89$$

Although other trial surfaces would have to be analysed to find the minimum factor of safety, the above calculation shows the slope to be unsafe ($F < 1·0$) and redesign would be needed.

5.3 *The 12 m deep cutting of Problem 5.2 is redesigned to include a berm as shown in Fig. 5.3. Find the new factor of safety.*

Here only experience can guide us on where to take our trial slip surfaces. As a start take O_1, vertically above the approximate mid-point of the berm, giving the slip surface shown in Fig. 5.3. Measure the radius R, angle subtended θ (allowing for tension cracks to the depth calculated in the previous problem), area A and distance d of the centroid from the vertical through O_1. Repeat the process for several other slip surfaces. For each arc the factor of safety

$$F = \frac{\text{resisting moment}}{\text{disturbing moment}} = \frac{c \times \text{length of arc} \times R}{W \times d}$$

Length of arc $= R\theta$

$W =$ weight of material tending to slip $= 1·92 \times 9·81\ A$
$$= 18·8\ A\ \text{kN}(A\ \text{in m}^2)$$

Then

$$F = \frac{cR^2\theta}{Wd} = \frac{50\ R^2\theta}{18·8\ Ad}$$

Table 5.2 *Data for critical circles*

Slope i	Angle of friction ϕ	Angles for setting out centre of critical circle		Depth factor D	Stability No. $\dfrac{c}{F_\gamma H}$
		ψ	θ		
90	0	47·6	30·2	—	0·261
	5	50·0	28·0	—	0·239
	10	53·0	27·0	—	0·218
	15	56·0	26·0	—	0·199
	20	58·0	24·0	—	0·182
	25	60·0	22·0	—	0·166
75	0	41·8	51·8	—	0·219
	5	45·0	50·0	—	0·195
	10	47·5	47·0	—	0·173
	15	50·0	46·0	—	0·152
	20	53·0	44·0	—	0·134
	25	56·0	44·0	—	0·117
60	0	35·3	70·8	—	0·191
	5	38·5	69·0	—	0·162
	10	41·0	66·0	—	0·138
	15	44·0	63·0	—	0·116
	20	46·5	60·4	—	0·097
	25	50·0	60·0	—	0·079
45	0	(28·2)	(89·4)	(1·062)	(0·170)
	5	31·2	84·2	1·026	0·136
	10	34·0	79·4	1·006	0·108
	15	36·1	74·4	1·001	0·083
	20	38·0	69·0	—	0·062
	25	40·0	62·0	—	0·044
30	0	(20·0)	(106·8)	(1·301)	(0·156)
	5	(23·0)	(96·0)	(1·161)	(0·110)
	5	20·0	106·0	1·332	0·110
	10	25·0	88·0	1·092	0·075
	15	27·0	78·0	1·038	0·046
	20	28·0	62·0	1·003	0·025
	25	29·0	50·0	—	0·009
15	0	(10·6)	(121·4)	(2·117)	(0·145)
	5	(12·5)	(94·0)	(1·549)	(0·068)
	5	11·0	95·0	1·697	0·070
	10	(14·0)	(68·0)	(1·222)	(0·023)
	10	14·0	68·0	1·222	0·023

Note. Figures in brackets are for most dangerous circle through the toe when a more dangerous circle exists which passes below the toe.

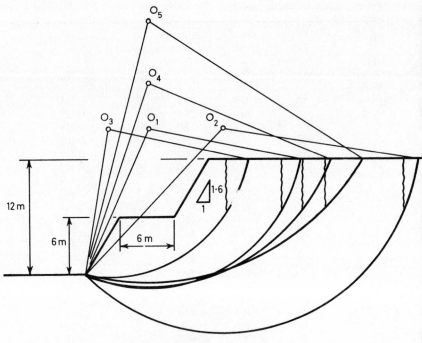

Fig. 5.3

If θ is measured in degrees instead of radians

$$F = \frac{50\,R^2}{18\cdot8\,Ad} \times \frac{\theta}{57\cdot3} = \frac{0\cdot0464\,R^2\theta}{Ad}$$

The results are shown in Table 5.3.

Table 5.3

Slip surface No.	Area A (m^2)	Radius, R (m)	Angle subtended, θ (deg)	Distance of centroid, d (m)	Factor of safety, F
1	169	16·8	84	4·9	1·33
2	449	21·5	111	3·4	1·56
3	78·4	15·5	65	6·2	1·49
4	189	21·3	70·5	6·1	1·29
5	206	27·4	59	7·4	1·35

Of the above, the lowest factor of safety is about 1·3 (for slip surface No. 4). It is possible that there may be a worse slip surface, and others should be tried. The assumption has been made that the worst slip surface passes through the toe of the slope. This may not be so, unless there is a strong stratum just below the bottom of the cutting which will prevent the slip extending below this level. The redesign of the slope has therefore produced a much improved factor of safety.

5.4 *A bank, 8 m high, has a slope of 30°. The soil has a density of 1·9 Mg/m³, cohesion of 14·5 kN/m², and angle of shearing resistance of 15°. Find the factor of safety for the trial slip surface shown in Fig. 5.4.*

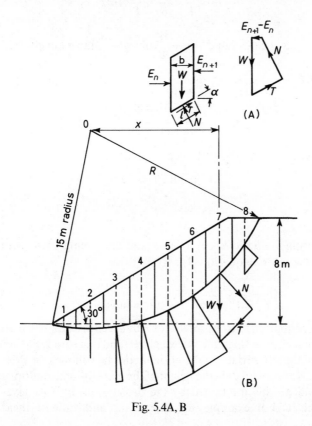

Fig. 5.4A, B

For this problem the method of slices is the most suitable. Consider unit length of slope. Divide the slip area into eight slices of equal width. The total width of the slip area scales 16·6 m, hence the width of the slices is 16·6/8 or 2·075 m. The force polygon for a slice is as shown in Fig. 5.4A. The interslice forces are indeterminate, but to simplify the analysis it may be assumed that they act horizontally.

Resolving vertically,

$$W = N \cos \alpha + T \sin \alpha$$

But
$$T = sl/F$$

The normal pressure on the base of the strip is

$$\sigma = \frac{N}{l} = \frac{W}{b} - \frac{s}{F} \tan \alpha$$

$$s = c + \sigma \tan \phi = c + \frac{W}{b} \tan \phi - \frac{s}{F} \tan \alpha \tan \phi$$

whence

$$s = \frac{c + \dfrac{W}{b} \tan \phi}{1 + (\tan \alpha \tan \phi)/F} \qquad (1)$$

Take moments about the centre of rotation O.

$$\Sigma W x = R \Sigma T = R \Sigma sl/F$$

Thus
$$F = \frac{R \Sigma sl}{\Sigma W x}$$

Putting $l = b \sec \alpha, x = R \sin \alpha$ and combining these with the expression for s (equation (1) above) gives:

$$F = \frac{1}{\Sigma W \sin \alpha} \Sigma \frac{(cb + W \tan \phi) \sec \alpha}{1 + (\tan \alpha \tan \phi)/F} \qquad (2)$$

This equation must be solved for F by successive approximations.

For each slice calculate the weight W and measure α, the inclination of the slip surface to the horizontal. The volume of a slice, 1 m thick, is approximately the height of the mid-ordinate multiplied by the width. This multiplied by the density and by 9·81 gives the weight W. For example, for slice 5, the mid-ordinate measures

Table 5.4A

(1) Slice No.	(2) $\alpha\,(deg)$	(3) $\sin\alpha$	(4) Height of slice, $y\,(m)$	(5) Weight, $W\,(kN)$	(6) $W\sin\alpha$ (kN)	(7) $cb + W\tan\phi$ (kN)	(8) $\dfrac{1+(\tan\alpha\tan\phi)/F}{\sec\alpha}$ $(F=1\cdot4)$	(9) $\dfrac{Col.(7)}{Col.(8)}$
1	-6	$-0\cdot105$	$0\cdot72$	$27\cdot9$	$-2\cdot9$	$37\cdot6$	$0\cdot975$	$38\cdot6$
2	0	0	2.10	$81\cdot2$	0	$51\cdot8$	$1\cdot000$	$51\cdot8$
3	$+8\cdot5$	$+0\cdot148$	$3\cdot21$	$124\cdot2$	$+18\cdot4$	$63\cdot4$	$1\cdot017$	$62\cdot3$
4	$+16\cdot25$	$+0\cdot280$	$3\cdot93$	$152\cdot0$	$+42\cdot6$	$70\cdot8$	$1\cdot014$	$69\cdot8$
5	$+25$	$+0\cdot423$	$4\cdot29$	$165\cdot9$	$+70\cdot2$	$74\cdot5$	$0\cdot987$	$75\cdot5$
6	$+33\cdot5$	$+0\cdot552$	$4\cdot41$	$170\cdot6$	$+94\cdot2$	$75\cdot8$	$0\cdot940$	$80\cdot6$
7	$+44$	$+0\cdot695$	$3\cdot93$	$152\cdot0$	$+105\cdot6$	$70\cdot8$	$0\cdot852$	$83\cdot1$
8	$+55$	$+0\cdot819$	$1\cdot74$	$67\cdot3$	$+55\cdot1$	$48\cdot1$	$0\cdot730$	$65\cdot9$
					$\Sigma = +383\cdot2$			$\Sigma = 527\cdot6$

4·29 m and the weight is therefore $4·29 \times 2·075 \times 1·90 \times 9·81 = 166$ kN. The angle α for this slice is $25°$. The weights are assumed to act at the centre of each slice, except for the end ones which are nearly triangular in shape. Some values of α will be negative.

The calculations are best set out in tabular form (Table 5.4A). Assuming a likely value of F in the term $(\tan \alpha \tan \phi)/F$ calculate F from equation (2). If this does not agree with the assumed value a closer approximation can be made.

In column (8) of Table 5.4A, F is assumed to be 1·4.

Summing columns (6) and (9) we get

$$F = 527·6/383·2 = 1·38,$$

which is near enough to the assumed value of 1·4.

In the *Swedish method* the procedure is simplified by assuming that the inter-slice forces cancel out and so may be ignored. The error in the value of F deduced in this way is slightly on the safe side.

Here again the calculations are set out in tabular form. Calculate the weights of the slices as before. For each slice draw a force triangle as shown in Fig. 5.4B to determine the tangential and normal components T and N. The values of these are entered in the table, with due regard to the sign of T. Alternatively the components can be calculated from $T = W \sin \alpha$ and $N = W \cos \alpha$.

Table 5.4B

	Forces in kilonewtons		
Slice No.	Weight W (as in Table 5.4A)	Tangential component T	Normal component N
1	27·9	− 3	28
2	81·2	0	81
3	124·2	+ 18	123
4	152·0	+ 43	146
5	165·9	+ 70	150
6	170.6	+ 94	142
7	152·0	+ 106	109
8	67·3	+ 55	39
		$\Sigma = + 383$	$\Sigma = 818$

Total disturbing force along any slip surface

$$T = 383 \text{ kN}$$

Maximum resisting force = cohesive resistance + frictional resistance

$$= cL + N \tan \phi$$

where L = length of arc = radius × angle subtended

$$= 15 \times 76 \times \frac{\pi}{180} = 19 \cdot 9 \text{ m}$$

Therefore,

$$\text{Resisting force} = 14 \cdot 5 \times 19 \cdot 9 + 818 \times 0 \cdot 268$$
$$= 289 + 219$$
$$= 508 \text{ kN}$$

These forces act at the same distance from O, thus the ratio of the resisting moment to the disturbing moment is the same as that of the corresponding forces.

$$\text{Factor of safety} = \frac{508}{383} = 1 \cdot 33$$

This is, of course, only the factor of safety for one particular slip surface. Several others should be tried in order to find the minimum factor of safety.

5.5 *The section of a cutting, 14 m deep, slope $1\frac{1}{2}$ horizontal to 1 vertical is as shown in Fig. 5.5. For a depth of 5 m below the surface, the soil has the following properties: density = 1·80 Mg/m³, c' = 25 kN/m², ϕ' = 10°. Below this, the soil properties are density = 1·95 Mg/m³, c' = 34 kN/m², ϕ' = 24°. The soil is saturated. The pore-water pressure on the slip surface, found from a flow-net investigation, is represented by the ordinates from the slip surface to the dotted curve. For the given trial slip surface, find the factor of safety of the slope under these conditions of steady seepage.*

The procedure is similar to that of the previous problem, but here there are two strata with different properties. Also, the pore-water pressure reduces the normal forces effective in mobilising friction.

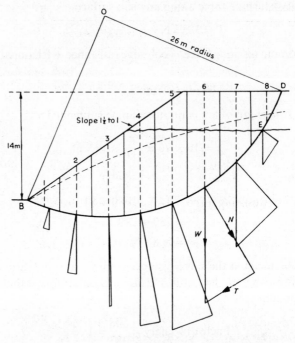

Fig. 5.5

The Bishop method of analysis leads to the equation

$$F = \frac{1}{\sum W \sin \alpha} \sum \frac{\{c'b + (W - ub) \tan \phi'\} \sec \alpha}{1 + (\tan \alpha \tan \phi')/F}$$

and the procedure is similar to that for the previous problem.

In the following solution an alternative method is employed, in which inter-slice forces are neglected.

The section is divided into eight slices. The total length scales 34·5 m, therefore the width of each slice is 34·5/8 or 4·31 m.

For example, consider slice No. 6.

The mid-ordinate of the strip scales 5·0 m in the upper stratum and 7·4 m in the lower.

$$W = 5 \times 4·31 \times 1·80 \times 9·81 + 7·4 \times 4·31 \times 1·95 \times 9·81$$
$$= 991 \text{ kN}$$

The force triangle gives $N = 855$ kN and $T = 515$ kN.

Table 5.5

		Forces in kilonewtons			
		Components			Effective
				Pore-water	normal
Slice	Weight	Tangential	Normal	force	force
No.	W	T	N	U	$N' = N - U$
1	196	− 55	180	90	90
2	519	− 90	510	225	285
3	781	15	780	310	470
4	965	180	945	365	580
5	1084	370	1020	385	635
6	991	515	855	390	465
7	721	500	535	305	230
					2755
8	302	250	175	75	100
		1685			

The ordinate to the dotted curve, representing the pore pressure head at the centre of the slice, measures 7·65 m.

Therefore the pressure = $7·65 \times 1·0 \times 9·81 = 75·0$ kN/m².

Length of chord of surface of sliding = 5·2 m.

Therefore pore-water force $U = 75·0 \times 5·2 = 390$ kN.

Effective normal force $N' = N - U = 855 - 390 = 465$ kN.

By using similar procedures for the remaining slices, Table 5.5 is completed.

Total disturbing force along the slip surface $\Sigma T = 1685$ kN.

Maximum resisting force $= C' + \Sigma N' \tan \phi'$

By measuring subtended angles, the arc DE is found to be 5·43 m and the arc BE = 35·6 m.

Therefore,
$$C' = 25 \times 5·43 + 34 \times 35·6$$
$$= 1346 \text{ kN}$$

For most of strip 8, $\phi' = 10°$; for the others, $\phi' = 24°$

$$\Sigma N' \tan \phi' = 2755 \tan 24° + 100 \tan 10°$$
$$= 2755 \times 0·445 + 100 \times 0·176$$
$$= 1244 \text{ kN}$$

129

Factor of safety

$$\frac{C' + \Sigma N' \tan \phi'}{\Sigma T} = \frac{1346 + 1244}{1685}$$

$$= 1 \cdot 54$$

Again, this is the factor of safety for one particular assumed circle. To find the minimum factor of safety several other circles must be similarly analysed.

5.6 *A vertical cut is to be made in clay soil for which tests give $\rho = 1 \cdot 76$ Mg/m³, $c = 36$ kN/m² and $\phi = 0°$. Find the maximum height for which the cut may be temporarily unsupported.*

Referring to Table 5.2, for $\phi = 0°$ and $i = 90°$, the stability number

$$N = \frac{c}{F \gamma H} = 0 \cdot 26$$

In this problem, $\gamma = 1 \cdot 76 \times 9 \cdot 81 = 17 \cdot 27$ kN/m³, and for the maximum unsupported height $F = 1$.
Therefore

$$H = \frac{c}{\gamma N} = \frac{36}{17 \cdot 27 \times 0 \cdot 26} = 8 \cdot 0 \text{ m}$$

With a factor of safety of, say, $1 \cdot 5$, the maximum unsupported height would be

$$\frac{8 \cdot 0}{1 \cdot 5} = 5 \cdot 3 \text{ m}$$

5.7 *Site investigation has shown that a soil has the following properties: $c = 24$ kN/m², $\phi = 15°$, $\rho = 1 \cdot 95$ Mg/m³. A cutting is to be made in this soil with a slope of 30° to the horizontal and a depth of 16 m. It is required to find the factor of safety of the slope against slip. It can be assumed that friction and cohesion are mobilised to the same proportion of their ultimate values.*

If friction were fully mobilised, the resultant at any point on the slip circle would be at 15° to the normal. In this condition ($i = 30°$, $\phi = 15°$) the stability number, N, from Table 5.2 is $0 \cdot 046$.

This gives a factor of safety, F, with respect to cohesive resistance

$$F = \frac{c}{N\gamma H} = \frac{24}{0.046 \times 1.95 \times 9.81 \times 16} = 1.7$$

The value of F to be used is less than this since friction is not fully mobilised. It must be found by trial, since the extent of mobilised resistance is unknown.

Assume $F = 1.4$ for both cohesion and friction. The mobilised angle of friction ϕ_1, is given by

$$\tan \phi_1 = \tan 15°/1.4$$

or, since the angle is small

$$\phi_1 = \frac{15}{1.4} = 10.7°$$

By interpolating the values given in Table 5.2, for $\phi_1 = 10.7°$, the stability number N is 0.07.

Therefore

$$F = \frac{c}{N\gamma H} = \frac{24}{0.07 \times 1.95 \times 9.81 \times 16} = 1.12$$

Since this does not agree with the assumed value 1.4, a new value should be tried, say 1.25. Following the same procedure this gives a factor of safety of 1.24, which is sufficiently close to the assumed value to be considered correct.

5.8 *An earth dam, of height 25 m is constructed of soil of which the properties are: $\rho = 2.05$ Mg/m^3; $c = 44$ kN/m^2 and $\phi = 20°$. The faces of the dam are at $30°$ to the horizontal. The water in the reservoir is drawn off very rapidly so that there is no time for appreciable drainage of water from the dam itself. Find the factor of safety immediately after drawdown.*

Using the approximate method suggested by Taylor, this is the condition known as 'sudden drawdown'.

The disturbing force depends on the full bulk density, but the normal forces mobilising friction are reduced in the ratio $(\gamma - \gamma_w)/\gamma$ which is the same as $(\rho - \rho_w)/\rho$. This is equivalent to reducing

131

tan ϕ, or the angle ϕ itself if it is small, in that ratio. The stability equation can therefore be used if the value of ϕ is reduced to

$$\frac{20(2\cdot05 - 1\cdot00)}{2\cdot05} = 10° \text{ approx.}$$

For $\phi = 10°$ and $i = 30°$, $N = 0\cdot075$, from Table 5·2.
   Therefore the factor of safety

$$F = \frac{c}{N\gamma H} = \frac{44}{0\cdot075 \times 2\cdot05 \times 9\cdot81 \times 25}$$
$$= 1\cdot17$$

This is the factor of safety with respect to cohesion. The true factor of safety, assumed the same for both friction and cohesion will be a little less than this, probably about 1·1.

If $F = 1\cdot1$, the mobilised angle of friction would be $10/1\cdot1 = 9\cdot5°$. The data in Table 5·2 does not permit of a more accurate determination of F.

A factor of safety of 1·1 is very low, and some modification of the design would be advisable.

5.9 *A cutting of depth 11 m is to be made in soil of which the density is 1·84 Mg/m³ and the cohesion 40 kN/m². There is a hard stratum under the clay at 13 m below the original ground surface. Assuming $\phi = 0°$ and allowing for a factor of safety of 1·5, find the slope of the cutting.*

The depth of the critical circle is limited by the hard stratum below the clay.

$$\text{The } depth \; factor \; D = \frac{\text{depth of hard stratum}}{\text{depth of cutting}}$$
$$= \frac{13}{11} = 1\cdot2$$

The stability number $N = \dfrac{c}{F\gamma H} = \dfrac{40}{1\cdot5 \times 1\cdot84 \times 9\cdot81 \times 11} = 0\cdot134$

Using Taylor's stability curves (Fig. 5.9) for $D = 1\cdot2$ and $\phi = 0°$, the required slope i is found to be about 22°.

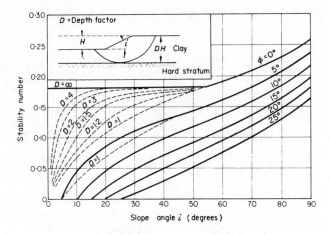

Fig. 5.9 Taylor's stability curves

5.10 *The section of an embankment is shown in Fig. 5.10A. For the given assumed slip surface determine the factor of safety with respect to cohesion, and also the true factor of safety assuming this to be the same for both cohesive and frictional resistance. Properties of soil:* $\rho = 1\cdot84 \ Mg/m^3$; $\phi = 17°$; $c = 15\cdot4 \ kN/m^2$. *Neglect the effect of tension cracks.*

For this problem, since conditions are relatively simple, the ϕ-circle method is suitable.

Angle AOD measures $75° = 1\cdot31$ radian.

Therefore arc AD $= 14\cdot6 \times 1\cdot31 = 19\cdot1$ m.

Area of ABD (by planimeter or by measurement) $= 57\cdot6 \ m^2$.

Its weight/unit length, W, is $57\cdot6 \times 1\cdot84 \times 9\cdot81 = 1040 \ kN$.

Replace cohesive force acting round arc AD by a force C acting parallel to chord AD and at a distance a from O such that

$$a = 14\cdot6 \times \frac{\text{arc AD}}{\text{chord AD}} = 14\cdot6 \times \frac{19\cdot1}{17\cdot8} = 15\cdot67 \ m$$

The centroid G of the area ABD is found by the cardboard template method.

Draw the ϕ-circle, centre O, of radius $14\cdot6 \sin 17°$ or $4\cdot27$ m.

From the intersection of the forces W and C draw a line tangent

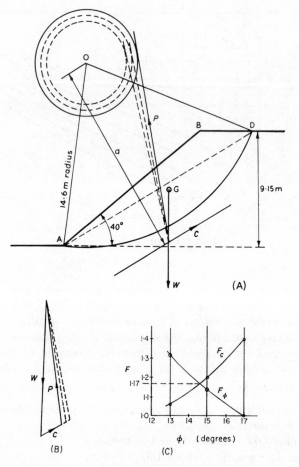

Fig. 5.10A, B, C

to the ϕ-circle. This represents the reaction P, which is the resultant of the normal and frictional forces on the surface AD.

Draw the force triangle to a large scale (Fig. 5.10B), then C scales 196 kN.

Unit cohesion mobilised $= 196/17\cdot8 = 11\cdot0$ kN/m^2.

Therefore the factor of safety with respect to cohesion $= 15\cdot4/11\cdot0 = 1\cdot4$.

To find the true factor of safety, assuming it the same for friction

Table 5.10

Mobilised friction angle ϕ_1 (deg.)	$R \sin \phi_1$ (m)	$F_\phi = \dfrac{\tan 17°}{\tan \phi_1}$	C (kN)	$c_1 = \dfrac{C}{17 \cdot 8}$ (kN/m^2)	$F_c = \dfrac{c}{c_1}$
17	4·27	1·00	196	11·0	1·40
15	3·78	1·14	228	12·8	1·20
13	3·28	1·32	260	14·6	1·05

as for cohesion, repeat the above construction for friction angles $\phi = 15°$ and $13°$. The relevant lines are shown in Fig. 5.10A. The results are as shown in Table 5.10.

Plot F_ϕ and F_c against ϕ_1 (Fig. 5.10C). The curves intersect at $F_\phi = F_c = 1 \cdot 17$. Hence the required factor of safety is $1 \cdot 17$.

5.11 *An embankment 9 m high has just been constructed at a slope of 25° to the horizontal. There is no external water pressure on the slope. Find the factor of safety for the trial slip circle of radius 21 m shown in Fig. 5.11, with its centre vertically above the centre of the slope. Properties of fill: $c' = 26 \cdot 4 \ kN/m^2$, $\phi' = 15°$, dry density $1 \cdot 76$ Mg/m^3, specific gravity of particles $2 \cdot 65$, average water content 15%. Assume that the average value of the pore-pressure parameter $\bar{B}$ is $0 \cdot 5$.*

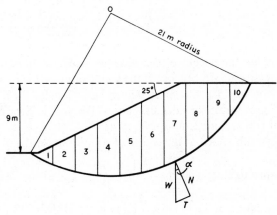

Fig. 5.11

135

If the Bishop analysis is used the term $(W - ub) \tan \phi'$ in the expression for F becomes $W(1 - \bar{B}) \tan \phi'$ (Problem 5.5).

Using the Swedish method the equation for F becomes

$$F = \frac{c'L + \Sigma W(\cos \alpha - \bar{B} \sec \alpha) \tan \phi'}{\Sigma W \sin \alpha}$$

and this method is employed in the following solution.

Dividing the slip area into 10 slices of width 3 m, the relevant data are calculated and entered in Table 5.11.

Table 5.11

Slice	α (deg)	Weight W (kN)	$W \sin \alpha$	$\bar{B} \sec \alpha$	$\cos \alpha - \bar{B} \sec \alpha$	$W(\cos \alpha - \bar{B} \sec \alpha)$
1	-25	68	-29	·552	·354	24
2	-18	206	-64	·526	·425	88
3	-9	331	-52	·506	·482	160
4	-2	430	-15	·500	·499	215
5	7	510	62	·504	·489	249
6	15	556	144	·518	·448	249
7	24	572	233	·547	·367	210
8	33	510	278	·596	·243	124
9	44	375	261	·695	·024	9
10	54	161	130	·851	$-·263$	-42
			$\Sigma = 948$			$\Sigma = 1286$

To calculate the weight of the slices we need the bulk density. The dry density is 1.76 Mg/m^3. If the soil is saturated with a moisture content of 15% the bulk density is $1.76 (1 + 0.15) = 2.02$ Mg/m^3. For example consider slice No. 4. The area is 21.66 m^2 and the weight is therefore $21.66 \times 2.02 \times 9.81 = 429$ kN.

The angle subtended at the centre of rotation is $96°$.

$$\text{Resistance to sliding} = c'L = 26.4 \times \frac{96}{180} \times \pi \times 21 = 929 \text{ kN}.$$

The summation of the $W \sin \alpha$ column in the table is 948 and that of the last column is 1286.

$$\text{Therefore } F = \frac{929 + 1286 \tan 15^\circ}{948} = 1 \cdot 34$$

This assumed circle is, of course, not necessarily the critical circle, and several other circles must be tried in order to find the minimum value of F.

If the Bishop method is employed the factor of safety for this circle is about $1 \cdot 45$. The discrepancy between the two values increases as the central angle of the arc increases, and is also greater for higher values of excess pore pressure.

5.12 *The earth bank shown in Fig. 5.12 borders a canal. The average soil properties are: $\rho = 2 \cdot 04$ Mg/m³; $\phi' = 30°$; $c' = 15$ kN/m². Calculate the factor of safety for the slip circle shown, using Bishop's method, the piezometric levels for points on the circle being represented by the chain line.*

The complete equation for this situation, in which water is in contact with the slope, is

$$F = \frac{1}{\Sigma(W_1 + W_2)\sin \alpha} \sum \left([c'b + \tan \phi'(W_1 + W_2 - bu_s \right.$$

$$\left. + X_n - X_{n+1})] \times \frac{\sec \alpha}{1 + [(\tan \alpha \tan \phi')/F]} \right)$$

where the symbols have the meanings shown in Fig. 5.12. The effect of the impounded water on the face of the slope is catered for by using the submerged unit weight in calculating W_2, and by expressing the pore pressure at a point (u_s) as an excess over the hydrostatic pressure which corresponds to the water level outside the slope. Only the inter-slice forces X_n, X_{n+1} appear in the expression for F, but it can also be shown that the equations

$$\Sigma(X_n - X_{n+1}) = 0$$

and

$$\Sigma(E_n - E_{n+1}) = -0 \cdot 5 \, \gamma_w \, d^2$$

have to be satisfied in a complete solution.

For many circumstances, and at least for first estimates, a reasonably accurate value for F is found by putting

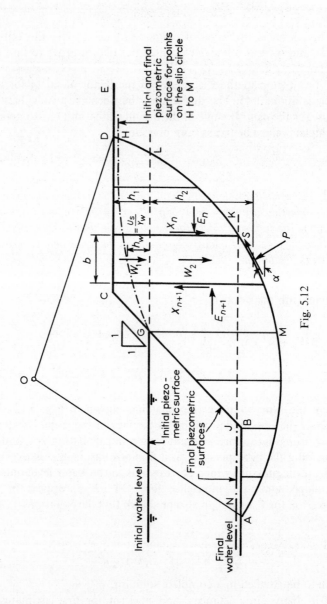

Fig. 5.12

138

Table 5.12

Slice No.	Dimensions (m) b	h₁	h₂	Slope (deg) α	φ'	$W_1 = \gamma b h_1$ (kN)	$W_2 = \gamma_{sub} b h_2$ (kN)*	$W_1 + W_2$ (kN)	$\sin \alpha$	$(W_1 + W_2)\sin\alpha$ $Col(i) \times Col(j)$ (kN)	h_w (m)	$u_s = 9{\cdot}81 h_w$ (kN/m²)	bu_s (kN)
(a)	(b)	(c)	(d)	(e)	(f)	(g)	(h)	(i)	(j)	(k)	(l)	(m)	(n)
1	2·50	1·70*	0·70*	+61·0	30	85·0	17·9	102·9	0·875	90·0	1·75	17·2	43·0
2	2·50	2·00	3·75	+42·0		100·0	95·6	195·6	0·669	130·9	1·60	15·7	39·3
3	2·50	2·00	5·50	+27·9		100·0	140·3	240·3	0·468	112·5	1·25	12·3	30·8
4	2·50	1·20	6·50	+16·7		60·0	165·8	225·8	0·287	64·8	0·50	4·9	12·3
5	2·50	0	5·75	+5·7		0	146·6	146·6	0·099	14·5	0	0	0
6	2·50	0	3·25	−5·7		0	82·9	82·9	−0·099	−8·2	0	0	0
7	2·50	0	1·50	−16·7		0	38·3	38·3	−0·287	−11·0	0	0	0
8	2·00	0	0·50	−26·6		0	10·2	10·2	−0·448	−4·6	0	0	0
										Σ 388·9			

*adjusted to give correct areas bh_1 and bh_2

139

Table 5.12 (Contd.)

$(W_1 + W_2 - bu_s)$ (kN)	$(W_1 + W_2 - bu_s) \times \tan\phi'$ (kN)	c' (kN/m²)	$c'b$ (kN)	Col(r)+ Col(p) (kN)	$\sec\alpha$	$\tan\alpha$	$\dfrac{\sec\alpha}{1 + \dfrac{\tan\phi'\tan\alpha}{F}}$ $F = 1.80$	$\dfrac{Col(v) \times}{Col(s)}$	$\dfrac{\sec\alpha}{1 + \dfrac{\tan\phi'\tan\alpha}{F}}$ $F = 2.25$	$\dfrac{Col(x) \times}{Col(s)}$
(o)	(p)	(q)	(r)	(s)	(t)	(u)	(v)	(w)	(x)	(y)
59.9	34.6	15	37.5	71.1	2.063	1.804	1.307	92.9	1.410	100.3
156.3	90.2			127.7	1.346	0.900	1.044	133.3	1.093	139.6
209.5	121.0			158.5	1.132	0.529	0.968	153.4	0.997	158.0
213.5	123.3			160.8	1.044	0.300	0.952	153.1	0.969	155.8
146.6	84.6			122.1	1.005	0.100	0.974	118.9	0.980	119.7
82.9	47.9			85.4	1.005	−0.100	1.038	88.6	1.031	88.0
38.3	22.1			59.6	1.044	−0.300	1.155	68.8	1.131	67.4
10.2	5.9		30.0	35.9	1.118	−0.501	1.332	47.8	1.283	46.1
								Σ 856.8		Σ 874.9

$$F_0 = \frac{\Sigma Col(w)}{\Sigma Col(k)} = \frac{856.8}{388.9} = 2.20; \quad F_1 = \frac{\Sigma Col(y)}{\Sigma Col(k)} = \frac{874.9}{388.9} = 2.25$$

$$F = \frac{1}{\Sigma(W_1 + W_2)\sin\alpha}\sum\Bigg([(c'b + \tan\phi'(W_1 + W_2 - bu_s)] \\ \times \frac{\sec\alpha}{1 + [(\tan\alpha\tan\phi')/F]}\Bigg)$$

This simplification will be used. A tabular solution is the most satisfactory (Table 5.12).

The unit weights are:

$$\gamma = 2{\cdot}04 \times 9{\cdot}81 = 20{\cdot}0 \text{ kN/m}^3$$

and

$$\gamma_{sub} = 1{\cdot}04 \times 9{\cdot}81 = 10{\cdot}2 \text{ kN/m}^3$$

The table is completed column by column, starting at the left with the geometrical parameters, and performing the operations described in the column headings. In column (*l*) h_w is the piezometric head above the external water level. When column (*v*) is reached, an estimate has to be made of a possible F value (this is shown as 1·80). A first calculated value for F, i.e. F_0, is obtained by calculating Σ column (*w*)/Σ column (*k*). This equals 2·20 in the table, and it differs significantly from the assumed 1·80. The modified value of $F = 2{\cdot}25$ is then used, column (*x*) and column (*y*), producing a second calculated value for F of $F_1 = 2{\cdot}25$. This corresponds exactly with the value used in making the calculation, and the table is therefore concluded.

In an actual site situation, many circles would be analysed, to ensure that $F = 2{\cdot}25$ is the minimum value. The consequences of an inadequate determination can be catastrophic.

5.13 *If the water level in the canal (of Problem 5.12) suddenly falls by 4·75 m, what is the effect on the factor of safety?*

The effect of rapid drawdown is to remove the stabilising effect of the water pressure on the face of the slope (JG) (Fig. 5.12). At the same time the soil in the bank, if it is not free draining, remains saturated and the pore pressures are modified in keeping with the change in total pressures.

Thus after drawdown, the soil is submerged only at the lower levels ABJ and the excess pore pressures are calculated from the new horizon JK. The piezometric surface in that part to the right

Table 5.13

Slice No.	Dimensions (m)			$W_1 = \gamma b h_1$ (kN)	$W_2 = \gamma_{sub} b h_2$ (kN)	$W_1 + W_2$ (kN)	$(W_1 + W_2)\sin\alpha$ (kN)	h_w (m)	u_s (kN/m²)	$b u_s$ (kN)
	b	h_1	h_2							
(a)	(b)	(c)	(d)	(g)	(h)	(i)	(k)	(l)	(m)	(n)
1	2·50	2·40	0	120·0	0	120·0	105·0	2·50	24·5	61·3
2	2·50	5·75	0	287·5	0	287·5	192·3	5·35	52·5	131·3
3	2·50	6·75	0·75	337·5	19·1	356·6	166·9	6·00	58·9	147·3
4	2·50	5·95	1·75	297·5	44·6	342·1	98·2	5·25	51·5	128·8
5	2·50	3·50	2·25	175·0	57·4	232·4	23·0	3·50	34·3	85·8
6	2·50	1·00	2·25	50·0	57·4	107·4	−10·6	1·00	9·8	24·5
7	2·50	0	1·50	0	38·3	38·3	−11·0	0	0	0
8	2·00	0	0·50	0	10·2	10·2	−4·6	0	0	0
							$\Sigma 559\cdot2$			

142

$(W_1 + W_2 - bu_s)$ (kN)	$\dfrac{sec\ \alpha}{1 + \dfrac{tan\ \phi'\ tan\ \alpha}{F}}$ $F = 1\cdot60$	$Col(v) \times Col(s)$	$\dfrac{sec\ \alpha}{1 + \dfrac{tan\ \phi'\ tan\ \alpha}{F}}$ $F = 1\cdot50$	$Col(x) \times Col(s)$
(o)	(v)	(w)	(x)	(y)
58·7	1·250	88·9	1·218	86·6
156·2	1·016	129·7	1·000	127·7
209·3	0·951	150·7	0·941	149·1
213·3	0·942	151·5	0·936	150·5
146·6	0·970	118·4	0·968	118·2
82·9	1·043	89·1	1·045	89·2
38·3	1·171	69·8	1·180	70·3
10·2	1·365	49·0	1·385	49·7
		$\Sigma 847\cdot1$		$\Sigma 841\cdot3$
		$F_0 = \dfrac{847\cdot1}{559\cdot2} = 1\cdot52$		$F_1 = \dfrac{841\cdot3}{559\cdot2} = 1\cdot50$

143

(GCDLMG) of the former water level, point G, will for a while remain the same. Over that part of the slope surface which has had water removed from it, the reduction in total pressure will be accompanied by an immediate equal reduction in pore pressure ($\bar{B} = 1$). The surface in this zone will follow the line of the slope JG.

The calculation proceeds as before (Table 5.13). The columns not shown are identical to those in Table 5.12. Tables 5.13 and 5.12 give the same computed values for $(W_1 + W_2 - bu_s)$, although obtained by different calculations, thus showing that on rapid drawdown for a material which is not free draining ($\bar{B} = 1$) the effective stresses remain unchanged. This implies constant strength under increased loading.

The factor of safety, for the selected slip circle, is reduced to 1·50.

5.14 *A slope in cohesionless soil stands at an angle of 25° to the horizontal. The soil properties are: $\phi' = 38°$; dry density = 1·70 Mg/m^3; $G_S = 2·65$, it is initially dry and of extensive area. During a period of prolonged rainfall, the water table rises progressively and then stabilises parallel to the ground surface at a depth of 2 m. What are the factors of safety against mass movement, before and during the rainfall, if the soil rests on a rock surface at an average depth of 4m?*

For a cohesionless slope the most likely form of failure surface is a plane, parallel to the ground surface.

Before rainfall

The factor of safety, when expressed as the ratio of

$$\frac{\text{forces resisting downslope movement}}{\text{forces assisting downslope movement}}$$

equals $\tan \phi'/\tan \beta$, in which β is the slope angle. Hence

$$F = \tan 38°/\tan 25° = 1·68$$

This is independent of the unit weight of the soil and the depth of the deposit. Failure is equally probable on any slip surface parallel to the ground.

After rainfall

Unit weight above the water table $= 1.70 \times 9.81$ kN/m³. Unit weight below the water table

$$\gamma_{\text{sat}} = \left[1.70 \left(1 - \frac{1}{2.65} \right) + 1.00 \right] \times 9.81 = 2.06 \times 9.81 \text{ kN/m}^3$$

A stable water table parallel to the ground surface produces steady seepage, also parallel to the ground surface. Equipotential lines are thus normal to the surface. The pore pressures are hence calculable for points on the slip surface (see Fig. 5.14).

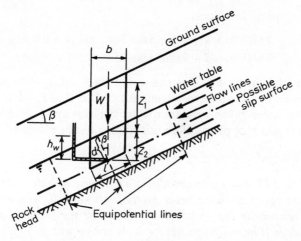

Fig. 5.14

The weight $W = (b z_1 \gamma + b z_2 \gamma_{\text{sat}})$

Downslope force $= W \sin \beta = b \sin \beta (z_1 \gamma + z_2 \gamma_{\text{sat}})$

Total normal force $= W \cos \beta = b \cos \beta (z_1 \gamma + z_2 \gamma_{\text{sat}})$

Pore water pressure $= \gamma_w h_w = \gamma_w z_2 \cos^2 \beta$

since $h_w = d \cos \beta$ and $d = z_2 \cos \beta$,

Pore water force $= l \gamma_w z_2 \cos^2 \beta = b \cos \beta \gamma_w z_2 = U$

145

Thus

$$\text{Effective normal force} = W \cos \beta - U$$
$$= b \cos \beta(\gamma z_1 + \gamma_{\text{sat}} z_2 - \gamma_w z_2)$$
$$= b \cos \beta(\gamma z_1 + \gamma_{\text{sub}} z_2)$$

$$\text{Shear resistance} = b \cos \beta(\gamma z_1 + \gamma_{\text{sub}} z_2) \tan \phi'$$

Hence
$$F = \frac{b \cos \beta(\gamma z_1 + \gamma_{\text{sub}} z_2) \tan \phi'}{b \sin \beta(\gamma z_1 + \gamma_{\text{sat}} z_2)}$$
$$= \frac{(\gamma z_1 + \gamma_{\text{sub}} z_2) \tan \phi'}{(\gamma z_1 + \gamma_{\text{sat}} z_2) \tan \beta}$$

Substituting the values:

$$F = \frac{9 \cdot 81(1 \cdot 70 \times 2 + 1 \cdot 06 z_2) \tan 38°}{9 \cdot 81(1 \cdot 70 \times 2 + 2 \cdot 06 z_2) \tan 25°} = \frac{0 \cdot 781 + 0 \cdot 828 z_2}{1 \cdot 585 + 0 \cdot 961 z_2}$$

It can be shown that this has a minimum value when z_2 is a maximum. In this problem maximum $z_2 = 2\ m$, thus $F = 1 \cdot 23$.

If the water table were to rise to the surface, $F = 0 \cdot 86$ and failure would take place before this stage could be reached.

5.15 *Fig. 5.15 shows a section through a natural hillside in which a thin, soft clay band underlies a purely frictional soil. Assuming no pore pressures in the frictional soil determine the factor of safety of the slope. The soil properties for rapid failure are:*

frictional soil $\phi' = 38°; \gamma = 18 \cdot 0\ kN/m^3$
soft clay $\phi_u = 0°; c_u = 40\ kN/m^2; \gamma = 20 \cdot 0\ kN/m^3$

Without the clay, the factor of safety of the slope would be

$$F = \frac{\tan 38°}{0 \cdot 5} = 1 \cdot 56$$

The clay presence will make shearing within it possible, and although a large-radius failure circle could be analysed, this problem can be examined in terms of planar failure surfaces. A possible mechanism is shown in Fig. 5.15, in which blocks ABCD and BCE move on surfaces DC and CE with interaction T on their common surface BC. The forces consist of:

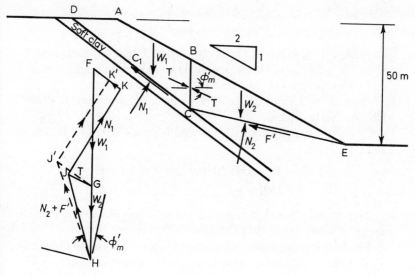

Fig. 5.15

W_1 = weight of ABCD = $(36 \times 52/2 - 16 \times 32/2) \times 18 = 12240$ kN,

W_2 = weight of BCE = $(20 \times 38/2) \times 20 = 7600$ kN,

N_1 and N_2, normal reactions to be determined but known in direction,

T the thrust between the blocks, inclined at an angle of shearing resistance to the common normal,

F' a frictional resistance on CE, which together with N_2 produces a resultant thrust inclined at an angle of shearing resistance to the normal,

C_1 a cohesive force = $(c_u \times$ length CD$)/F$.

The problem is best solved by drawing a force diagram. Set off lines

$$FG = W_1 = 12240 \text{ kN parallel to its line of action}$$
$$GH = W_2 = 7600 \text{ kN on FG extended}$$

Assume a value for F, the factor of safety, say 1·50. The angle of friction mobilised is then

147

$$\phi'_m = \tan^{-1}\left(\frac{\tan 38°}{1·50}\right) = 27·5°$$

and this will be taken as the line of thrust T and the direction of F' and N_2 combined. Hence, set off HJ and GJ in their appropriate directions. Length GJ represents the value of the thrust T.

From point J, draw JK parallel to force N_1 and from F, draw FK parallel to force C.

C_1 is represented by length FK and it scales 3700 kN. But the available force

$$C_1 = 40 \times 63/1·50 \text{ (the factor of safety)}$$
$$= 1680 \text{ kN}$$

This is less than that required for stability. Hence the actual factor of safety is less than the assumed value.

Further trials using the same construction lead to the diagram FGHJ'K'F which closes with $F = 1·25$, the assumed value.

Other possible inclinations for CE would have to be examined to determine the absolute minimum value for the factor of safety.

A check should also be made to ensure that failure on the interface CD takes place in the clay and not in the frictional soil.

In this example $\tan^{-1}(FK'/J'K') = 11°$, which is less than $\tan^{-1}(\tan 38°/1·25) = 32°$, hence failure would occur in the soft clay, and the construction is valid.

5.16 *When tested to large slip displacements in a reversal shear box test, a stiff fissured clay showed a cohesion intercept of zero and a residual angle of shearing resistance $\phi'_r = 22°$. At what limiting slope angle would natural slopes be expected to stand in this soil if its unit weight is $19·3 \text{ kN}/m^3$?*

In the long term, slips in relatively flat natural clay slopes may be expected to occur as shallow sheet sliding on failure surfaces parallel to the ground. Movements take place most frequently during wet climatic conditions, when the water table is at, or near, the ground surface and with downslope seepage.

For the latter condition:

$$F = \frac{c' + (\gamma_{sat} - \gamma_w)z\cos^2\beta\tan\phi'}{\gamma_{sat}\,z\sin\beta\cos\beta}$$

For this problem, it is appropriate to use the residual strength parameters of the soil.

Substituting

$$c' = c'_r = 0 \qquad \phi' = \phi'_r = 22° \qquad F = 1·0$$

$$1 = \frac{(19·3 - 9·8) \tan 22°}{19·3 \tan \beta}$$

From which $\tan \beta = 0·1989$ and $\beta = 11°\ 15'$. The natural slope would be about $11°$.

CHAPTER SIX

Stability of retaining structures

The methods generally adopted for the determination of earth pressures are based on one of the two classical theories—those of Coulomb and Rankine. Careful attention should be paid to the assumptions made in these theories, and to the consequent limitations in their application. As in the preceding chapter the symbol γ represents the *weight* per unit volume that is, the mass density $\times$ 9·81.

6.1 *A retaining wall, with a vertical back of height 8 m, supports cohesionless soil of density 1·75 Mg/m³, and angle of shearing resistance, $\phi = 30°$. The surface of the soil is horizontal. Find the magnitude and direction of the thrust per metre of wall:*

   (a) *by Rankine's theory,*

   (b) *by Rankine, modified for wall friction (assume angle of friction,*
     $\delta = 20°$).

(a) For the conditions given here (vertical wall and horizontal fill surface), Rankine's theory disregards the friction between the soil and the back of the wall.

The coefficient of active earth pressure K_a is equal to the ratio of the principal stresses. From the Mohr circle, this ratio is

$$\frac{1 - \sin \phi}{1 + \sin \phi} \quad \text{or} \quad \tan^2\left(45° - \frac{\phi}{2}\right)$$

Thus

$$K_a = \frac{1 - \frac{1}{2}}{1 + \frac{1}{2}} = \frac{1}{3}$$

The thrust
$$P_a = \tfrac{1}{2} K_a \gamma H^2$$

where γ is the weight per unit volume

$$= 1.75 \times 9.81 = 17.17\ \text{kN/m}^3$$

Therefore $P_a = \frac{1}{2} \times \frac{1}{3} \times 17.17 \times 8^2$

$$= 183\ \text{kN per metre run acting horizontally.}$$

(*b*) Wall friction can be allowed for thus: multiply the Rankine thrust by an empirical coefficient α varying from 0.90 for $\delta = 15°$ to 0.80 for $\delta = 30°$ to give the horizontal component of the resultant thrust.

Thus $\qquad\qquad\qquad P_a \cos \delta = 183\ \alpha$

By interpolation $\alpha = 0.87$ for $\delta = 20°$ ($\cos \delta = 0.94$)

$$P_a = \frac{183 \times 0.87}{0.94} = 169\ \text{kN per metre}$$

The thrust acts downwards at $20°$ to the normal to the wall, since this is the angle of friction assumed.

6.2 *A wall, 9·5 m high, retains cohesionless soil of which the surface slopes upwards at 15° to the horizontal. The density of the soil is 1·9 Mg/m³ and $\phi = 32°$. Find the thrust on the wall per metre run using Rankine's method.*

Rankine's theory assumes that the resultant pressure on the wall acts parallel to the earth surface. The value depends on the ratio of the conjugate stresses shown in Fig. 6.2, namely the resultant stress p_r on a vertical plane and the vertical stress $\gamma z \cos \beta$

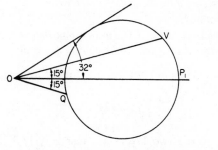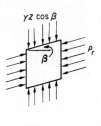

Fig. 6.2

on a plane parallel to the earth surface. To find the ratio of the conjugate stresses, draw a circle of any radius and a tangent to it at $32°$ to the axis OP_1. Draw lines OV and OQ, inclined at $15°$ above and below the axis; these represent the stresses $\gamma z \cos \beta$ and p_r respectively. Then OQ/OV is the ratio of conjugate stresses and is found by scaling to be 0.35.

The weight per unit volume $\gamma = 1.9 \times 9.81$

$$= 18.64 \text{ kN/m}^3$$

At the base of the wall the stress OV is

$$18.64 \times 9.5 \times \cos 15° = 171 \text{ kN/m}^2$$

The pressure on the wall at this level is, therefore, $171 \times 0.35 = 60 \text{ kN/m}^2$ obtained by multiplying the vertical stress at the base of the wall on a plane inclined at $15°$ to the horizontal, by the ratio of the conjugate stresses.

The thrust on the wall per metre of length is obtained by multiplying the mean pressure by the height.

Thrust on the wall

$$\tfrac{1}{2} \times 60 \times 9.5 = 285 \text{ kN/metre run}$$

This thrust acts parallel to the surface.

6.3 *A retaining wall with vertical back is 8 m high. The density of the top 3 m of fill is 1·75 Mg/m³ and the angle of shearing resistance 30°; for the lower 5 m the values are 1·85 Mg/m³ and 35° respectively. There is a surcharge load on the horizontal surface of the fill equivalent to 1·2 Mg/m² uniformly distributed. Find the magnitude and point of application of the thrust on the wall per metre run*

(a) *if the fill is well drained,*

(b) *if the fill is waterlogged after a storm (assume the saturated densities of the two strata 1·9 and 2·0 Mg/m³ respectively).*

For the top 3 m $K_a = 0.33$ as in Problem 6.1; for the lower part,

$$K_a = \frac{1 - \sin 35°}{1 + \sin 35°} = 0.27$$

The unit weights, γ, of the two layers are respectively $1.75 \times 9.81 = 17.17$ and $1.85 \times 9.81 = 18.15 \text{ kN/m}^3$.

Due to the surcharge the pressure at any depth is increased by $1.2 \times 9.81\ K_a = 11.8\ K_a$ that is, $3.9\ kN/m^2$ for the top stratum and 3.2 for the lower.

(a) Pressure due to fill at depth $3\ m = 0.33 \times 17.17 \times 3 = 17.2\ kN/m^2$.

Additional pressure due to $5\ m$ of lower material $= 0.27 \times 18.15 \times 5 = 24.5\ kN/m^2$.

The pressure distribution diagram is as shown in Fig. 6.3A.

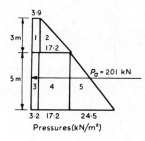

Fig. 6.3A

Total thrust = area of pressure distribution diagram.
The calculations are best set out in tabular form (Table 6.3A).

Table 6.3A

No.	Area of pressure diagram (kN)	Height of centroid above base (m)	Moment about base (kN m)
1	3.9×3 $= 11.7$	6.5	76
2	$\frac{1}{2} \times 17.2 \times 3 = 25.8$	6.0	155
3	3.2×5 $= 16.0$	2.5	40
4	17.2×5 $= 86.0$	2.5	215
5	$\frac{1}{2} \times 24.5 \times 5 = 61.3$	1.67	102
	200.8		588

The magnitude of the thrust is therefore 201 kN per metre of wall, and it acts at a height of 588/201, or 2.9 m, above the base.

(b) When the fill is waterlogged the submerged unit weights become $(1.9 - 1)\ 9.81 = 8.83$ and $9.81\ kN/m^3$ respectively. The corresponding active pressures are:

153

due to 3 m of top stratum: $0.33 \times 8.83 \times 3 = 8.8 \, \text{kN/m}^2$, and
due to 5 m of bottom stratum: $0.27 \times 9.81 \times 5 = 13.2 \, \text{kN/m}^2$.

There is in addition a hydrostatic pressure varying from 0 at the top to $1.0 \times 9.81 \times 8$, or $78.5 \, \text{kN/m}^2$, at the bottom. The pressure distribution diagrams are now as shown in Fig. 6.3B

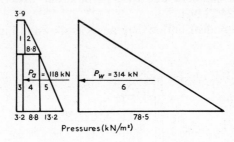

Fig. 6.3B

From Table 6.3B the thrusts per metre of wall are 118 kN due to earth pressure and 314 kN due to the water—total 432 kN.

The height of the point of application of this thrust can be obtained as before by taking moments, but since the hydrostatic pressure is predominant the resultant thrust will act very nearly at one-third the height up from the base.

Table 6.3B

No.	Area of pressure diagram (kN)
1	$3.9 \times 3 \quad = \quad 11.7$
2	$\frac{1}{2} \times 8.8 \times 3 \quad = \quad 13.2$
3	$3.2 \times 5 \quad = \quad 16.0$
4	$8.8 \times 5 \quad = \quad 44.0$
5	$\frac{1}{2} \times 13.2 \times 5 = \quad 33.0$
	117.9
6 (*hydrostatic*)	$\frac{1}{2} \times 78.5 \times 8 = 314.0$
	431.9

6.4 *The fill behind a retaining wall has the profile shown in Fig. 6.4. The properties of the cohesionless fill are: density, 1·75 Mg/m³, $\phi = 30°, \delta = 20°$. Find the active thrust per metre.*

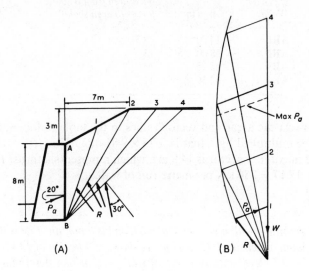

Fig. 6.4

In this problem, the semi-graphical method of using trial wedges is the most appropriate, because the surface is irregular and none of the classical theories can be applied analytically.

Choose several trial planes of rupture such as B1, B2, etc., as shown in Fig. 6.4A.

The forces acting on each wedge are:

(i) its weight W = area × 1·75 × 9·81 kN.

(ii) the reaction R on the plane of sliding, acting at an angle ϕ to the normal to the plane.

(iii) the thrust on the wall (P_a). This thrust acts at an angle δ to the normal to the wall.

The directions of all three forces acting on the wedge are known, and the magnitude of W can also be determined. The triangle of forces for each wedge can thus be drawn, and this procedure determines the thrust graphically (Fig. 6.4B). By plotting the values of P_a for all the trial wedges, the maximum value can be found. This represents the active thrust required.

The results are tabulated as in Table 6.4:

155

Table 6.4

Wedge	Area (m^2)	Thrust vector (measured from triangle of forces to area scale)
AB1	14·00	9·3
AB2	28·00	13·2
AB3	45·25	14·8
AB4	62·50	11·7

To convert the areas and vector values in the table to forces, they must be multiplied by γ, that is, $1·75 \times 9·81$ or $17·17$.

The maximum vector is $14·8 \ m^2$, which represents a thrust P_a of $14·8 \times 17·17 = 254 \ kN$ per metre run of wall.

6.5 *A retaining wall has a vertical back and is 8 m high. The soil is a sandy loam of density 1·75 Mg/m^3. It shows a cohesion of 13 kN/m^2 and $\phi = 20°$. Neglect any effect of wall friction and determine the thrust on the wall. The upper surface of the fill is horizontal.*

When the material exhibits cohesion, the pressure on the wall at depth z is given by

$$p_a = K_\phi \gamma z - 2c\sqrt{K_\phi}$$

where

$$K_\phi = \frac{1 - \sin \phi}{1 + \sin \phi} = 0·49 \text{ for } \phi = 20°$$

$$\sqrt{K_\phi} = 0·70.$$

The weight per unit volume $\gamma = 1·75 \times 9·81 = 17·17 \ kN/m^3$.

When the depth z is small, the expression for pressure is negative because of the effect of cohesion. In theory, this means that for some depth (known as the *critical depth*) the soil is in tension, or tending to support itself and draw away from the wall.
At the top ($z = 0$),

$$p_a = -2c\sqrt{K_\phi} = -26 \times 0·7 = -18·2 \ kN/m^2$$

The negative sign denotes tension.

156

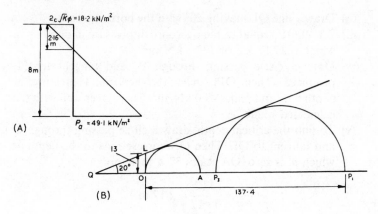

Fig. 6.5

At the bottom ($z = 8$ m),

$$p_a = -18\cdot2 + 0\cdot49 \times 17\cdot17 \times 8$$
$$= -18\cdot2 + 67\cdot3$$
$$= +49\cdot1 \text{ kN/m}^2$$

The pressure distribution is as shown in Fig. 6.5A. The *critical depth*, z_c, over which the above expression gives tension, is found by equating p_a to zero.

Thus

$$z_c = \frac{2c}{\gamma\sqrt{K_\phi}} = \frac{2 \times 13}{17\cdot17 \times 0\cdot70} = 2\cdot16 \text{ m}$$

Theoretically the area of the upper triangle to the left of the pressure axis represents a tensile force which should be subtracted from the compressive force on the lower part of the wall to obtain the resultant thrust. Since tension cannot be applied physically between the soil and the wall this tensile force is neglected.

From the area of the pressure triangle, the total thrust on the wall is

$$P_a = 0\cdot5 \times 49\cdot1(8 - 2\cdot16) = 143 \text{ kN per metre of wall.}$$

This problem can also be solved graphically by means of the Mohr circle: (Fig. 6.5B).

(i) Set up OL vertically, equal to the cohesion, 13 kN/m².

157

(ii) Draw a line QL making $20°$ with the horizontal axis.

(iii) Set off OP_1 equal to the overburden pressure at depth 8 m, which is $17·17 \times 8$ or $137·4$ kN/m^2.

(iv) Draw a circle passing through P_1 and tangent to QL produced. Then OP_3 gives the horizontal pressure at depth 8 m, and scales $49·0$ kN/m^2. This agrees well with the calculated value.

(v) To find the critical depth, draw a circle passing through O and tangent to QL. Then OA corresponds to the depth at which p_a is zero. OA scales $37·2$, therefore,

$$z_c = \frac{37·2}{17·17} = 2·17 \text{ m}$$

6.6 *Find the resultant thrust on the wall of Problem 6.5 if drains are blocked and water builds up behind the wall until the water table is at 3 m above the bottom of the wall.*

In some previous problems of this chapter the soil behind the wall has been assumed to be uniform throughout the depth. If there is non-uniformity caused by varying strata (as in Problem 6.3) or by the presence of water, a simple triangular pressure distribution cannot be assumed, and the problem becomes more complex.

Below the water table, the active earth pressure is reduced because the soil acts with its submerged density, but in addition a hydrostatic pressure is acting.

Down to a depth of 5 m from the surface, conditions are as in Problem 6.5. The pressure on the wall at 5 m, taking into account the tension above the critical depth, is

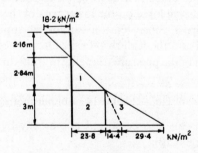

Fig. 6.6

$$0.49 \times 17.17 \times (5 - 2.16) = 23.8 \text{ kN/m}^2$$

Below 5 m from the surface the soil acts with its submerged density. It will be assumed that the given density of 1.75 Mg/m^3 is that of the soil in a moist but unsaturated condition. Below the water table the soil is saturated and its density is probably 10 to 15 per cent higher. Assume that it is 2.0 Mg/m^3. Then the submerged density will be $2 - 1 = 1$ Mg/m^3, corresponding to a weight per unit volume of 9.81 kN/m^3.

The pressure to be added to the 23.8 kN/m^3 is thus 0.49×9.81 for every metre of depth. At the base of the wall the total pressure is

$$23.8 + 0.49 \times 9.81 \times 3 = 38.2 \text{ kN/m}^2$$

The hydrostatic pressure at the base for 3 m of head is $9.81 \times 3 = 29.43$ kN/m^2.

Fig. 6.6 shows the pressure distribution diagram. Its area gives the total thrust on the wall. As in the previous example the triangular area to the left of the axis of the pressure diagram represents tension and is therefore neglected.

In the normal triangular pressure distribution the total thrust acts at one-third of the height. In a distribution such as this, moments of each area must be taken about the base of the wall and the centroid of the whole established.

Table 6.6

No.	Area of pressure diagram (kN)	Height of centroid (m)	Moment of area about base of wall
1	$\frac{1}{2} \times 23.8 \times 2.84 = 33.8$	3·95	133·5
2	$23.8 \times 3 \quad = 71.4$	1·50	107·1
3	$\frac{1}{2} \times 43.8 \times 3 \quad = 65.6$	1·00	65·6
	170·8 kN		306·2 kN m

Height of centroid above base $= 306.2/170.8 = 1.79$ m.

Total thrust $= 171$ kN per metre of wall, acting at 1.8 m above the base.

6.7 *A retaining wall 9 m high supports a filling of non-fissured clay of which the density is 1·9 Mg/m³, c = 28·5 kN/m² and φ = 0. Find the thrust on the wall per metre run taking the cohesion on the back of the wall as 2/3 of that of the clay.*

When $\phi = 0$ the pressure p_a at depth z, neglecting wall cohesion, is given by

$$p_a = \gamma z - 2c$$

It can be shown that when the wall cohesion c_w is taken into account the expression becomes

$$p_a = \gamma z - 2c\sqrt{\left(1 + \frac{c_w}{c}\right)}$$

To find the critical depth z_c put $p_a = 0$ at $z = z_c$

Then
$$z_c = \frac{2c}{\gamma}\sqrt{\left(1 + \frac{c_w}{c}\right)}$$
$$= \frac{2 \times 28\cdot5}{1\cdot9 \times 9\cdot81}\sqrt{\left(1 + \frac{2}{3}\right)}$$
$$= \frac{57 \times 1\cdot291}{18\cdot64} = 3\cdot95 \text{ m.}$$

At depth 9 m, $p_a = 18\cdot64 \times 9 - 57 \times 1\cdot291$
$$= 167\cdot8 - 73\cdot6$$
$$= 94\cdot2 \text{ kN/m}^2$$

Neglecting the tension above the critical depth as in the two previous problems,

Thrust $= \frac{1}{2} \times 94\cdot2(9 - 3\cdot95) = 238 \text{ kN/m run.}$

6.8 *A retaining wall 10 m high with the earth face vertical, supports cohesive soil of bulk density, 1·9 Mg/m³, cohesion, 15 kN/m² and angle of shearing resistance, 15°. Find the thrust per metre run of wall, allowing for friction and cohesion on the back of the wall. The values of wall friction and cohesion can be assumed to be the same as those for the soil.*

In this problem the method of trial wedges is the most suitable because of the complexity of the force systems. Choose trial planes of rupture, B1, B2, B3, etc. Since the soil is cohesive, the wedge areas are assumed to be reduced by tension cracks of depth

$$z_c = \frac{2c}{\gamma\sqrt{K_\phi}}$$

where

$$K_\phi = \frac{1 - \sin\phi}{1 + \sin\phi} = 0.59 \text{ for } \phi = 15°$$

and

$$\gamma = 1.9 \times 9.81 = 18.64 \text{ kN/m}^3$$

Therefore

$$z_c = \frac{2 \times 15}{18.64 \times 0.77} = 2.1 \text{ m}$$

The forces acting on each wedge are:

   (i) weight of wedge, W = area × 18·64 kN
  (ii) cohesive force on wall, $C_w = 15(10 - 2.1) = 118$ kN for each wedge.
 (iii) cohesive force on plane of rupture, $C = 15 \times$ length kN
 (iv) reaction on plane, R, acting at ϕ to the normal
  (v) thrust on the wall, P_a acting at angle δ to the normal to the wall (here, δ has been assumed equal to ϕ).

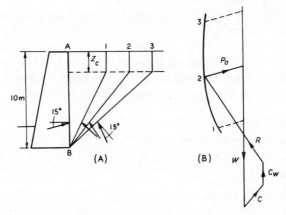

Fig. 6.8

The magnitudes and directions of (i), (ii) and (iii) are known, and the directions of (iv) and (v). Hence the force polygon can be completed and P_a scaled off. The object is to find the greatest value of P_a which then represents the thrust to be used in designing the wall.

The values for three trial wedges are shown in Table 6.8.

Table 6.8

Wedge	Area (m^2)	Weight $W(kN)$	Length $L(m)$	Cohesive force on plane $C = cL(kN)$	Thrust $P_a(kN)$ (from diagram)
AB1	24·2	451	8·8	132	140
AB2	39·3	733	10·2	153	220
AB3	54·5	1016	11·9	179	215

For clarity, only one of the force polygons, that for the wedge AB2, is shown in Fig. 6.8B. From the curve joining the ends of the P_a vectors the maximum value of the thrust is found to be approximately 225 kN per metre of wall.

In addition, for clays subject to tension cracks it is usually recommended that calculated pressures be increased to allow for the development of a hydrostatic head of water over the depth of the crack or half the height of the wall, whichever is less.

Thus, the thrust due to water pressure is

$$\tfrac{1}{2} \times 9\!\cdot\!81 \times z_c^2 = \tfrac{1}{2} \times 9\!\cdot\!81 \times 2\!\cdot\!1^2 = 22 \text{ kN}$$

This value is independent of the trial wedge assumed. Its incorporation in the force diagram displaces the locus 1, 2, 3 horizontally 22 kN to the left. The maximum P_a is thus augmented by $22 \times \sec 15°= 23$ kN, giving a total maximum thrust of 248 kN.

Alternate Solution

This problem can also be solved by the use of the coefficients tabulated in *Civil Engineering Code of Practice No. 2: Earth Retaining Structures*.

From the table, for $\delta = \phi$ and $\phi = 15°$,

$$K_\phi = 0\!\cdot\!50 \text{ and } K_{AC} = 1\!\cdot\!85$$

The horizontal pressure p_a is found from the equation

$$p_a = \gamma z K_\phi - c K_{AC}$$

At the base of the wall,

$$p_a = 18 \cdot 64 \times 10 \times 0 \cdot 50 - 15 \times 1 \cdot 85$$
$$= 93 \cdot 2 - 27 \cdot 75 = 65 \cdot 45 \text{ kN/m}^2$$

Critical depth z_c is found from

$$18 \cdot 64 z_c \times 0 \cdot 50 = 27 \cdot 75$$

whence $\qquad z_c = 2 \cdot 98$, say 3 m

Height of wall under pressure is

$$H - z_c = 10 - 3 = 7 \text{ m}$$

Therefore

$$\text{Horizontal component of thrust} = \tfrac{1}{2} \times 65 \cdot 45 \times 7$$
$$= 229 \text{ kN/m}$$

Actual thrust (at 15° to normal) is

$$\frac{229}{\cos 15^\circ} = \frac{229}{0 \cdot 97} = 236 \text{ kN/m}$$

6.9 *At the front face of a retaining wall, the toe of the wall is 3 m below ground level. The horizontal component of the active thrust on the wall is 226 kN per metre run and the vertical component of the load on the base is 423 kN per metre. The soil is cohesionless and has a density of 1·75 Mg/m³; $\phi = 27^\circ$. Find the passive resistance against the front of the wall, neglecting wall friction. Find also the factor of safety with respect to forward movement of the wall, taking into account the resistance to sliding on the base (angle of friction, 20°).*

Using Rankine's theory for passive resistance,

$$K_p = \frac{1 + \sin \phi}{1 - \sin \phi} = 2 \cdot 66 \text{ for } \phi = 27^\circ$$

The passive resistance per metre is

$$P_p = \tfrac{1}{2} K_p \gamma H^2 = \tfrac{1}{2} \times 2 \cdot 66 \times 1 \cdot 75 \times 9 \cdot 81 \times 3^2 = 205 \text{ kN}$$

Total resistance to sliding = passive resistance against the toe + friction on the base:

$$= 205 + 423 \tan 20°$$

$$= 359 \text{ kN per metre}$$

Factor of safety against sliding, therefore, is

$$\frac{\text{Total resistance}}{\text{Displacing force}} = \frac{359}{226} = 1·6$$

6.10 *The earth face of a 9·5 m high retaining wall has a batter of 4 vertical to 1 horizontal. The soil is cohesive and has the following properties: density, 1·9 Mg/m³; $\phi = 10°$; cohesion, 24 kN/m²; friction angle between soil and wall, 10°. Find the passive resistance to the movement of the wall towards the fill.*

In cohesive soil, the surface of rupture which develops when the passive resistance is overcome is not plane. Fig. 6.10A shows *one* trial slip surface, of which BZ is assumed to be a circular arc of radius 8·5 m and ZD is a plane making an angle of $45° - \phi/2$ or $40°$ to the horizontal.

The problem is worked out in three stages:

(a) determination of the resistance to displacement of the wedge YZD;
(b) determination of the resistance P_c of the whole block ABZY caused by cohesion along the slip surface and along the back of the wall;
(c) determination of the resistance P_w caused by the weight of the block.

(a) The total passive force on YZ, which scales 7·5 m, is

$$E_w + E_c = \tfrac{1}{2}\gamma(YZ)^2 \tan^2(45° + \phi/2) + 2cYZ \tan(45° + \phi/2)$$

$$E_w = \tfrac{1}{2} \times 1·9 \times 9·81 \times 7·5^2 \tan^2 50°$$

$$= 745 \text{ kN acting at one-third the height}$$

$$E_c = 2 \times 24 \times 7·5 \tan 50°$$

$$= 429 \text{ kN acting half way up, since the pressure due to cohesion is uniform.}$$

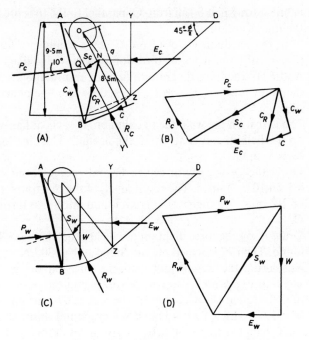

Fig. 6.10

Next we study the equilibrium of the portion ABZY.

(b) The cohesive forces are:

On the curve BZ, $C = c \times$ straight length BZ

$$= 24 \times 5\cdot8 = 139 \text{ kN}$$

On the wall,

$$C_w = c \times \text{AB} = 24 \times 9\cdot8 = 235 \text{ kN}$$

(i) As in Problem 5.10, the force C acts parallel to the chord BZ at a distance a from O such that:

$$c \times \text{chord BZ} \times a = c \times \text{arc BZ} \times \text{radius}$$

$$a = \frac{\text{arc BZ}}{\text{chord BZ}} \times \text{radius} = \frac{5\cdot93}{5\cdot8} \times 8\cdot5 = 8\cdot7 \text{ m}$$

165

(ii) A line is drawn at 8·7 m from O, parallel to BZ to represent the line of action of C.

(iii) Find the resultant C_R of C and C_w by a triangle of forces (Fig. 6.10B) and mark its direction on the wedge diagram.

(iv) Add E_c to the force diagram to find the resultant S_c. From the point N where E_c and C_R meet, draw the line of action of S_c.

(v) The thrust on the wall due to cohesion, P_c, acts at half-way up the height, and is at 10° to the normal. This line intersects S_c in Q.

(vi) Draw the ϕ-circle with centre O and radius $R \sin \phi = 8\cdot5 \sin 10° = 1\cdot48$ m. The resultant R_c of the reaction forces on BZ must be tangent to this circle and must pass through Q.

(vii) Draw R_c on the force diagram parallel to the direction thus found. Then P_c is scaled off and found to be 630 kN.

(c) Considering the weight and ignoring cohesion we get the forces shown in Fig. 6.10C. The area of ABZY and the position of its centroid are found (see Chapter 5). The area is 59·7 m^2 and the weight W is $59\cdot7 \times 1\cdot9 \times 9\cdot81 = 1113$ kN. Compound this with E_w, which was calculated to be 745 kN, to give a resultant S_w. Find where S_w and P_w intersect. (Note that both E_w and P_w act at one-third of their respective heights from the bottom.) The resultant, R_w, acts through this point and is tangent to the ϕ-circle. The force diagram (Fig. 6.10D) is completed and P_w scales 1310 kN.

The total passive resistance is therefore $P_c + P_w$.

$$630 + 1310 = 1940 \text{ kN per metre of wall}$$

This is, of course, only the passive resistance for a particular assumed slip surface. To obtain the maximum resistance several other slip surfaces should be tried. In practice, however, one trial such as the above gives a reasonable indication of the passive resistance to be expected.

6.11 *A cofferdam constructed of cantilever sheet piling, retains soil to a height of 6·6 m (Fig. 6.11). The soil is uniform and has an angle of friction of 30°. Find the depth to which the piles should be driven, assuming that two-thirds of the theoretical passive resistance is developed on the embedded length.*

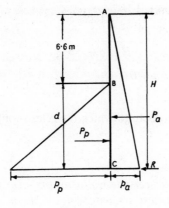

Fig. 6.11

Let H be the total length of the piles, and d the embedded length. The earth pressure coefficients are:

$$\text{(active)} \; K_a = \frac{1 - \sin 30°}{1 + \sin 30°} = \frac{1}{3}$$

$$\text{(passive)} \; K_p = \frac{1}{K_a} = 3 \; \text{(theoretically)}$$

The value of K_p developed is assumed to be two-thirds of this, or 2.

The pressures on the pile at the bottom are:

$$\text{(active)} \, p_a = \tfrac{1}{3}\gamma H$$

$$\text{(passive)} \, p_p = 2\gamma d$$

The total thrusts are, therefore,

$$P_a = \tfrac{1}{2} \times \tfrac{1}{3}\gamma H^2 = \gamma H^2/6$$

and

$$P_p = \tfrac{1}{2} \times 2\gamma d^2 = \gamma d^2$$

The forces P_a and P_p are balanced by additional passive resistance near the bottom of the piling, and it is assumed that this resistance, R, acts as a line force along the bottom edge.

Take moments about C, noting that γ cancels out:

$$H^2/6 \times H/3 = d^2 \times d/3$$

167

whence $\dfrac{H}{d} = 1\cdot82$

but $H = d + 6\cdot6$

thus $\dfrac{d + 6\cdot6}{d} = 1\cdot82$ or $d = 8\cdot05$ m

which is the depth to which the piles should be driven.

6.12 *An anchored sheet-pile wall is of the form shown in Fig. 6.12. The soil is cohesionless, its density is 1·9 Mg/m³ and $\phi = 30°$. Find the fraction of the theoretical maximum passive resistance on the embedded length BC which must be mobilised for equilibrium. Use the 'free earth support' method.*

Find also the force in one of the anchors, assuming that they are spaced at 2·5 m centres horizontally.

The first part of this problem can be solved without using the value of the density of the soil, but this is required for the second part. The working will be more easily understood if the active and passive forces are evaluated. The earth pressure coefficient K_a is $\frac{1}{3}$, as in Problem 6.11.

$$P_a = \tfrac{1}{2} \times \tfrac{1}{3} \times 18\cdot64 \times 9\cdot6^2 = 286 \text{ kN}$$

acting at 9·6/3 or 3·2 m from the bottom.

Let P_p be the resultant passive force, acting at 3·6/3 or 1·2 m from the bottom.

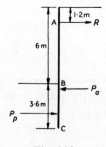

Fig. 6.12

Take moments about the anchor A

$$286(\tfrac{2}{3} \times 9\cdot6 - 1\cdot2) = P_p(\tfrac{2}{3} \times 3\cdot6 + 6 - 1\cdot2)$$

$$286 \times 5\cdot2 = 7\cdot2\, P_p$$

$$P_p = 207 \text{ kN}$$

$$\tfrac{1}{2}K_p \times 18\cdot64 \times 3\cdot6^2 = 207$$

$$K_p = 1\cdot71$$

For $\phi = 30°$ the maximum value of $K_p = 1/K_a = 3$.

Therefore the necessary passive resistance is $1\cdot71/3$ or $0\cdot57$ of the maximum.

Force in anchor $R = 286 - 207 = 79\,\text{kN}$ per metre of wall. Hence the force in one anchor (spacing $2\cdot5$ m) $= 2\cdot5 \times 79 = 198$ kN.

6.13 *An anchored sheet-pile wall supports a mass of soil of height 5·5 m, with horizontal surface. The soil is cohesionless and $\phi = 30°$. The anchor ties are 1·2 m below the top. Assuming 'free earth support,' find approximately the minimum length of the piles for stability. Neglect friction on the surface of the piling.*

As in the previous examples $K_a = \tfrac{1}{3}$ and $K_p = 3$.
Active thrust $P_a = \tfrac{1}{2} \times \tfrac{1}{3} \times \gamma(d + 5\cdot5)^2$.
Passive resistance $P_p = \tfrac{1}{2} \times 3 \times \gamma d^2$.
Take moments about A and note that γ cancels out

$$\tfrac{3}{2}d^2(5\cdot5 - 1\cdot2 + \tfrac{2}{3}d) = \tfrac{1}{6}(d + 5\cdot5)^2 \left[\tfrac{2}{3}(d + 5\cdot5) - 1\cdot2\right]$$

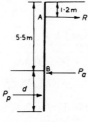

Fig. 6.13

This simplifies to the cubic equation:

$$d^3 + 5 \cdot 42d^2 - 8 \cdot 87d - 13 \cdot 99 = 0$$

This equation has to be solved by trial or by plotting.
The value of d is approximately 2·1 m.
Therefore the minimum length of piling for stability is
$5 \cdot 5 + 2 \cdot 1 = 7 \cdot 6$ m

6.14 *An excavation, 7·5 m deep, is to be made in cohesionless soil for which the density is 1·85 Mg/m³ and $\phi = 28°$. The sides of the excavation are to be supported by anchored sheet piling, with anchor ties 1·2 m below the surface. Assuming 'fixed earth support' and using the equivalent beam method, determine the minimum length of the piles for equilibrium.*

As in previous cases the density term γ cancels out in the solution, but it will clarify the working if the pressures and forces are fully worked out. The 'equivalent beams' are shown in Fig. 6.14A. For cohesionless soil the point of contraflexure C is commonly assumed to be at $0 \cdot 1h$ below B, in this case 0·75 m.

$$K_a = \frac{1 - \sin 28°}{1 + \sin 28°} = \frac{1 - 0 \cdot 469}{1 + 0 \cdot 469} = 0 \cdot 361$$

$$K_p = \frac{1}{K_a} = 2 \cdot 77$$

The weight of the soil per unit volume, γ, is $1 \cdot 85 \times 9 \cdot 81 = 18 \cdot 15$ kN/m³.

Referring to the pressure distribution diagram, Fig. 6.14B,

Active pressure at C $= 0 \cdot 361 \times 18 \cdot 15 \times 8 \cdot 25 = 54$ kN/m²

Active pressure at D $= 54 + 0 \cdot 361 \times 18 \cdot 15x$

$$= 54 + 6 \cdot 55x$$

Passive pressure at C $= 2 \cdot 77 \times 18 \cdot 15 \times 0 \cdot 75 = 37 \cdot 7$ kN/m²

Passive pressure at D $= 37 \cdot 7 + 2 \cdot 77 \times 18 \cdot 15x$

$$= 37 \cdot 7 + 50 \cdot 3x$$

Beam EC:

Active force $P_a = \frac{1}{2} \times 54 \times 8\cdot25 = 222\cdot8$ kN

acting at $8\cdot25/3$ or $2\cdot75$ m from C.

Passive force $P_p = \frac{1}{2} \times 37\cdot7 \times 0\cdot75 = 14\cdot1$ kN

acting at $0\cdot75/3$ or $0\cdot25$ m from C.

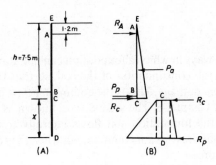

Fig. 6.14

Take moments about A

$$R_c(8\cdot25 - 1\cdot2) = 222\cdot8(8\cdot25 - 1\cdot2 - 2\cdot75) - 14\cdot1(8\cdot25 - 1\cdot2 - 0\cdot25)$$

whence

$$R_c = 122 \text{ kN}$$

Beam CD: The forces are obtained from the areas of rectangles and triangles in the pressure diagram. Take moments about D:

$$122x + 54\frac{x^2}{2} + 6\cdot55\frac{x^3}{6} - 37\cdot7\frac{x^2}{2} - 50\cdot3\frac{x^3}{6} = 0$$

Dividing by x and simplifying gives a quadratic equation from which $x = 4\cdot7$ m. The depth of embedment is therefore $4\cdot7 + 0\cdot75 = 5\cdot45$ m, and the minimum length of the piles is $5\cdot45 + 7\cdot5 = 12\cdot95$ m.

CHAPTER SEVEN

Stability of foundations

There are two ways in which a foundation can fail. It may settle too much, due to the consolidation of the soil, so that the supported structure suffers damage. This is the commoner type of failure, and is discussed in Chapter 8. The second type, known as shear failure, occurs when the foundation soil flows laterally from under the footing. Such failures are not common, but when they do occur they can be disastrous.

The term *ultimate bearing capacity* is defined as the load per unit area which causes the collapse of the foundation due to plastic shear failure. The term *safe bearing pressure* refers to the value of the ultimate bearing capacity reduced by a load factor or factor of safety. The *safe bearing pressure* is the value used in design when the effect of settlement is negligible, and the foundation need be protected only against shear failure. The *allowable bearing pressure* to be used in design takes into account the danger of both shear failure and settlement.

Although the mechanism of the shear failure of soil under a footing is of the same form as in the failure of a slope (Chapter 5), the study of foundation failure by means of the slip circle is now seldom adopted. Methods based on theoretical studies of elastic and plastic failure, supported by experimental results, are generally used.

The basic methods of attack on problems of bearing capacity are most easily introduced by considering strip footings, which are long in relation to their width and thus present a two-dimensional problem. The problems in the first part of this chapter are concerned with the bearing capacity of strip footings. The empirical extension to the three-dimensional problems of rectangular and circular footings is relatively simple. These cases are exemplified in the later part of the chapter.

In the later part of the chapter also, the conditions controlling the choice of a factor of safety are examined. For small footings only shear failure is likely to govern design and a small factor of safety applied to the ultimate bearing capacity gives the allowable bearing pressure. More frequently, especially for larger footings, the allowable bearing pressure adopted must be such that a predetermined maximum value of the settlement is not exceeded. The reciprocal of the product of cohesion and the coefficient of compressibility have been used by Skempton to define ranges of factors of safety for various simplified conditions. These factors of safety can be used to assess the allowable bearing pressure on a wide range of clay soils. For clays, calculations are usually made on the basis of shear strength in undrained tests, since this reflects the strength immediately after the first loading.

7.1 *The foundation material on a site consists of a deep stratum of clay. Samples tested in the undrained condition gave average values, over the depth to be significantly stressed by the foundation, of $c = 60 \, kN/m^2$ and $\phi = 0°$. What is the ultimate bearing capacity for a strip footing laid on the surface?*

It is usual in determining the safety of foundations on clay soils to accept the undrained condition as representing the most dangerous stage. From theoretical analyses, various researchers have shown

Table 7.1 *Bearing Capacity of a Strip Footing laid on the Surface of a Homogeneous Clay with no Overburden.*

Authority	Bearing capacity factor N_c	Nett ultimate bearing capacity $q = cN_c$ (kN/m^2)
Prandtl ⎱ Skempton ⎰ Meyerhof	5·14	308
Fellenius	5·50	330
Terzaghi	5·70	342

that the ultimate bearing capacity q of a soil loaded on the surface by a strip footing is a simple multiple of the cohesion, that is, $q = cN_c$ where N_c is the bearing capacity factor. Table 7.1 shows the variation between the views of experimenters.

The estimate of the bearing capacity, therefore, varies from 308 to 342 kN/m². When these are divided by a factor of safety, the range is well within conditions of site variation.

7.2 *A saturated cohesive soil was tested by unconfined compression, and the following values of the compressive strength obtained: 39·3, 43·4, 37·2, 44·8, 48·3, 42·7, 40·7 kN/m².*

Make an estimate of the bearing capacity of the soil loaded by a strip footing on the surface.

The mean unconfined compression strength of the soil is 42 kN/m². Since the state of unconfined compression is represented in the Mohr circle diagram by a circle tangent to the vertical axis, $(\sigma_3 = 0)$, and a saturated clay, tested rapidly, has $\phi = 0°$, the shear strength or cohesion is half the compressive strength.

Using Terzaghi's estimate of ultimate bearing capacity:

$$q = cN_c = 0·5 \times 42 \times 5·7 \text{ kN/m}^2$$

Thus the ultimate bearing capacity is 120 kN/m².

7.3 *In a saturated clay a strip footing is to be laid at a depth of 2 m below the surface. Unconfined compression tests gave an average value of $c_u = 54$ kN/m². The bulk density is 1·76 Mg/m³. What are the nett and total ultimate bearing capacities?*

The weight of the soil on either side of the strip footing clearly increases the ability of the soil to withstand the pressure of the footing without plastic failure. Terzaghi, whose bearing capacity factors depend only on the value of ϕ and on the assumption of a rough base, gives the value of $N_q = 1$ when $\phi = 0$ (Fig. 7.3). γz is the pressure exerted by the weight of the column of soil, where γ is $1·76 \times 9·81$ kN/m³ and z is the foundation depth.

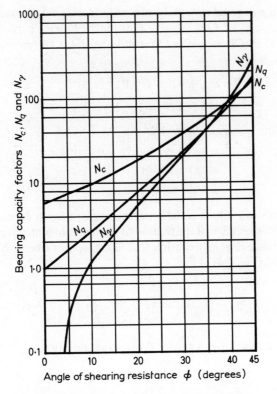

Fig. 7.3. Bearing capacity factors (Terzaghi)

Thus

$$q = cN_c + \gamma z N_q$$
$$= 54 \times 5 \cdot 7 + 17 \cdot 3 \times 2 \times 1$$
$$= 342 \text{ kN/m}^2$$

The nett ultimate bearing capacity, that is, the pressure additional to the original pressure in the soil at that depth is, therefore, cN_c or 308 kN/m².

7.4 *In a saturated cohesive soil a strip footing 1·5 m wide is to be laid at a depth of 4 m. Estimate the ultimate bearing capacities from the theories of Terzaghi and Skempton.* $(c_u = 138\,kN/m^2, \gamma = 1·76 \times 9·81\,kN/m^3.)$

According to Terzaghi, when $\phi = 0°$,

$$N_c = 5·7; \quad N_q = 1; \quad N_\gamma = 0$$

$$\begin{aligned} q &= cN_c + \gamma z N_q \\ &= 138 \times 5·7 + 1·76 \times 9·81 \times 4 \times 1 \\ &= 787 + 69 \\ &= 856\,\text{kN/m}^2. \end{aligned}$$

Skempton's values of the bearing capacity factors depend on the ratio of the breadth of the footing to the depth at which it is laid. In this instance depth/breadth is 2·7. Skempton's value of N_c is thus about 7·2 (Fig. 7.4).

$$\begin{aligned} q &= cN_c + \gamma z \\ &= 138 \times 7·2 + 69 \\ &= 1063\,\text{kN/m}^2 \end{aligned}$$

or roughly 24% greater than Terzaghi's estimation.

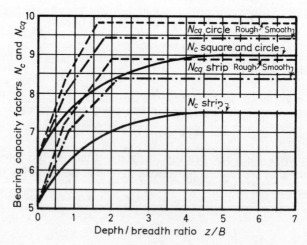

Fig. 7.4. Bearing capacity factors for clay (Meyerhof and Skempton)

7.5 *A strip footing, 1·2 m wide, is to be laid at a depth of 2 m in soil having a bulk density of 1·70 Mg/m³. The soil is of the c-φ type, with a cohesion of 26 kN/m² and an angle of shearing resistance of 28°. Determine the ultimate and nett bearing capacities from Terzaghi's bearing capacity factors.*

When ϕ becomes significant, excessive settlements under working loads are more probable than the danger of failure by shear. If ϕ is greater than zero, then the whole of Terzaghi's equation is needed. This equation reads

$$q = cN_c + \gamma z N_q + 0.5\,\gamma B N_\gamma$$

From the published figures for Terzaghi's work, the factors for $\phi = 28°$ are (Fig. 7.3):

$$N_c = 32; \quad N_q = 16; \quad N_\gamma = 16$$

Thus

$q = 26 \times 32 + 1.70 \times 9.81 \times 2 \times 16 + 0.5 \times 1.70 \times 9.81 \times 1.2 \times 16$

$\approx 1526 \text{ kN/m}^2$

Vertical pressure at foundation level before construction of the foundation $= 1.70 \times 9.81 \times 2 = 33 \text{ kN/m}^2$

Hence, the nett bearing capacity

$$q_{\text{nett}} = 1526 - 33 = 1493 \text{ kN/m}^2$$

In this problem the foundation is placed at a depth of about 1·7 times the breadth and use of the Terzaghi bearing capacity factors, which are generally acceptable up to a depth/breadth ratio of 1, will thus lead to a significant underestimate of the bearing capacity.

7.6 *A strip footing, 1·5 m wide, rests on the surface of dry cohesionless material with $\phi = 37°$, $\gamma = 1·70 \times 9·81$ kN/m³ and $G_s = 2·65$. Flooding causes the water table to rise to the surface temporarily. By what percentage is the bearing capacity of the foundation reduced?*

Reduction in bearing capacity due to flooding is of importance only in cohesionless materials. In cohesive soils a sudden and temporary flooding will have little effect on the bearing capacity. In cohesionless soils, flooding has little effect on the angle of shearing resistance, but the effective pressure which gives the soil its resistance to shear is much reduced.

For a cohesionless material with surface loading, only the last term of the general equation is required, and $N_\gamma = 55$, according to Terzaghi.

Originally, $q = 0.5\, B\gamma N_\gamma = 0.5 \times 1.5 \times 1.70 \times 9.81 \times 55$
$$= 688 \text{ kN/m}^2$$

Flooded, the pressure exerted by the weight of the now saturated soil is reduced by (1.0×9.81) kN/m^2 for each metre of depth below the water table. This is the pore pressure which when subtracted from the total pressure gives the effective pressure producing shear strength. The necessary allowance is made by using the submerged unit weight in the bearing capacity equation.

The saturated unit weight $= \{1.70(1 - 1/2.65) + 1.00\} \times 9.81$
$$= 2.06 \times 9.81 \text{ kN/m}^3$$

Hence $q = 0.5 \times 1.5\,(2.06 - 1.00) \times 9.81 \times 55$
$$= 429 \text{ kN/m}^2$$

The reduction in bearing capacity is 38%. As a general working rule it is often assumed that in most granular soils about half the bearing capacity is lost as a result of flooding.

7.7 *A cohesionless material with an angle of shearing resistance of $\phi = 30°$ carries a strip footing 1·2 m wide at a depth of 7 m. The bulk density is 1·71 Mg/m^3. Determine the ultimate bearing capacity.*

In this problem, the depth/breadth ratio is 5·8 and use of the Terzaghi coefficients, which relate to surface, or near surface, conditions would lead to a gross underestimate of the bearing capacity.

In Meyerhof's theory, which shows reasonable agreement with experiment and recorded results on foundations, the values of the bearing capacity factors depend on a variety of conditions not considered by Terzaghi. Meyerhof's equation may be written in the same form as that of Terzaghi

$$q = cN_c + p_0 N_q + 0.5\,\gamma B N_\gamma$$

but N_c, N_q and N_γ depend on the depth and shape of the foundation as well as on ϕ and the roughness of the base. The quantity p_0 has also to be derived as part of the solution.

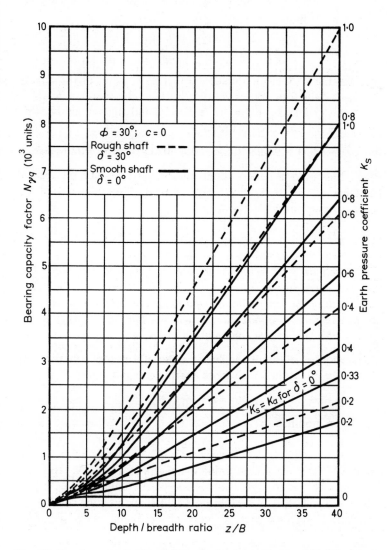

Fig. 7.7. Bearing capacity factors for cohesionless soils ($\phi = 30°$) (Meyerhof)

For the problem under consideration $c = 0$, hence

$$q = p_0 N_q + 0.5\gamma BN_\gamma$$

To avoid the complication of determining p_0 each time, Meyerhof has combined the effects of N_γ and N_q into a bearing capacity factor $N_{\gamma q}$ (Fig. 7.7), so that

$$q = 0.5\gamma BN_{\gamma q}$$

The value of $N_{\gamma q}$ is a function of the depth/breadth ratio and of the value of the earth pressure coefficient K_s acting on the vertical surface of the foundation (so that horizontal pressure $= K_s \gamma z$).

In this problem, for $\phi = 30°$, $z/B = 5.8$ and an assumed $K_s = K_a$ (active earth pressure coefficient $= 0.33$) $N_{\gamma q} \doteqdot 300$.

$$q = 0.5 \times 1.71 \times 9.81 \times 1.2 \times 300 = 3020 \text{ kN/m}^2 = 3.02 \text{ MN/m}^2$$

To this could be added a contribution for friction on the vertical surfaces of the foundation and the below ground parts of the structure supported by the strip.

7.8 *A shallow strip footing is founded in clay at a depth of 0.9 m. It must carry safely a bearing pressure of 130 kN/m². Determine the width of the strip footing required, if the building is not likely to be sensitive to differential settlement. The bulk density of the soil is 1.82 Mg/m³ and cohesion is 45.8 kN/m².*

Meyerhof's analysis of the special case of a purely cohesive clay led to the equation for ultimate bearing capacity:

$$q = cN_c + p_0 N_q$$

which he modified to

$$q = cN_{cq} + K_s \gamma z$$

where N_{cq} is a factor combining the effects of N_c and N_q. Its value depends on the configuration of the plastic failure zone, and on the width and depth of the footing (Fig. 7.4). In this latter expression, Meyerhof suggests that K_s may generally be taken as unity. Hence

$$q = cN_{cq} + \gamma z$$

Since the building is not sensitive to differential settlement it is reasonable to assume a factor of safety which will protect against shear failure — say 3.

Allowable bearing pressure $= \dfrac{cN_{cq}}{3} + \gamma z = 130$ kN/m² as a given condition.

Multiplying by the factor of safety, 3, to find the ultimate bearing capacity,

$$3 \times 130 = 45 \cdot 8 \, N_{cq} + 1 \cdot 82 \times 9 \cdot 81 \times 0 \cdot 9 \times 3$$

This derivation underlines the fact that only the nett bearing capacity should be divided by the factor of safety, the added strength afforded by the pressure due to the weight of soil being present in full even at the safe loading.

$$\text{From the equation, } N_{cq} = 7 \cdot 5$$

Meyerhof's figures show that for this value of N_{cq} with a strip footing, the ratio of depth to breadth is 1·0. The breadth of the strip footing theoretically required is, therefore, only $0 \cdot 9 / 1 \cdot 0 = 0 \cdot 9$ m.

7.9 *A strip footing, 1·5 m wide, in c-ϕ soil, is laid at 9 m below the surface. The soil has a bulk density of 1·84 Mg/m³, c = 83·8 kN/m² and ϕ = 15°. Determine the ultimate bearing capacity.*

With a depth/breadth ratio of 6, a solution requires use of the general equation

$$q = cN_c + p_0 N_q + 0 \cdot 5 \gamma B N_\gamma$$

where the bearing capacity factors are those determined by Meyerhof for deep foundations. For *full friction* developed on the vertical faces of the foundation, his coefficients are given by Fig. 7.9.

$$\text{For} \quad \phi = 15° : N_c = 35; \quad N_q = 10; \quad N_\gamma = 6$$

The ultimate bearing capacity (base resistance only) is

$$q = (83 \cdot 8 \times 35) + (p_0 \times 10) + (0 \cdot 5 \times 1 \cdot 84 \times 9 \cdot 81 \times 1 \cdot 5 \times 6)$$
$$= 2933 + 10 p_0 + 81 = 3014 + 10 p_0 \ (\text{kN/m}^2)$$

181

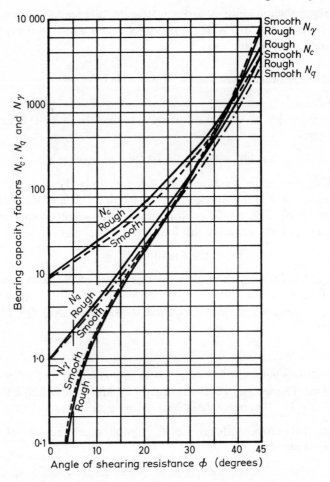

Fig. 7.9. Bearing capacity factors for deep strip foundations (Meyerhof)

p_0 is the average horizontal pressure acting against the vertical face of the foundation over the height affected by plastic failure. This height (measured from base level) is given by

$$h = \frac{e^{\theta \tan \phi} B}{2 \sin \{(\pi/4) - (\phi/2)\}} \qquad \text{in which } \theta = \{(5\pi/4) - (\phi/2)\}$$

182

Substituting $\phi = 15°$ and $B = 1.5$ m in the above expressions

$$h = 3.41 \text{ m}$$

The average horizontal pressure is thus

$$p_0 = \gamma(z - 0.5h)K_s$$
$$= (1.84 \times 9.81)(9 - 3.41/2)K_s = 131.68\,K_s \text{ kN/m}^2$$

K_s is the horizontal earth pressure coefficient acting against the vertical face of the foundation. This will be taken as equal to the active earth pressure coefficient K_a (assuming the soil to be purely frictional).

Hence $$K_s = \frac{1 - \sin\phi}{1 + \sin\phi} = 0.59$$

and $$p_0 = 131.68 \times 0.59 = 78 \text{ kN/m}^2$$

from which $q = 3014 + 780 = 3794$ kN/m²   say   3·8 MN/m²

To this base resistance could be added a further resistance due to friction and adhesion on the vertical face of the foundation.

7.10 *The properties of a soil, as measured by undrained shear tests, are $c = 96\ kN/m^2$ and $\phi = 0$. A load of 3000 kN must be carried by a square footing at a depth of 3 m. The bulk density of the soil is $1.92\ Mg/m^3$. The clay is overconsolidated. Determine the required dimension of the footing.*

The reciprocal of the product of the coefficient of compressibility (m_v) and the cohesion for a soil of this strength is likely to be in the region of 100–200. From Skempton's table of factors of safety for clay foundations (Table 7.10), there is a choice of factors from 3 to 24 depending on the nett settlement permitted. If we assume that a nett settlement of 25 mm should be allowed for, some rough estimate of the size of the footing is required. Assuming approximately 320 kN/m² as the allowable bearing pressure, the footing will be just over 3 m square. The factor of safety is thus from the table in the range from 3 to 6. If the value of m_v is known or can be determined, a more exact estimation of factor of safety might be made, but the extra investigation required may not be worth the accuracy finally obtained. Such decisions are engineering

Table 7.10 *Factors of Safety on Clay* (*Skempton*)

Type of Soil	Overconsolidated						Normally consolidated					
$1/m_v c$	200			100			50			25		
Permissible settlement (mm)	25	75	150	25	75	150	25	75	150	25	75	150
Breadth of footing (m) $1\frac{1}{2}$	(3)	(3)	(3)	3	(3)	(3)	6	(3)	(3)	12	4	(3)
3	3	(3)	(3)	6	(3)	(3)	12	4	(3)	24	8	4
6	6	(3)	(3)	12	4	(3)	24	8	4	48	16	8
12	12	4	(3)	24	8	4	48	16	8	96	32	16

judgements and are based as much on experience as on calculation. A factor of safety of 4 would seem to be a suitable one for preliminary investigation.

A square or circular footing can carry a greater stress per square metre than can a strip footing. Terzaghi estimates that at least 30% can be added to the bearing capacity as measured by cohesion. Thus nett ultimate bearing capacity

$$q = 1.3 \times 5.7c = 711 \text{ kN/m}^2$$

Applying the factor of safety of 4 to the nett ultimate bearing capacity, the nett allowable bearing pressure is 178 kN/m². To this must be added the pressure exerted by the weight of 3 m of soil, or $1.92 \times 9.81 \times 3 = 56.5$ kN/m².

Thus the allowable bearing pressure is

$$178 + 57 = 235 \text{ kN/m}^2$$

The area required is

$$\frac{3000}{235} = 12.8 \text{ m}^2$$

The side of the square footing is, therefore, 3·58 m.

Checking back to the assumption made, we find that this is somewhat larger than the 3 m assumed in order to adopt a factor of safety. Since the factor of safety increases with the width of the footing for a given settlement in clay, a second derivation might be made, using a larger factor.

7.11 *A bridge abutment is 4 m wide and lies in stiff, over-consolidated clay at a depth of 3 m from the surface. Determine the length of the foundation for a load of 10 MN applied at an inclination of 10° to the vertical. The cohesion of the clay is 134 kN/m² (1·72 Mg/m³ bulk density).*

At an inclination of 10° the load on the foundation with a horizontal base causes a reduction in the bearing capacity below that obtained in earlier problems when the loads were all assumed to be vertical. Meyerhof has developed a theory backed by experimental results. For a purely cohesive soil he gives the vertical ultimate bearing capacity as

$$q = cN_{cq}$$

in which N_{cq} has the values shown in Fig. 7.11.

For this problem $z/B = 3/4 = 0.75$

From the graph, with $z/B = 0$, $N_{cq} = 4$

$z/B = 1$, $N_{cq} = 6$, without allowance for adhesion

$z/B = 1$, $N_{cq} = 8$, with allowance for full adhesion, $c_a = c = 134$ kN/m²

For $z/B = 0.75$, using linear interpolation $N_{cq} = 5.5$ or 7

Hence $q = 737$ kN/m², without allowance for adhesion

and $q = 938$ kN/m², with allowance for full adhesion.

The allowable bearing pressure, using a factor of safety of 6, is say $737/6 = 123$ kN/m²

185

This gives, as a rough estimate, a length of footing of

$$\frac{10000}{123 \times 4} = 20\cdot3 \text{ m}$$

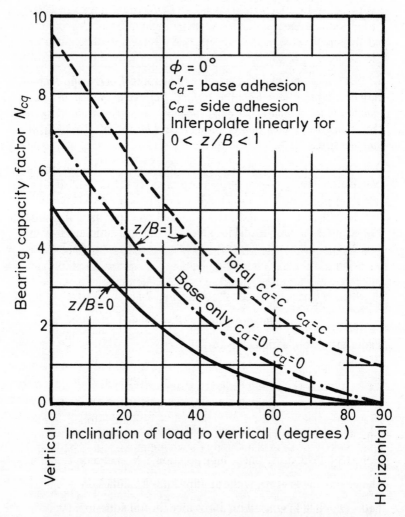

Fig. 7.11. Bearing capacity factors for inclined loads (Meyerhof)

or, if full adhesion is allowed for

$$\frac{10000 \times 6}{938 \times 4} = 16\cdot0\,\text{m}$$

The bearing capacity of a rectangular footing is higher than that of a strip by a factor of $(1 + 0\cdot2\,B/L)$ (Skempton for vertically loaded foundations) but in view of the inclination of the loading and the small value of the ratio in this instance, the effect can be ignored.

7.12 *A foundation material is tested in the consolidated-undrained state and the following properties deduced:* $c_{cu} = 9\cdot6\ kN/m^2$; $\phi_{cu} = 20°$; $\gamma = (1\cdot93 \times 9\cdot81)\,kN/m^3$. *This material carries a circular pier, 4·5 m in diameter at a depth of 2·5 m. The load on the pier is concentric and of a value of 3100 kN. What will be the final value of the safety factor after most of the consolidation has taken place?*

The consolidation of a thick clay stratum occupies many years. At the end, the properties, when the clay is loaded rapidly, are those measured in the consolidated-undrained tests of small samples.

For $\phi = 20°$ Terzaghi's bearing capacity factors are:

$$N_c = 18; \quad N_q = 9; \quad N_\gamma = 4$$

For a circular foundation, the factors 1·3 and 0·3 are used in the first and final terms in place of 1·0 and 0·5 respectively, which refer to a strip footing.

The nett ultimate bearing capacity, deducting γz, is

$$\begin{aligned}q &= 1\cdot3cN_c + \gamma z(N_q - 1) + 0\cdot3B\gamma N_\gamma \\ &= 1\cdot3 \times 9\cdot6 \times 18 + 1\cdot93 \times 9\cdot81 \times 2\cdot5 \times 8 \\ &\quad + 0\cdot3 \times 4\cdot5 \times 1\cdot93 \times 9\cdot81 \times 4 \\ &= 706\ kN/m^2\end{aligned}$$

Add to this an allowance for adhesion of the soil against the shaft of the pier. The value of the cohesion on the shaft is likely to be less than c and may be reduced to, say, one-half.

Ignoring the frictional resistance (due to ϕ) on the shaft, the nett capacity is thus

$$Q = 706\pi \times 2\cdot25^2 + 4\cdot5\pi \times 2\cdot5 \times \frac{1}{2} \times 9\cdot6$$

$$= 11400 \text{ kN}$$

The nett load applied by the foundation is

$$3100 - 1\cdot93 \times 9\cdot81 \times 2\cdot5\pi \times 2\cdot25^2$$
$$= 2350 \text{ kN}$$

And the factor of safety is at least

$$\frac{11400}{2350} = 5$$

a value which is acceptable if the settlement of the pier can be tolerated.

7.13 *A footing, 6 m long by 1·2 m wide is to be laid at a depth of 2 m. The soil has a bulk density of 1·8 Mg/m^3, c = 47·9 kN/m^2 and ϕ = 8°. Find the allowable bearing pressure if the footing is in clay whose coefficient of compressibility m_v is 0·000522 m^2/kN. Only a small settlement can be permitted.*

Skempton gives

$$N_c(\text{rectangle}) = (1 + 0\cdot2B/L)N_c(\text{strip})$$

This factor, for the present problem, is $(1 + 0\cdot2 \times 0\cdot2)$, which is 1·04.

The reciprocal of the product of c and m_v is

$$1/(47\cdot9 \times 0\cdot522 \times 10^{-3}) = 40$$

This places the material in the softer or normally-consolidated type, and the factor of safety for a 25 mm settlement is in the region of 8.

Using Terzaghi's coefficients (Fig. 7.3)

$$N_c = 9 \quad N_q = 2\cdot5 \quad N_\gamma = 0\cdot8$$
$$q = cN_c(1\cdot04) + \gamma z(N_q - 1) + 0\cdot5 B\gamma N_\gamma$$

$$= 47 \cdot 9 \times 9 \times 1 \cdot 04 + 1 \cdot 8 \times 9 \cdot 81 \times 2 \times 1 \cdot 5$$
$$+ 0 \cdot 5 \times 1 \cdot 2 \times 1 \cdot 8 \times 9 \cdot 81 \times 0 \cdot 8$$
$$= 510 \, \text{kN/m}^2$$

which is the nett *ultimate bearing capacity* for a shallow foundation.

The *allowable bearing pressure*, taking into account the pressure of the overburden (2 m deep) is

$$\frac{510}{8} + 1 \cdot 8 \times 9 \cdot 81 \times 2$$
$$= 99 \, \text{kN/m}^2$$

The total load, therefore, is $6 \times 1 \cdot 2 \times 99 = 713$ kN. Since the depth/breadth ratio is $2/1 \cdot 2 = 1 \cdot 7$, the foregoing estimate will be conservative. A more precise analytical solution would require an application of expressions of the type introduced by Meyerhof.

7.14 *A column of a warehouse shed is to be founded on a square footing. Because of the presence of services and nearby foundations, the footing cannot be greater than 2 m square. At what depth should it be placed to carry safely a load of 1800 kN? The clay weighs $(1 \cdot 92 \times 9 \cdot 81)$ kN/m³ and is overconsolidated, with a cohesion of 112 kN/m².*

Assuming 25% increase in ultimate bearing capacity over that for a strip footing, the nett ultimate bearing capacity of the square footing is

$$q = 1 \cdot 25 c N_c = 1 \cdot 25 \times 112 N_c = 140 N_c$$

With overconsolidated clay and an allowable settlement of 75 mm, which is not unacceptable for a warehouse shed, the factor of safety is about 3 (Table 7.10). Using this we have as the allowable bearing pressure, the nett ultimate divided by the factor of safety plus the overburden pressure.

$$\frac{1800}{2^2} = \frac{140 N_c}{3} + 18 \cdot 8 z$$

or $$23 \cdot 9 = 2 \cdot 5 N_c + z$$

Skempton's value of N_c for a square footing on clay depends on

189

Table 7.14
(B = 2 m)

z/B	1·0	1·5	2·0	3·0
N_c (*Fig.* 7.4)	7·7	8·1	8·4	8·8
$2 \cdot 5 N_c$	19·3	20·3	21·0	22·0
z	2·0	3·0	4·0	6·0
$2 \cdot 5 N_c + z$	21·3	23·3	25·0	28·0

the depth at which the footing is founded. The equation is, thus, most quickly solved by trial and error after a rough calculation to investigate the approximate value of z.

By plotting the values in the last line against z it is found that a value of 23·9 corresponds to a depth of foundation of about 3·3 m.

Check:
$$\frac{z}{B} = \frac{3 \cdot 3}{2} = 1 \cdot 65$$

Thus $N_c = 8 \cdot 2$ (from Fig. 7.4)

$2 \cdot 5 \times 8 \cdot 2 + 3 \cdot 3$ should equal 23·9.

This is only 0·1 in error, which is acceptable.

7.15 *A structural loading of 398 kN is to be applied by a stanchion to a square footing. Because of structural requirements and the configuration of the ground, the stanchion must be founded at 3 m below ground level. The soil (c = 48 kN/m²) has a bulk density of 1·98 Mg/m³. The factor of safety to be used is 3. Find the dimensions of the square footing to give a safe bearing pressure.*

Since it is likely that the width of the footing will be less than its founding depth of 3 m, the design should not be based on the assumption of a shallow foundation if economies are to be made. The influence of depth will have to be taken into account.

From Fig. 7.4, Skempton gives

$$N_c(\text{square}) = 7\cdot7 \text{ for } z/B = 1\cdot0 \text{ i.e. } B = 3\cdot0 \text{ m}$$
$$= 8\cdot1 \text{ for } z/B = 1\cdot5 \text{ i.e. } B = 2\cdot0 \text{ m}$$
$$= 8\cdot3 \text{ for } z/B = 2\cdot0 \text{ i.e. } B = 1\cdot5 \text{ m}$$

Now $\qquad q = cN_c + \gamma z$ (ultimate bearing capacity)

and $\qquad\qquad\qquad q_{\text{nett}} = cN_c$

If the weight of the foundation, stanchion below ground and backfill over the foundation is taken as being approximately equal to the weight of soil they replace, then the structural loading of 398 kN is the nett loading.

Safe nett bearing pressure $= \dfrac{cN_c}{3} = \dfrac{398}{B^2}$

and thus $N_c = \dfrac{398 \times 3}{48 \times B^2}$

For	$B = 1\cdot5$ m	N_c required $= 11\cdot07$
	$= 2\cdot0$ m	$= 6\cdot23$
	$= 1\cdot8$ m	$= 7\cdot69$
	$= 1\cdot7$ m	$= 8\cdot62$
	$= 1\cdot74$ m	$= 8\cdot22$

Comparison with the figures given earlier shows that the latter breadth of 1·74 m (z/B = 1·72) gives a satisfactory solution.

Using Meyerhof's values of N_{cq} (Fig. 7.4), the required foundation size is 1·64 m square (ignoring any contribution to the bearing capacity due to adhesion).

7.16 *Decide whether the following proposed construction is safe from the possibility of shear failure. Several stanchions are in line and spaced 3 m apart. The stanchions are based 5 m below the surface, and each may carry 2 MN maximum load. The strip footing on which they are founded is to be 1·2 m wide. The soil below and above the footing has a c_u of 144 kN/m², $\phi_u = 0°$ and is of unit weight 17·7 kN/m³.*

The strip footing has a proposed depth/breadth ratio of $5/1\cdot2 = 4\cdot17$ and can therefore be considered deep.

The ultimate bearing capacity according to Skempton is

$$q = cN_c + \gamma z$$

For $z/B = 4\cdot2$, $N_c = 7\cdot5$ (Fig. 7.4)

Hence nett ultimate bearing capacity $= 7\cdot5 \times 144 = 1080\,\text{kN/m}^2$.

If it is assumed that the weight of the foundation, stanchions below original ground level and backfill equals the weight of the soil removed in establishing the foundation, then the nett applied load $= 2000$ kN per 3 metre run of foundation.

$$\text{The nett applied bearing pressure} = \frac{2000}{3 \times 1\cdot2} = 556\ \text{kN/m}^2$$

$$\text{The factor of safety} = \frac{1080}{556} = 1\cdot94$$

This would normally be considered too low and the foundation would have to be increased in width. For a factor of safety of 3, the width required is approximately $= 1\cdot2 \times 3/1\cdot94 = 1\cdot86$ m, say $2\cdot0$ m.

The modified z/B ratio $= 5/2\cdot0 = 2\cdot50$, and revised $N_c = 7\cdot2$. Hence revised nett ultimate bearing capacity $= 7\cdot2 \times 144 = 1036$ kN/m^2 and this gives a factor of safety of $\dfrac{1036 \times 3\cdot0 \times 2\cdot0}{2000} = 3\cdot11$

which is satisfactory.

7.17 *If the strip foundation of Problem 7·16 applies its load at the bottom of a large excavated basement, how wide should it be?*

This must be considered as a surface foundation, no matter how deep the basement, because the basement is large and neglecting the presence of the basement slab, the term γz is zero.

Hence $N_c = 5\cdot14$ (Skempton)

and $q_{\text{nett}} = 5\cdot14 \times 144 = 740$ kN/m^2

With $F = 3$,

maximum safe nett bearing pressure $= 740/3 = 247 \text{ kN/m}^2$

and required width of strip foundation $= \dfrac{2000}{3 \times 247} = 2 \cdot 70 \text{ m}$

7.18 *A small circular tank is to be designed to carry a depth of water of 2 m. The tank is to be 5 m diameter and its empty weight, including the base, is almost 500 kN. The borehole log is shown in Fig. 7.18. Make an estimate, preparatory to more exact design, of whether this proposal is feasible. Use a factor of safety of 4.*

If the clay stratum had the alternative strength properties $c_u = 5 \cdot 2 \text{ kN/m}^2$, $\phi_u = 0°$, at what depth should the tank be founded to avoid the possibility of a shear failure?

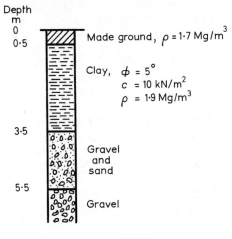

Fig. 7.18

$\gamma_{\text{clay}} = 1 \cdot 9 \times 9 \cdot 81 = 18 \cdot 6 \text{ kN/m}^3$ and $\gamma_{\text{fill}} = 1 \cdot 7 \times 9 \cdot 81 = 16 \cdot 7 \text{ kN/m}^3$

The base of the tank must be founded below the made ground and below frost level. Assume 1·1 m below the ground surface.

The pressure of soil at this depth

$$\Sigma \gamma z = 0 \cdot 5 \times 16 \cdot 7 + 0 \cdot 6 \times 18 \cdot 6 = 19 \cdot 5 \text{ kN/m}^2$$

For $\phi = 5°$,

$N_c = 7 \cdot 0$; $N_q = 1 \cdot 7$; $N_\gamma = 0$ (Terzaghi, shallow foundation)
Use 1·3 as coefficient for cN_c (circular base)

193

Nett ultimate bearing pressure $= 1{\cdot}3\,cN_c + \Sigma\gamma z(N_q - 1)$

$$= 1{\cdot}3 \times 70 + 19{\cdot}5 \times 0{\cdot}7$$

$$= 104{\cdot}7\ \text{kN/m}^2$$

Safe bearing pressure $= \dfrac{104{\cdot}7}{4} + 19{\cdot}5 = 45{\cdot}7\ \text{kN/m}^2$

Thus the load which can be safely carried on a circular base 5 m diameter $= 2{\cdot}5^2\pi \times 45{\cdot}7 = 897\ \text{kN}$

The load it is proposed to apply $=$ weight of tank $+$ weight of 2 m water

$$= 500 + 10 \times 2 \times 2{\cdot}5^2\pi = 893\ \text{kN}$$

The design is therefore feasible.

It is worthwhile making a more detailed study, with perhaps some minor alterations. The bulb of pressure of significant stresses applied by the tank is likely to extend to a depth of 7 or 8 m below the base of the tank. This would take it into the sand and gravel, which would give stability. The clay is on the other hand very soft and the higher stresses are applied within it. This indicates the necessity to investigate the amount and rate of possible settlement, and the selection of an allowable bearing pressure using a higher factor of safety.

For the alternative clay condition:
The load applied by tank and water $= 893\ \text{kN}$
This applies a gross pressure of $893/6{\cdot}25\pi = 45{\cdot}5\ \text{kN/m}^2$
The ultimate nett bearing capacity of the clay

$$= 1{\cdot}3\,cN_c = 1{\cdot}3 \times 5{\cdot}2 \times 5{\cdot}7\ \text{(Terzaghi)}$$

$$= 38{\cdot}5\ \text{kN/m}^2$$

The safe nett bearing pressure $(F = 4) = 9{\cdot}6\ \text{kN/m}^2$
Relief of pressure required from excavation

$$= 45{\cdot}5 - 9{\cdot}6 = 35{\cdot}9\ \text{kN/m}^2$$

Thus $\Sigma\gamma z = 35{\cdot}9 = \text{fill} + d$ metres of clay

$$35{\cdot}9 = 0{\cdot}5 \times 16{\cdot}7 + 18{\cdot}6\,d$$

from which $d = 1{\cdot}5$ m approximately.

At this depth of 2·0 m below ground level, the base of the tank applies only about $10\ \text{kN/m}^2$ as a nett bearing pressure.

7.19 *An estimate is required for the load which can be carried by a pile in soil having a cohesion of 72 kN/m², γ = (1·90 × 9·81) kN/m³, and φ = 10°. The pile is driven through 15 m of this material, and is 400 mm square in cross-section.*

The bearing capacity is found in the same way as for a larger footing.

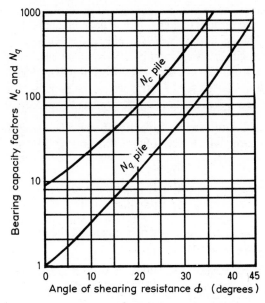

Fig. 7.19. Bearing capacity factors for piles (Meyerhof)

Meyerhof has given semi-empirical figures for N_c and N_q (Fig. 7.19) for driven piles with 60° points.

The ultimate bearing capacity ($N_c = 25$; $N_q = 3\cdot2$) is

$$cN_c + \gamma z N_q = 72 \times 25 + 18\cdot6 \times 15 \times 3\cdot2 = 2693 \text{ kN/m}^2$$

This must be multiplied by the area, as usual. In piled foundations, however, the skin friction on the shaft of the pile is of importance. Experiments have shown that for rough concrete, the adhesion is about 0·8c or a little more, and for steel piles, somewhat less, say 0·6–0·8c. An additional allowance for adhesion on the shafts of piers can also be made in this way, and may prove to be important in design.

195

The total ultimate bearing capacity is the pressure on the square end plus the adhesion. Here, the frictional component is neglected.

$$2693 \times 0\cdot4^2 + 4(0\cdot4 \times 15) \times 0\cdot8 \times 72 = 1765 \text{ kN.}$$

The application of a suitable factor of safety gives the allowable load.

7.20 *A group of piles (spaced on line at 1 m centres), is square in plan, the dimension being 4 m. The piles are 9 m long and are driven in material with a cohesion of 89 kN/m². The value of $\phi = 5°$ and $\gamma = (1\cdot95 \times 9\cdot81) kN/m^3$. The piles are 250 mm in diameter. Determine the minimum factor of safety which can be relied upon against tilting collapse by shear failure of the group. ($N_c = 15, N_q = 1\cdot7$).*

The nett ultimate bearing capacity of one pile, using the bearing capacity factors which were obtained from Fig. 7·19 is

$$\begin{aligned} q &= cN_c + \gamma z N_q \\ &= 89 \times 15 + 19\cdot1 \times 9 \times 1\cdot7 \\ &= 1627 \text{ kN/m}^2 \end{aligned}$$

The total ultimate load per pile, including the effect of adhesion on the periphery of each pile, is

$$1627 \times \text{c.s. area of pile} + (0\cdot8c) \times \text{surface area of each pile.}$$
$$= 1627(\pi \times 0\cdot125^2) + (0\cdot8 \times 89)(9\pi \times 0\cdot25)$$
$$= 583 \text{ kN.}$$

The piles are spaced so that there are 25 in the group. The total ultimate load represented by 25 piles each carrying 583 kN is 14575 kN.

But the ultimate bearing capacity of a group of piles is obtained by treating it as a square footing:

$$cN_c + \gamma z N_q = 89 \times 9\cdot1 + 19\cdot1 \times 9 \times 1\cdot6 = 1085 \text{ kN/m}^2$$

where $N_c = 7 \times 1\cdot3$; $N_q = 1\cdot6$ (Fig. 7.3).

The total ultimate bearing capacity, taking into account adhesion on the periphery of the group, is

1085 × c.s. area of pile group + adhesion × surface area of pile group

$$= 1085 \times 4^2 + (0.8 \times 89) \times 4 \times 9 \times 4$$
$$= 27613 \, \text{kN}.$$

Terzaghi and Peck point out that the total design load (safe load on each pile multiplied by the number of piles) should not be greater than one-third of the calculated total load for the group if collapse failure is to be avoided.

The design load for this group, therefore, should not be greater than $27613/3 = 9204$ kN. If this figure is divided into the total ultimate load obtained by multiplying the ultimate bearing load per pile by the number of piles, the result is

$$\frac{14575}{9204} = 1.6$$

This is the minimum factor of safety. Whether this is acceptable depends on the sensitivity of the structure to movement or to the danger of non-homogeneous soil conditions under different parts of the foundation. An increase in the factor of safety can be obtained by a lengthening of the piles to allow of a greater contribution from adhesion.

7.21 *A square section pile, 0·40 m side, is driven into a saturated clay deposit to a depth of 20 m. The undrained shear strength of the clay at toe level and for several metres beyond is 30 kN/m² and its average value over the length of embedment is 20 kN/m². Estimate the maximum safe load that can be placed on the pile.*

The ultimate carrying capacity is

$$Q_f = c_u N_c A_b + \gamma D N_q A_b + c_a A_s S$$
$$= \text{load carried by base} + \text{load carried by shaft}$$

where

c_u = undrained shear strength at base level and beyond

A_b = area of base

A_s = area of shaft

S = shape coefficient = $\begin{cases} 1 & \text{for parallel-sided pile} \\ 1 \cdot 2 & \text{for tapered pile} \end{cases}$

c_a = mean adhesion on shaft

and the other symbols have the customary meanings. Hence

$$Q_f = c_u N_c B^2 + \gamma D N_q B^2 + 4 c_a BD$$

For $\phi = 0°$,

$$N_c = 9 \qquad \text{(Skempton–deep foundation)}$$

$$N_q = 1$$

To a close approximation the self-weight of the pile is γDB^2, thus the applied load at failure will be

$$
\begin{aligned}
Q_f(\text{applied}) &= 9 c_u B^2 + 4 c_a BD \\
&= 30 \times 9 \times 0{\cdot}4^2 + 20 \times 0{\cdot}7 \times 4 \times 0{\cdot}4 \times 20
\end{aligned}
$$

(the adhesion factor being taken as 0·7)

$$= 43 + 448 = 491 \text{ kN}$$

Adopting an overall factor of safety of 2·5 gives $Q_{\text{safe}} = 196$ kN. Adopting partial factors of safety of 3 (end bearing) and 1·5 (shaft resistance) to allow for differing degrees of mobilisation at the same settlement

$$Q_{\text{safe}} = \frac{43}{3} + \frac{448}{1{\cdot}5} = 313 \text{ kN}$$

Use the lesser value of 196 kN.

7.22 *A cast-in-situ bored pile is formed in a clay stratum, with a base diameter of 1·84 m; a shaft diameter of 0·92 m; a shaft length of 15·0 m. The undrained shear strength of the clay at base level is 120 kN/m² and its mean value over the shaft length is 95 kN/m². What is its safe working load if partial safety factors of 3 (on end bearing) and 2 (on shaft resistance) are used?*

As in the previous problem:

$$Q_f = c_u N_c A_b + \gamma D N_q A_b + c_a A_s S$$

and for $\phi = 0°$

$$N_c = 9 \quad N_q = 1 \quad S = 1$$

Assuming as an approximation that the self-weight of the soil removed equals the weight of the pile

$$Q_f \text{(applied)} = 120 \times 9 \times (\pi/4) \times (1\cdot84)^2 + 95 \times 0\cdot45 \times \pi \times 0\cdot92$$
$$\times (15\cdot0 - 2 \times 1\cdot84) \times 1$$
$$= 2872 + 1399 = 4271 \text{ kN}$$

In this calculation the adhesion factor has been taken as $0\cdot45$ for a bored pile and adhesion has been ignored over a length $= 2 \times$ base diameter.

$$Q_{safe} = \frac{2872}{3} + \frac{1399}{2} = 957 + 700 = 1657 \text{ kN}$$

7.23 *A square section concrete pile is driven into a deposit of dense sand to a depth of 15 m. If the sand has a ϕ' value of 40°, and a unit weight of 20·1 kN/m³, and the pile is of 0·40 m side, determine the load which would produce bearing capacity failure of the pile.*

$$Q_{nf} = p'(N_q - 1)A_b + 0\cdot4\,\gamma'BN_\gamma A_b + K_s p'_m \tan \delta'\, A_s$$

in which

Q_{nf} is the nett failure load,

p' is the effective overburden pressure at toe level, and p'_m is its mean value over the embedded length,

A_b is the toe area,

γ' is the effective (i.e. submerged) unit weight of the soil,

B is the width of the pile,

K_s is the coefficient of earth pressure acting horizontally against the shaft,

δ' is the skin friction angle,

N_q and N_γ are bearing capacity factors.

In this formulation it is assumed that the weight of the pile equals the weight of soil displaced by it on installation, and that the sand is subjected to a water table at ground level.

For this deep foundation the term $0\cdot4\,\gamma'BN_\gamma A_b$ will be small and will be ignored.

Substituting values

$$Q_{nf} = (20\cdot1 - 9\cdot8)\,15\,(N_q - 1)(0\cdot4)^2 + K_s(20\cdot1 - 9\cdot8)\,15/2$$
$$\times \tan \delta' \times 4 \times 0\cdot4 \times 15$$
$$= 24\cdot7(N_q - 1) + 1854\cdot0\,K_s \tan \delta'$$

199

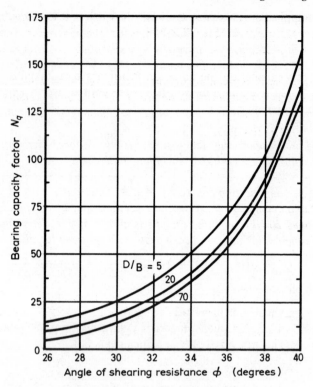

Fig. 7.23. Bearing capacity factors for piles in frictional soils.
(Berezantsev; Tomlinson)

Table 7.23

Type of pile	K_s		δ'
	Loose	Dense	
Steel	0·5	1·0	20°
Concrete	1·0	2·0	0·75 ϕ'
Timber	1·5	3·0	0·67 ϕ'

For $\phi' = 40°$; $N_q = 140$ from values by Berezantsev (Fig. 7.23). K_s from Table 7.23 = 2·0; δ' from Table 7.23 = 0·75 ϕ'. Hence $Q_{nf} = 3433 + 2141 = 5574$ kN or 5·5 MN.

200

7.24 *A site exploration discloses an extensive fine sand deposit with the water table at a depth of 2 m. Standard penetration tests at five plan positions gave the typical values of N shown in the Table. What size of foundation, sited at a depth of 1·5 m below ground level, is required to carry a load of 7·4 MN with a factor of safety against ultimate failure of 3? The unit weights of the sand are 17·8 kN/m³ and 19·4 kN/m³, above and below the water table respectively.*

If the water table can rise to ground surface, what effect will this have on the required size of foundation?

Table 7.24

Depth below ground level (m)	1·5	2·5	3·5	4·5	5·5	6·5	7·5	8·5
N	15	18	23	25	29	35	40	42

Assume the foundation to be square and of size 5 m. The relevant N values will be those over a depth of D to $D + B$ metres below ground level, where D is the foundation depth and B is the foundation width. This range is 1·5 m to 6·5 m.

The recorded N values are first corrected for the overburden depth at which the respective tests were made. Using Fig. 7.24A, for example, the $N = 15$ at a depth of 1·5 m is corrected to 36. The set of values over the range of interest is 36, 35, 37, 36, 35 and 40 giving a mean value $N = 36$.

This is only one of a number of methods of correction. The results vary according to the procedure used.

The penetration values were measured in a fine saturated sand and further modification is needed to allow for pore pressure generation during the test.

$$\text{Final corrected } N \text{ value} = N' = \tfrac{1}{2}(N - 15) + 15$$
$$= \tfrac{1}{2}(36 - 15) + 15 = 25$$

From Fig. 7.24B for $N' = 25$;

$$\phi' = 35° \quad N_\gamma = 38 \quad N_q = 32$$

Using the bearing capacity formula:

$$q_{nf} = 0.4\gamma B N_\gamma + p'_0(N_q - 1)$$

201

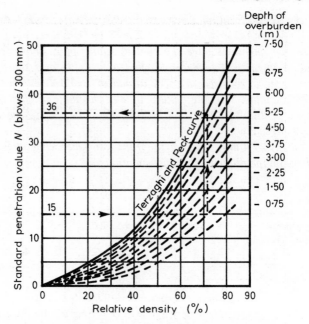

Fig. 7.24A. Correction of standard penetration results
for effect of overburden (Thorburn)

in which

q_{nf} = nett ultimate bearing capacity,

p_0' = effective overburden pressure at foundation level,

and the other symbols have the usual meanings.

$$p_0' = 17\cdot8 \times 1\cdot5 = 26\cdot7 \text{ kN/m}^2 \quad \text{(the water table being}$$
$$\text{below foundation level).}$$

In the first term, γ will be taken equal to the submerged unit weight (because the water table is near foundation level).

Substituting in the formula:

$$q_{nf} = 0\cdot4 \times (19\cdot4 - 9\cdot8) \times 5 \times 38 + 26\cdot7\,(32 - 1)$$
$$= 729\cdot6 + 827\cdot7 = 1557 \text{ kN/m}^2$$

The maximum nett safe bearing pressure is $1557/3 = 519 \text{ kN/m}^2$ and if the weight of foundation plus backfill equals the weight of soil excavated, the maximum load that can be applied by the

202

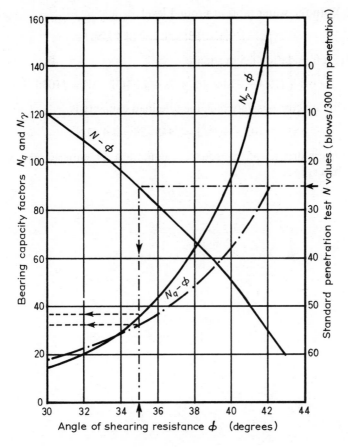

Fig. 7.24B. Bearing capacity factors and SPT values (Peck, Hanson and Thorburn)

foundation is $519 \times 5^2 = 13$ MN. This is greater than that required. Therefore assume a reduced breadth of 4 m and repeat the calculation.

Revised $N' = 36$, hence values for N_q, N_y remain the same.

$$q_{nf} = 0.4 \times (19.4 - 9.8) \times 4 \times 38 + 26.7(32 - 1) = 1411 \text{ kN/m}^2$$

and the safe load capacity of the modified foundation is $1411 \times 4^2/3 = 7.5$ MN, which is sufficiently close to the required value of 7.4 MN to permit adoption of a 4 m square foundation.

With the water table at ground level

$$p'_0 = (19{\cdot}4 - 9{\cdot}8) \times 1{\cdot}5 = 14{\cdot}4 \text{ kN/m}^2$$

Try a foundation 4·5 m square:

$$q_{nf} = 0{\cdot}4 \times (19{\cdot}4 - 9{\cdot}8) \times 4{\cdot}5 \times 38 + 14{\cdot}4(32 - 1) = 1103 \text{ kN/m}^2$$

With a factor of safety of 3, the safe load capacity is

$$1103 \times 4{\cdot}5^2/3 = 7445 \text{ kN} = 7{\cdot}4 \text{ MN}$$

Therefore a 4·5 m square foundation is satisfactory with submergence.

GROUP 3

Limitation of Deformation

CHAPTER EIGHT

Deformation and settlement

A knowledge of the way in which foundation loads are transmitted to the soil supporting a foundation, and the distribution of stresses within the soil are of fundamental importance to the design engineer. Such knowledge enables estimates to be made of possible settlements and allowable bearing pressures, and permits the planning of adequate site explorations, apart from its function of providing design data for the structural proportioning of the foundation. The problems in this chapter fall into three categories – the estimation of stresses, consolidation settlements, and immediate settlements.

Most of the methods currently used for studying stress distributions within soil masses are based on elastic theory or empirical modifications to precise mathematical solutions of elasticity. The assumptions, unless stated otherwise, are therefore that the soil is

(1) semi-infinite in extent,
(2) isotropic,
(3) homogeneous,
(4) elastic and obeys Hooke's law.

Natural soils seldom comply with any of these assumptions, but the absence of acceptable alternatives makes their use a practical necessity. Calculated stress distributions should be taken as a guide to the order of magnitude of the effects.

Solutions to many problems are available in texts on the theory of elasticity, and the purely analytical approaches can be found there. In this chapter we are concerned solely with the application of existing solutions to foundation problems.

In the second group of problems, results from stress calculations

are applied to the estimation of the amount of settlement of
foundations due to the consolidation of a compressible clay layer.
Because of the relatively low permeability of such a soil the full
consolidation settlement may only develop a long time after the
structure is completed and fully loaded. One must therefore
consider the time element when calculating such settlements.

It is customary practice to base calculations of settlement,
as a function of time, on the results of consolidation tests made
on small specimens of the soils concerned. The results of these tests
are expressed in terms of the coefficient of compressibility, from
which final consolidation settlements are calculated, and the
coefficient of consolidation, on which the rate of development of
settlement depends.

In the third category, procedures for calculating settlements
which take place immediately on loading are introduced. For
clays, these settlements, when added to the long-term settlements
due to consolidation, give the total movements. For cohesionless
soils these immediate settlements are synonymous with the long-
term movements.

8.1 *Determine the distribution of vertical stress on horizontal planes
to a depth of 12 m in the line of action of a concentrated vertical
load of 800 kN acting normally on the upper plane surface of a
semi-infinite, elastic, isotropic and homogeneous continuum.*

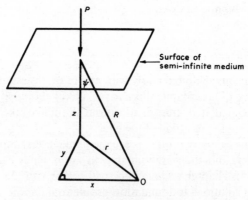

Fig. 8.1

This is the commencing point for the solution of many problems relating to stresses caused by foundation loads. The solution published by Boussinesq in 1885 gives:

Vertical direct stress on horizontal planes at depth z (point 0, see Fig. 8.1) is

$$\widehat{zz} = \frac{3Pz^3}{2\pi R^5} \quad \text{or} \quad \frac{3P}{2\pi z^2} \cos^5 \psi$$

The equation is generally used in the form

$$\widehat{zz} = K \frac{P}{z^2}$$

in which

$$K = \frac{3}{2\pi} \frac{1}{\left[1 + \left(\frac{r}{z} \right)^2 \right]^{5/2}} = \frac{3z^5}{2\pi R^5}$$

This dimensionless influence factor K has been evaluated for values of r/z, and details are given in Table 8·1A.

In the problem $P = 800$ kN; $r = 0$ for the axial stresses. Hence

$$K = 0·4775 \text{ (from the table)}$$

and the results are given in Table 8.1B

These results should be plotted by the student.

Table 8.1A *Influence Factors for Vertical Pressure caused by a Point Load*

$\frac{r}{z}$	Influence factor K	$\frac{r}{z}$	Influence factor K	$\frac{r}{z}$	Influence factor K
0·00	0·4775	1·00	0·0844	2·00	0·0085
0·10	0·4657	1·10	0·0658	2·10	0·0070
0·20	0·4329	1·20	0·0513	2·20	0·0058
0·30	0·3849	1·30	0·0402	2·30	0·0048
0·40	0·3294	1·40	0·0317	2·40	0·0040
0·50	0·2733	1·50	0·0251	2·50	0·0034
0·60	0·2214	1·60	0·0200	2·60	0·0029
0·70	0·1762	1·70	0·0160	2·70	0·0024
0·80	0·1386	1·80	0·0129	2·80	0·0021
0·90	0·1083	1·90	0·0105	2·90	0·0018

Table 8.1B

z (m)	z^2 (m^2)	$\widehat{zz} = KP/z^2$ (kN/m^2)
0	0	∞
2	4	96
4	16	24
6	36	11
8	64	6
10	100	4
12	144	3

8.2 *For the case given in Problem 8.1, determine the distribution of vertical stress on a horizontal plane at a depth of 2 m below the surface to a distance of 4 m from the line of action of the load.*

The calculation is best set out in tabular form (Table 8.2).

Table 8.2

z (m)	r (m)	$\dfrac{r}{z}$	K	$\widehat{zz} = \dfrac{KP}{z^2} = 200\,K$ (kN/m^2)
(a)	(b)	(c)	(d)	(e)
2	0	0	0·4775	96
	0·8	0·4	0·3294	66
	1·6	0·8	0·1386	28
	2·4	1·2	0·0513	10
	3·2	1·6	0·0200	4
	4·0	2·0	0·0085	2

The problem is axially symmetrical and the results given in Col. (e) in Table 8.2 therefore apply for all radial directions. The student should plot these results.

8.3 *A circular foundation rests on the horizontal upper surface of a semi-infinite soil mass whose properties comply with the usual elasticity requirements and carries a load of 800 kN. The contact pressure is uniform and the foundation flexible. The base of the foundation is frictionless. The diameter of the foundation is 3 m. Determine the vertical stress distribution on horizontal planes along the central axis of the foundation to a depth of 12 m below the surface.*

In deriving the Boussinesq solution for a point load the upper boundary condition is that there are no shearing stresses in the plane of the surface and there are no normal surface stresses (other than at the point of application of the load). The surface is therefore not restrained by boundary stresses from deforming vertically and radially.

In this problem, since the base is frictionless and perfectly flexible the same boundary conditions are applicable. The Boussinesq solution can therefore be used, suitably integrated for the distributed load. Consider an element of the foundation shown in plan in Fig. 8.3 bounded by the radial lines OA, OB and the circumferential lines at distance r and $(r + dr)$ from the centre O.

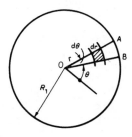

Fig. 8.3

The load on the elemental area $= qr\,d\theta\,dr$, where q is the contact pressure intensity.

This load will produce stresses on the axis O according to the Boussinesq relationships. Thus for the vertical stress $d\widehat{zz}$ we obtain

$$d\widehat{zz} = \frac{3qr\,d\theta\,dr\,z^3}{2\pi R^5}$$

in which $R^2 = r^2 + z^2$. Hence

211

$$d\widehat{zz} = \frac{3qrz^3 \, d\theta \, dr}{2\pi(r^2 + z^2)^{5/2}}$$

The total stress is obtained by integrating this according to the equation

$$\widehat{zz} = \int_0^{2\pi} \int_0^{R_1} \frac{3qrz^3 \, d\theta \, dr}{2\pi(r^2 + z^2)^{5/2}}$$

Since in this problem q is independent of r and θ, and θ is independent of all other quantities, the equation simplifies to

$$\widehat{zz} = 3qz^3 \int_0^{R_1} \frac{r \, dr}{(r^2 + z^2)^{5/2}}$$

$$= q - \frac{q}{[1 + (R_1/z)^2]^{3/2}}$$

$$= qK$$

where

$$K = \left[1 - \frac{1}{[1 + (R_1/z)^2]^{3/2}} \right]$$

This influence factor is tabulated in Table 8.3A.

Table 8.3A *Influence Factors for Vertical Pressure under Centre of Uniformly Loaded Circular Area of Diameter D*

$\dfrac{D}{z}$	Influence factor K	$\dfrac{D}{z}$	Influence factor K	$\dfrac{D}{z}$	Influence factor K
0·00	0·0000	2·00	0·6465	4·00	0·9106
0·20	0·0148	2·20	0·6956	6·00	0·9684
0·40	0·0571	2·40	0·7376	8·00	0·9857
0·60	0·1213	2·60	0·7733	10·00	0·9925
0·80	0·1996	2·80	0·8036	12·00	0·9956
1·00	0·2845	3·00	0·8293	14·00	0·9972
1·20	0·3695	3·20	0·8511	16·00	0·9981
1·40	0·4502	3·40	0·8697	20·00	0·9990
1·60	0·5239	3·60	0·8855	40·00	0·9999
1·80	0·5893	3·80	0·8990	200·00	1·0000

To obtain the vertical pressure at a given depth under the centre of the circular loaded area, multiply the appropriate influence factor by the contact pressure q.

In the problem
$$D = 2R_1$$
$$R_1 = 1.5 \text{ m}$$
$$q = \frac{800}{\pi \times 1.5^2} = 113 \text{ kN/m}^2$$

The results of the calculation are given in Table 8.3B and it is instructive to compare them with those in Table 8.1B.

Table 8.3B

Depth below centre z (m)	$\dfrac{D}{z}$	K	$\widehat{zz} = qK$ (kN/m^2)
0	∞	1.0000	113
1	3	0.8293	94
2	1.5	0.4880	55
4	0.75	0.1791	20
6	0.50	0.0869	10
8	0.375	0.0505	6
10	0.300	0.0328	4
12	0.250	0.0230	3

8.4 *A rectangular raft foundation imposes a contact pressure of 155 kN/m² on the surface of a foundation soil. Determine the distribution of vertical stress on horizontal planes below the centre of the foundation to a depth of 18 m. The raft is 36 m × 24 m in size.*

This problem could be attempted in a similar way to that adopted for Problem 8.3. The integrations become involved and they have in fact been performed by various workers.

The problem will therefore be solved using the curves produced by Fadum and shown in Fig. 8.4. The curves relate to the pressure under a corner of a rectangular foundation, but they can nevertheless be used for this problem by considering the raft foundation to consist of four separate foundations of size 18 m × 12 m abutting with their common corner at the centre of the 36 m × 24 m foundation. The contribution of each of the four foundations is evaluated separately and then summed since the principle of superposition is applicable.

213

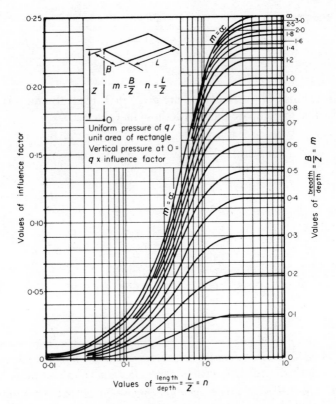

Fig. 8.4. Fadum's chart

In this problem the four foundations are identical, so that only one need be considered and the resultant stresses multiplied by four. The calculations are set out in Table 8.4.

Table 8.4

Depth below corner z (m)	$n = \dfrac{L}{z}$	$m = \dfrac{B}{z}$	Influence factor I_f	Vertical Stress $4 \times q \times I_f$ (kN/m^2)
(a)	(b)	(c)	(d)	(e)
0	∞	∞	0·250	155
2	9·00	6·00	0·248	154
4	4·50	3·00	0·246	153
6	3·00	2·00	0·238	148
8	2·25	1·50	0·225	140
9	2·00	1·33	0·217	135
10	1·80	1·20	0·210	130
11	1·64	1·09	0·200	124
12	1·50	1·00	0·193	120
13	1·38	0·92	0·185	115
14	1·29	0·86	0·175	109
15	1·20	0·80	0·170	105
16	1·13	0·75	0·162	100
17	1·06	0·71	0·156	97
18	1·00	0·67	0·146	91

8.5 *A rectangular foundation subjects the subgrade to a nett contact pressure of 215 kN/m², uniform over its area. The foundation is 24 m × 12 m in size. Determine the vertical stress for a point located outside the plan area of the foundation at O (Fig. 8.5) at a depth of 8 m.*

Fadum's graphs can also be used for this type of problem. Thus the stress at O is obtained by considering area AEOH to be loaded and

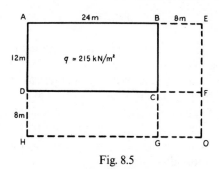

Fig. 8.5

then deducting for the effect of area DCBEOH. The latter is obtained by considering areas DFOH + BEOG − CFOG, each of which has a common corner at point O.

Table 8.5

Area	L (m)	B (m)	$n = \dfrac{L}{z}$	$m = \dfrac{B}{z}$	I_f	Vertical stress (kN/m²)
+ AEOH	32	20	4·0	2·5	+ 0·243	+ 52·3
+ CFOG	8	8	1·0	1·0	+ 0·176	+ 37·8
− DFOH	32	8	4·0	1·0	− 0·205	− 44·1
− BEOG	20	8	2·5	1·0	− 0·203	− 43·7

The answer is thus 2·3 kN/m² (compression). $\Sigma = +2·3$

8.6 *A rectangular foundation is perfectly flexible and carries a load of 360 kN/m² on its upper surface. It is 4·5 m × 3 m in size. Determine the vertical pressure at a depth of 6 m below a point A situated as shown in Fig. 8.6. Assume the foundation to be weightless.*

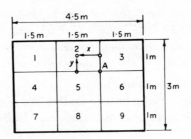

Fig. 8.6

Because of the flexibility the contact pressure distribution will be the same as the distribution of load to the top of the foundation. This problem will be solved by numerical integration of Boussinesq's solution for the point load. For this purpose the foundation is divided into a convenient number of areas (9 in the example). The distributed load is considered to act as a series of separate point loads with their points of application at the load centroid of the individual areas.

216

The load acting on each area is thus

$$\delta P = 1 \cdot 5 \times 1 \times 360 = 540 \text{ kN}$$

The Boussinesq solution is applied to each area in turn and the results summed as shown in Table 8.6.

Table 8.6

Area No.	Load centroid co-ordinate y (m)	Load centroid co-ordinate x (m)	Radius $r = \sqrt{(x^2 + y^2)}$ (m)	$\dfrac{r}{z}$	K (from Table 8.1A)
1	$+0 \cdot 5$	$+2 \cdot 25$	$2 \cdot 30$	$0 \cdot 38$	$0 \cdot 3408$
2	$+0 \cdot 5$	$+0 \cdot 75$	$0 \cdot 90$	$0 \cdot 15$	$0 \cdot 4516$
3	$+0 \cdot 5$	$-0 \cdot 75$	$0 \cdot 90$	$0 \cdot 15$	$0 \cdot 4516$
4	$-0 \cdot 5$	$+2 \cdot 25$	$2 \cdot 30$	$0 \cdot 38$	$0 \cdot 3408$
5	$-0 \cdot 5$	$+0 \cdot 75$	$0 \cdot 90$	$0 \cdot 15$	$0 \cdot 4516$
6	$-0 \cdot 5$	$-0 \cdot 75$	$0 \cdot 90$	$0 \cdot 15$	$0 \cdot 4516$
7	$-1 \cdot 5$	$+2 \cdot 25$	$2 \cdot 70$	$0 \cdot 45$	$0 \cdot 3011$
8	$-1 \cdot 5$	$+0 \cdot 75$	$1 \cdot 68$	$0 \cdot 28$	$0 \cdot 3954$
9	$-1 \cdot 5$	$-0 \cdot 75$	$1 \cdot 68$	$0 \cdot 28$	$0 \cdot 3954$

$$\Sigma K = 3 \cdot 5799$$

The stress due to an element of load is

$$\delta P \frac{K}{z^2}$$

The total stress is therefore

$$\widehat{zz} = \sum \delta P \frac{K}{z^2}$$

and since in this example δP and z are the same for each element

$$\widehat{zz} = \frac{\delta P}{z^2} \sum K$$

$$= \frac{540 \times 3 \cdot 5799}{6 \times 6} = 54 \text{ kN/m}^2$$

The student should check this value using Fig. 8.4.

When δP is not the same for each element

$$\widehat{zz} = \frac{1}{z^2} \sum \delta P K$$

217

8.7 *A long strip footing of width 2 m carries a load of 500 kN/m run. It can be assumed flexible and smooth on its undersurface. Calculate the maximum vertical stress at a depth of 5 m below the foundation using an approximate distribution method.*

There are a number of such methods available and generally speaking their accuracy increases as the distance from the loaded area increases. The use of two will be demonstrated here.

The first method, due to Kogler, assumes that the vertical stress is zero beyond the limits delineated by lines radiating from the edges of the base and inclined at an angle of 55° to the vertical. The stress is then assumed to vary as shown in Fig. 8.7A.

From the diagram $L = B + 2z \tan 55°$.

Since the total upward force must equal the force applied by the foundation the solution for $\hat{z}\hat{z}$ can be obtained.

In this problem $B = 2$m, $q = 500/2 = 250$ kN/m², $z = 5$m.

Consider unit length of the footing. For equilibrium

$$q \times B \times 1 = \hat{z}\hat{z}_{\max} B \times 1 + \hat{z}\hat{z}_{\max} z \tan 55° \times 1$$

Hence

$$\hat{z}\hat{z}_{\max} = \frac{qB}{(B + z \tan 55°)}$$

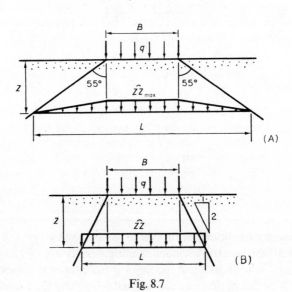

Fig. 8.7

218

$$\widehat{zz}_{max} = \frac{q}{[1 + (z/B)\tan 55°]}$$

$$= \frac{250}{[1 + (5/2)\tan 55°]}$$

$$= 55 \text{ kN/m}^2$$

The second method, which is even simpler to apply, assumes the distribution shown in Fig. 8.7B.

In this case $L = B + z$.

Applying this to the problem given

$$\widehat{zz} = qB/(B + z)$$

$$= 250 \times 2/(2 + 5)$$

$$= 71 \text{ kN/m}^2$$

The theoretically correct value is 62 kN/m^2.

The degree of correspondence is not always as good and therefore care must be exercised in using these empirical rules.

8.8 *A square foundation is to carry a total vertical load of 5·4 MN. Calculate the distribution of vertical pressure with depth on the central axis of the foundation assuming the permissible contact pressure to be 150 kN/m^2, 337·5 kN/m^2, 1·35 MN/m^2. Also determine this distribution for a point load and for the case of 150 kN/m^2 contact pressure calculated using the 1:2 slope approximate method of Problem 8.7.*

These calculations have been performed using the Boussinesq coefficients for the point load and Fadum's charts for the distributed loads. The answers are given in Table 8.8 for depths up to 18 m.

When using the approximate methods one must remember that the spread occurs in two directions. Thus for the 2:1 slope method the area carrying the load at depth z is given by $(B + z)^2$, where B is the foundation side.

The results show that there is close agreement in the calculated values for depths in excess of 8 m or so, excluding the 1:2 slope method. If the latter is included, similar results are obtained for depths of 12 m or more. A point of great practical importance follows from this in that one can see that increasing the foundation

Table 8.8

Depth below foundation (m)	Point load	Vertical stress (kN/m^2) produced by			
		150 kN/m^2 pressure	337·5 kN/m^2 pressure	1·35 MN/m^2 pressure	150 kN/m^2 pressure 1:2 slope method
0	∞	150	338	1350	150
2	645	129	238	470	84
4	161	83	117	158	54
6	72	53	58	71	38
8	40	39	38	38	28
10	26	23	27	27	21
12	18	17	17	17	17
14	13	14	14	14	14
16	10	11	10	10	11
18	8	8	8	8	9
Size of square foundation (m)	0	6	4	2	6

area from 4 m² to 36 m² does not significantly affect the stresses beyond 8 m depth *if the total load being supported is kept constant.* This is of course the well-known principle of St Venant, frequently encountered in theoretical elasticity. It follows that, if settlement is produced by the consolidation of a deep stratum, the movements cannot be reduced by decreasing the allowable bearing pressure and making the foundation larger. The total load being supported is the governing factor.

8.9 *An excavation 3 m wide × 6 m long is to be made to a depth of 2·4 m below ground level in a soil of bulk density 2000 kg/m³. What effect will this have on the vertical pressure distribution over a depth of 6 m below the centre point of the foundation?*

Before excavation the vertical pressure will be constant on any horizontal plane and equal to

$$\gamma z = 2000 \times 9·81 z \, \text{N/m}^2$$

Table 8.9

Depth below original ground level (m)	Depth below formation level (z_m) Col. (a) $-2\cdot4$ (m)	Fadum's $m = \dfrac{L}{z_m} = \dfrac{3}{z_m}$	Fadum's $m = \dfrac{B}{z_m} = \dfrac{1\cdot5}{z_m}$	Influence factor I_f	Change in stress $= 4 \times I_f$ $\times -47$ (kN/m²)	Original stress due to overburden Col. (a) × 19·6 (kN/m²)	Final stress after excavation Col. (g) + Col. (f) (kN/m²)
(a)	(b)	(c)	(d)	(e)	(f)	(g)	(h)
0	$-2\cdot4$	—	—	—	—	0	0
2·4	0	∞	∞	0·250	-47	47	0
3·6	1·2	2·50	1·25	0·218	-41	71	30
4·8	2·4	1·25	0·625	0·147	-28	94	66
6·0	3·6	0·83	0·417	0·100	-19	118	99

The results are shown in Fig. 8.9.

where z equals the depth in metres below ground level.

After excavation the stress conditions are altered in the vicinity of the hole. If one accepts that the Boussinesq equations are valid for loadings applied at shallow depths below the surface, then the desired stress distribution can be determined.

Before excavation, vertical pressure at a depth of 2·4 m is

$$2000 \times 9 \cdot 81 \times 2 \cdot 4 = 47088 \text{ N/m}^2$$
$$\doteqdot 47 \text{ kN/m}^2$$

After excavation, pressure at this level is zero. Excavation can therefore be likened to the application of a negative (i.e. upward) contact pressure at formation level of 47 kN/m². The calculation appears in Table 8.9.

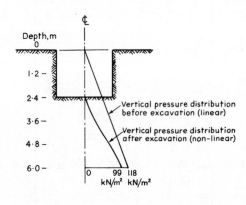

Fig. 8.9

8.10 *A rectangular raft foundation is 12 m × 15 m in size and it carries a total load of 24 MN. It rests within a uniform sand deposit which is underlain by a compressible clay stratum 3·2 m thick. The properties of the sand stratum are*

Dry density 1950 kg/m³
Specific gravity of sand particles 2·65
Moisture content of sand above the water-table 9%
Water-table is at a depth of 4·3 m below the ground surface
Thickness of sand stratum 6·4 m.

The contact pressure may be assumed uniform over the whole area of the raft.

(a) *Using the graphs of Figure 8.4, determine the depth at which the raft should be founded to limit the increase in vertical stress in the clay to 75 kN/m². The validity of the Boussinesq solution may be assumed for shallow subsurface foundations.*

(b) *With the foundation at the depth determined at (a), what is the maximum total vertical pressure at the bottom of the clay layer if the bulk density of the clay is 2020 kg/m³?*

(a) The average contact pressure at the interface between the soil and foundation is

$$24 \times 10^3 \div 12 \times 15 = 133 \, \text{kN/m}^2$$

The bulk density of the sand above the water-table is

$$1950 \times 1 \cdot 09 = 2126 \, \text{kg/m}^3$$

Before construction of the foundation the vertical pressure at depth D metres in the sand stratum would be solely attributable to the presence of the overburden and would be equal to

$$2126 \times 9 \cdot 81 \, D \, \text{N/m}^2 = 20 \cdot 86 \, D \, \text{kN/m}^2$$

for *values of D less than 4·3*, i.e. to water-table level.

The *increase* in the vertical stress in the clay is produced by the nett pressure acting at foundation level. The nett pressure is defined as the difference between the pressure applied by the foundation (including its self weight and anything placed above its base level) and the pressure previously existing at foundation level. In this problem the former pressure is the contact pressure of 133 kN/m² and the latter pressure is the previous overburden pressure of $20 \cdot 86 \, D$ kN/m², in which D now represents the depth of the foundation.

Therefore nett pressure $= (133 - 20 \cdot 86 \, D) \, \text{kN/m}^2$ for $D \leq 4 \cdot 3$

With the raft at an approximate depth of $133 \div 20 \cdot 86 = 6 \cdot 38$ m the nett pressure and hence the increase in vertical stress in the clay would both be zero. The actual foundation depth required will therefore be significantly less than 6·38 m.

To determine the required foundation depth, calculations will

223

be performed using three trial values and the actual solution found by interpolation.

Thus with the raft at depth   0 m the nett pressure is 133 kN/m^2
with the raft at depth 1·5 m the nett pressure is 102 kN/m^2
with the raft at depth   3 m the nett pressure is   70 kN/m^2

The maximum vertical stress increase in the clay will occur at its upper surface, i.e. nearest to the foundation, and under the centre of the raft. This surface is 6·4 m from the original ground level. The calculation is best set out in tabular form as shown opposite.

By graphical interpolation, the depth at which the raft should be placed to limit the vertical stress increase in the clay to 75 kN/m^2 is found to be 2·3 m. The last line of Table 8.10 shows a confirmatory calculation. This depth places the raft above the water-table depth of 4·3 m and the calculation made for the nett pressure is therefore valid. If this were not the case, an appropriate allowance would need to be made for the different bulk density of the sand below the water-table.

  (b) With the foundation at depth 2·3 m the distance z to the bottom of the clay layer becomes $(6·4 + 3·2 - 2·3) = 7·3$ m.

Then $n = 1·03$
$$m = 0·82$$
$$I_f = 0·162; \quad 4\,I_f = 0·648$$

The maximum *increase* in vertical stress at the bottom of the clay is therefore $0·648 \times 85 = 55$ kN/m^2.

To obtain the maximum total vertical pressure, the pre-existing overburden pressure must be added to this value.

The bulk density of the sand above the water-table has already been calculated and that of the clay is given. The bulk density of the sand below the water-table may be obtained as follows.

Dry density $= 1950$ kg/m^3

This will not change on saturation, therefore the volume of solids in 1 m^3 of saturated sand is

$$1950 \div (2·65 \times 1000) = 0·736 \text{ m}^3$$

and hence the void ratio

$$e = \frac{1 - 0·736}{0·736} = 0·359$$

Table 8.10

Assumed depth of foundation D (m)	Distance of clay surface below foundation z (m)	Fadum's $n = \dfrac{Length}{z} = \dfrac{7 \cdot 5}{z}$ (See Fig. 8.4)	Fadum's $m = \dfrac{Breadth}{z} = \dfrac{6}{z}$ (See Fig. 8.4)	Influence factor I_f (See Fig. 8.4)	Influence factor $\times 4$ $4I_f$	Nett pressure (kN/m^2)	Increase in vertical stress $Col(g) \times Col(f)$ (kN/m^2)
(a)	(b)	(c)	(d)	(e)	(f)	(g)	(h)
0	6·4	1·17	0·94	0·182	0·728	133	96·8
1·5	4·9	1·53	1·22	0·206	0·824	102	84·1
3·0	3·4	2·21	1·76	0·230	0·920	70	64·4
2·3	4·1	1·83	1·46	0·220	0·880	85	74·8

The saturated bulk density is thus

$$= \frac{G_S + e}{1 + e} \rho_w = \frac{2 \cdot 65 + 0 \cdot 36}{1 \cdot 36} \times 1000 = 2213 \text{ kg/m}^3$$

The pre-existing overburden pressure is

$$\{(2126 \times 4 \cdot 3) + (2213 \times 2 \cdot 1) + (2020 \times 3 \cdot 2)\} 9 \cdot 81 \text{ N/m}^2 = 199 \text{ kN/m}^2$$

The maximum total vertical pressure at the bottom of the clay layer is therefore

$$55 + 199 = 254 \text{ kN/m}^2$$

8.11 *If the foundation described in Problem 8.3 delivers the 800 kN load to the soil surface with a contact pressure that varies linearly from a maximum at the centre of the foundation to a value of zero at the perimeter determine the effect on the previously calculated stresses.*

As in the previous problem the stress is obtained by integrating the expression

$$\widehat{zz} = \int_0^{2\pi} \int_0^{R_1} \frac{3qrz^3 \, \mathrm{d}\theta \, \mathrm{d}r}{2\pi(r^2 + z^2)^{5/2}}$$

but in this instance q is a function of r. It is however still independent of θ.

One must therefore start the solution by establishing the relationship between q and r. If the maximum contact pressure (i.e. at the centre) is denoted by q_{max} then

$$q = q_{max}\left(1 - \frac{r}{R_1}\right)$$

The varying contact pressure must support the total applied load P, hence

$$P = \int_0^{2\pi} \int_0^{R_1} q_{max}\left(1 - \frac{r}{R_1}\right) r \, \mathrm{d}\theta \, \mathrm{d}r$$

$$= 2\pi q_{max} \int_0^{R_1} \left(1 - \frac{r}{R_1}\right) r \, \mathrm{d}r$$

$$= \frac{\pi R_1^2}{3} q_{max}$$

Thus $\quad q_{max} = \dfrac{3P}{\pi R_1^2} = 3$ times the average pressure $\left(\dfrac{P}{\pi R_1^2}\right)$

Therefore $\qquad q = \dfrac{3P}{\pi R_1^2}\left(1 - \dfrac{r}{R_1}\right)$

Substituting in the first equation gives

$$\widehat{zz} = \int_0^{2\pi} \int_0^{R_1} \frac{3}{2\pi} \frac{3P}{\pi R_1^2}\left(1 - \frac{r}{R_1}\right)\frac{rz^3}{[r^2 + z^2]^{5/2}}\, d\theta\, dr$$

$$= \frac{9Pz^3}{\pi R_1^2} \int_0^{R_1} \frac{r(R_1 - r)}{R_1[r^2 + z^2]^{5/2}}\, dr$$

$$= \frac{3P}{\pi R_1^2}\left\{1 - \left[1 + \left(\frac{R_1}{z}\right)^2\right]^{-1/2}\right\}$$

$$\widehat{zz} = \frac{P}{\pi R_1^2}[K] = q_{avge}[K]$$

in which the influence factor $[K] = \left\{3 - 3\left[1 + \left(\dfrac{R_1}{z}\right)^2\right]^{-1/2}\right\}$

The evaluation of the vertical stress components is given in Table 8.11, q_{avge} having the value $113\ kN/m^2$ as in Problem 8.3.

The results are seen to be identical to those of Problem 8.3 for depths in excess of 4 metres. Within practical limits the actual distribution of the contact pressure over a foundation does not significantly affect the stresses produced in the supporting medium some distance from the foundation level.

Table 8.11

Depth below centre (m) z	$\dfrac{D}{z} = \dfrac{2R_1}{z}$	K	$\widehat{zz} = q_{avge} K$ (kN/m^2)
0	∞	3·0000	339
1	3·000	1·3359	151
2	1·500	0·6000	68
4	0·750	0·1910	22
6	0·500	0·0896	10
8	0·375	0·0514	6
10	0·300	0·0332	4
12	0·250	0·0232	3

Table 8.12A

Distance from centre of foundation (m)	Breadth B (m)	Length L (m)	$n = \dfrac{L}{z}$	$m = \dfrac{B}{z}$	Element I_f	Resultant I_f	Resultant $I_f \times 2$	Vertical stress = Col(h) × 400 (kN/m²)
(a)	(b)	(c)	(d)	(e)	(f)	(g)	(h)	(j)
0	1·5	+1·5	0·250	0·250	+0·028	0·056	0·112	44·8
1	1·5	+1·5 +2·5	0·250 0·417	0·250	+0·028 +0·043	0·052	0·104	41·6
2	1·5	+0·5 +3·5	0·083 0·583	0·250	+0·009 +0·052	0·043	0·086	34·4
3	1·5	−0·5 +4·5	0·083 0·750	0·250	−0·009 +0·062	0·034	0·068	27·2
4	1·5	−1·5 +5·5	0·250 0·917	0·250	−0·028 +0·065	0·022	0·044	17·6
5	1·5	−2·5 +6·5 −3·5	0·417 1·083 0·583	0·250	−0·043 +0·068 −0·052	0·016	0·032	12·8

8.12 *Two square foundations of side 3 m are positioned with their centres 5 m apart and their edges parallel, on the horizontal upper surface of a soil. They each carry a vertical load (including their self-weight) of 3·6 MN. Determine the distribution of vertical stress on the horizontal plane at a depth of 6 m, on a line joining their centres. The contact pressures may be assumed uniform.*

This problem presents an exercise in determining the combined effects of two foundations. Since the basic approach customarily adopted assumes linear elasticity the answer is obtained by an application of the principle of superposition, from which the result is merely the algebraic sum of the effects produced by each foundation acting separately.

$$\text{The average contact pressure} = \frac{3\cdot6 \times 10^3}{3 \times 3} = 400 \text{ kN/m}^2$$

Because the foundations are identical in size and loading it will suffice to perform detailed stress calculations in respect to only one of them. The approach will be that of Fig. 8.4. Because of symmetry about the line joining the centres of the foundations, one half-width will be considered and the result doubled. In addition, following the kind of calculation shown in Fig. 8.5, the result will be obtained as the algebraic sum of the results for two rectangular loaded areas.

The depth z is 6 m throughout the ensuing calculation set out in Table 8.12A, which gives the stresses (Col.(j)) due to the load on one

Table 8.12B

Distance from centre of one foundation (m)	Vertical stress due to load on the foundation indicated in Col.(a) (kN/m²)	Vertical stress due to load on both foundations (kN/m²)
(a)	(b)	(c)
0	44·8	44·8 + 12·8 = 57·6
1	41·6	41·6 + 17·6 = 59·2
2	34·4	34·4 + 27·2 = 61·6
3	27·2	27·2 + 34·4 = 61·6
4	17·6	17·6 + 41·6 = 59·2
5	12·8	12·8 + 44·8 = 57·6

foundation at various distances from the centre of that foundation (Col.(a)).

The resultant vertical stresses due to the loads on both foundations are then obtained as shown in Table 8.12B.

It will be noted from Table 8.12B that *for the particular depth of 6 m*, to which the calculations relate, the soil between the foundations is more heavily stressed than that lying directly beneath the foundations. The effect of the interaction of the two foundations can be clearly seen by comparing the values of Col(b) with those of Col.(c).

8.13 *A point load of 500 kN is applied at a depth of 5 m below the surface of a soil the Poisson's ratio of which is 0·50. Plot the distribution of vertical stress below the load in its line of action, to a depth of 15 m. Compare this with the Boussinesq solution.*

To solve this problem we make use of Table 8.13A.

Table 8.13A *Influence Factors for Vertical Pressure caused by a Vertical Point Load acting below the Surface at Depth d. Poisson's Ratio = 0·50.*

z/d \ r/d	0	0·2	0·4	0·6	1·0	1·4	2·0	2·5	3·0
1·0	—	0·115	0·103	0·086	0·051	0·026	0·008	0·003	0·001
1·2	6·067	0·150	0·194	0·094	0·050	0·027	0·010	0·004	0·001
1·4	1·574	0·934	0·338	0·144	0·055	0·029	0·011	0·005	0·002
1·6	0·732	0·577	0·328	0·174	0·065	0·033	0·013	0·006	0·003
1·8	0·431	0·378	0·268	0·172	0·073	0·037	0·015	0·007	0·004
2·0	0·289	0·266	0·212	0·154	0·076	0·040	0·017	0·009	0·004
2·2	0·209	0·197	0·168	0·133	0·075	0·042	0·019	0·010	0·005
2·4	0·160	0·153	0·136	0·114	0·071	0·043	0·020	0·011	0·006
2·6	0·126	0·123	0·112	0·097	0·066	0·042	0·021	0·012	0·007
2·8	0·103	0·101	0·093	0·083	0·061	0·041	0·022	0·013	0·008
3·0	0·086	0·084	0·079	0·072	0·055	0·039	0·022	0·014	0·008

To obtain the vertical pressure at a given depth z multiply the appropriate factor for the desired z/d ratio and radial distance ratio r/d by the point load P and divide by d^2.

The calculations are set out in Table 8.13B.

$$r = 0 \quad \text{(axis being considered)}$$
$$d = 5 \text{ m}$$

Table 8.13B

z (m)	$\dfrac{z}{d}$	Influence factor	$\widehat{zz}$ (kN/m²)	$(z_m)^2$ (m²)	$\widehat{zz}$ by Boussinesq (kN/m²)
(a)	(b)	(c)	(d)	(e)	(f)
5	1·0			0	
6	1·2	6·067	121	1	239
7	1·4	1·574	31	4	60
8	1·6	0·732	15	9	27
9	1·8	0·431	9	16	15
10	2·0	0·289	6	25	10
11	2·2	0·209	4	36	7
12	2·4	0·160	3	49	5
13	2·6	0·126	3	64	4
14	2·8	0·103	2	81	3
15	3·0	0·086	2	100	2

therefore

$$\frac{r}{d} = 0 \text{ and } \frac{P}{d^2} = \frac{500}{25} = 20 \text{ kN/m}^2$$

Column (d) is obtained by multiplying Col. (c) by 20. Col. (f) is calculated using the Boussinesq factor 0·4775 (centre-line case, Table 8.1A) and multiplying this by P/z_m^2, where z_m is the depth below the point of application of the load, i.e.

$$z_m = z - 5$$

A comparison of Cols. (d) and (f) shows an overestimate of about 50% in the Boussinesq values over a great part of the depth investigated.

8.14 *A vertical pile 10 m long carries a load of 1 MN of which 400 kN is carried by point bearing and the remainder by side friction. The material in which the pile is embedded can be assumed to have a Poisson's ratio of 0·50. Calculate the vertical stress at a position 6·7 m below the point of the pile at a horizontal radial distance of 2 m. The friction force is uniformly distributed along the length of the pile.*

To solve this we make use of Tables 8.13A and 8.14.

$$r = 2 \text{ m} \qquad z = 10 + 6\!\cdot\!7 = 16\!\cdot\!7 \text{ m}$$
$$d = 10 \text{ m} \quad z/d = 1\!\cdot\!67$$
$$r/d = 0\!\cdot\!20$$

From Table 8.13A the influence factor = 0·497.

The stress due to the point load is

$$0\!\cdot\!497 \times \frac{400}{10^2} = 2\!\cdot\!0 \text{ kN/m}^2$$

From Table 8.14 the influence factor = 0·273.
The stress due to the uniformly distributed friction load is

$$0\!\cdot\!273 \times \frac{(1000 - 400)}{10^2} = 1\!\cdot\!6 \text{ kN/m}^2$$

The total vertical stress is

$$2\!\cdot\!0 + 1\!\cdot\!6 = 3\!\cdot\!6 \text{ kN/m}^2$$

Table 8.14 *Influence Factors for Vertical Pressure caused by a Uniformly Distributed Vertical Line Load acting from the Surface to Depth d. Poisson's Ratio = 0·50.*

z/d \ r/d	0	0·2	0·4	0·6	1·0	1·4	2·0	2·5	3·0
1·0	—	0·750	0·337	0·189	0·067	0·025	0·006	0·002	0·001
1·2	1·42	0·649	0·329	0·193	0·076	0·032	0·009	0·003	0·001
1·4	0·540	0·440	0·289	0·186	0·082	0·037	0·012	0·005	0·002
1·6	0·339	0·305	0·235	0·169	0·084	0·041	0·015	0·006	0·003
1·8	0·239	0·224	0·188	0·147	0·082	0·044	0·017	0·008	0·004
2·0	0·180	0·172	0·151	0·125	0·077	0·045	0·019	0·010	0·005
2·2	0·141	0·136	0·124	0·107	0·072	0·045	0·021	0·011	0·006
2·4	0·114	0·111	0·103	0·091	0·065	0·043	0·022	0·012	0·007
2·6	0·094	0·093	0·087	0·079	0·059	0·041	0·022	0·013	0·008
2·8	0·080	0·078	0·074	0·068	0·054	0·039	0·023	0·014	0·008
3·0	0·068	0·067	0·064	0·060	0·049	0·037	0·022	0·014	0·009

To obtain the vertical pressure at a given depth z multiply the appropriate factor for the desired z/d ratio and radial distance ratio r/d by the total value of the distributed line load P_f and divide by d^2.

8.15 *During a site investigation for a building project samples of a saturated silty clay were obtained and subjected to laboratory tests to determine its consolidation characteristics. Increments of pressure were applied in an oedometer to a specimen 76·2 mm in diameter which was originally 19 mm thick. In general each increment was double the preceding one and was maintained for at least 24 hours until movement ceased. Changes in thickness were determined as a function of time and applied pressure. A maximum pressure of 856 kN/m²*
was used, after which the pressure was released and the sample allowed to swell in the presence of water, for a period of 48 hours. The final water content was then determined and found to be 38·7%. The results of the measurements of final settlements under each pressure are given in Table 8.15A. The specific gravity of the soil particles was 2·70.

Table 8.15A

Pressure (kN/m^2)	Final dial gauge reading (mm)
(a)	(b)
0	5·588
26·75	5·232
53·5	4·958
107	4·602
214	3·962
428	3·414
856	2·784
0	5·222

Determine the void ratio–log effective pressure relationship, together with the compression index and the coefficient of compressibility for the various pressure ranges.

The first requirement is therefore a calculation of the void ratio at the end of each pressure stage. This can be done working from the final water content value and a knowledge of the changes in thickness at each stage.

The final void ratio for the saturated material is

$$wG_s = 0.387 \times 2.70 = 1.045$$

233

The thickness at this stage is

$$19\cdot000 - (5\cdot588 - 5\cdot222) = 18\cdot634 \text{ mm}$$

At any stage the thickness h corresponds to a volume which is related to $1 + e$. The rate of change of void ratio with thickness is given by

$$\frac{\delta e}{\delta h} = \frac{1 + e}{h}$$

and therefore

$$\delta e = (1 + e)\frac{\delta h}{h}$$

Substituting the known final values of e and h

$$\delta e = \frac{2\cdot045}{18\cdot634}\delta h = 0\cdot1097\ \delta h$$

This relationship permits calculation of the changes in void ratio from known changes in thickness, Col.(e) gives values of the latter and Col.(f) gives values of the former quantity (Table 8.15B).

Column (g) can then be completed, starting at the bottom with the previously calculated final void ratio and subtracting or adding the change in void ratio for each stage as appropriate. The

Table 8.15B

Range of pressure p (kN/m^2)	Pressure increment δp (kN/m^2)	Incre- mental change in thickness $\delta h\,(mm)$	Change in void ratio $\delta e =$ $0\cdot1097\ \delta h$	Void ratio at end of stage e	$a_v = \dfrac{\delta e}{\delta p}$ (m^2/kN)
(c)	(d)	(e)	(f)	(g)	(h)
0 − 26·75	+ 26·75	− 0·356	− 0·0391	1·046	0·00146
26·75 − 53·5	+ 26·75	− 0·274	− 0·0301	1·016	0·00113
53·5 − 107	+ 53·5	− 0·356	− 0·0391	0·977	0·00073
107 − 214	+ 107	− 0·640	− 0·0702	0·907	0·00066
214 − 428	+ 214	− 0·548	− 0·0601	0·847	0·00028
428 − 856	+ 428	− 0·630	− 0·0691	0·778	0·00016
856 − 0	− 856	+ 2·438	+ 0·2674	1·045	—

relationship between e and $\log p$ can now be drawn, resulting in Fig. 8.15A.

By definition the Compression Index

$$C_c = -\frac{\delta e}{\delta(\log_{10} p)}$$

where δe is the change in void ratio resulting from a change in pressure δp. Since the loads have been doubled in each stage of the test beginning with 26·75 kN/m², $\delta(\log_{10} p)$ is 0·3010. The changes δe can be obtained from Table 8.15B or Fig. 8.15A and the values of C_c determined. These are given in Table 8.15C, Col.(c).

The ratio $-\delta e/\delta p$ can be obtained by determining the gradient of the $e - p$ curve (Fig. 8.15B), or approximately by taking the ratio of these quantities appearing in Table 8.15B. The results appear in Col.(h) Table 8.15B.

The coefficient of compressibility m_v is defined by the equation

$$m_v = -\frac{1}{1 + \bar{e}}\frac{de}{dp} = \frac{1}{1 + \bar{e}}a_v$$

It can therefore be evaluated by dividing the values of a_v or de/dp by the expression $1 + \bar{e}$, in which $\bar{e}$ is taken to be the mean void ratio during the interval represented by dp. The results of this calculation appear as Col.(f) in Table 8.15C.

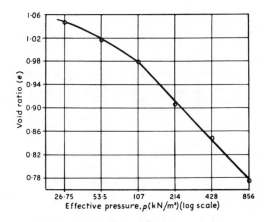

Fig. 8.15A

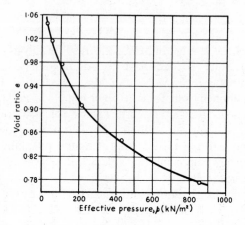

Fig. 8.15B

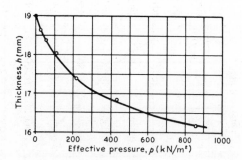

Fig. 8.15C

Table 8.15C

Effective pressure p (kN/m²)	Change in void ratio δe	Compression index $C_c = \dfrac{-\delta e}{0.3010}$	$1 + \bar{e}$	Slope of curve $-\delta e/\delta p$ (m²/kN)	Coefficient of compressibility $m_v = \dfrac{1}{1+\bar{e}}\dfrac{\delta e}{\delta p}$ (m²/kN)	Thickness h (mm)	Slope of curve $-\dfrac{dh}{dp}$ (mm.m²/kN)	Coefficient of compressibility $m_v = \dfrac{1}{h}\dfrac{dh}{dp}$ (m²/kN)
(a)	(b)	(c)	(d)	(e)	(f)	(g)	(h)	(i)
0								
	−0·0391		2·065	0·00146	0·000707	18·822	0·0133	0·000707
26·75		0·100						
	−0·0301		2·031	0·00113	0·000556	18·507	0·0102	0·000551
53·5		0·130						
	−0·0391		1·997	0·00073	0·000366	18·192	0·0067	0·000368
107		0·233						
	−0·0702		1·942	0·00066	0·000340	17·694	0·0060	0·000339
214		0·200						
	−0·0601		1·877	0·00028	0·000149	17·100	0·0026	0·000152
428		0·230						
	−0·0691		1·813	0·00016	0·000088	16·511	0·0015	0·000091
856								

A comparison of Col. (f) and (i) shows the similarity of the results achieved using these alternative approaches (see also Fig. 8.15D).

Alternatively it can be shown that m_v is given by $(1/h)(dh/dp)$ and this can be determined from a thickness—effective pressure graph (Fig. 8.15C). These values for m_v are also given in Table 8.15C (Col. (i)).

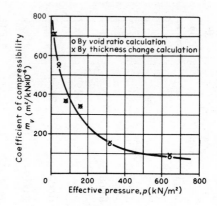

Fig. 8.15D

8.16 *During one of the loading stages on a clay subjected to one-dimensional consolidation the data given in Table 8.16 was obtained. The value of the coefficient of consolidation is required making allowance for secondary consolidation effects according to the method introduced by Taylor and Merchant.*

This method makes use of the fact that up to about 50% of total consolidation the theoretical U_v/T_v curve for a uniform pressure distribution, such as that assumed to apply in the oedometer test, is very nearly a parabola having the equation

$$U_v = \frac{2}{\sqrt{\pi}}\sqrt{T_v} = 1\cdot13\sqrt{T_v}$$

It follows from this that when $\sqrt{T_v}$ is plotted against U_v a straight line graph is obtained with a slope of 1·13. Because settlement is related to U_v and time is related to T_v a similar diagram

Table 8.16

Time from start of loading t (min)	Thickness of specimen h (mm)	Total change in thickness δh (mm)
(a)	(b)	(c)
0	19·202	0
0·25	19·075	0·127
1·0	18·821	0·381
2·25	18·654	0·548
4·0	18·512	0·690
6·25	18·423	0·779
9·0	18·364	0·838
12·25	18·318	0·884
16·0	18·288	0·914
20·25	18·278	0·924
120	18·199	1·003
1440	18·123	1·079

is produced when $\sqrt{t}$ is plotted against settlement, or thickness of specimen. This has been done in Fig. 8.16.

To determine the coefficient of consolidation a straight line is drawn through the first few points of the curve covering a range of 50% or slightly more of the total change in thickness, giving line OH in the figure. In the example chosen this line goes approximately through the origin of coordinates. This is not always the case and sometimes a zero error is indicated.

Line OJ is then drawn in so that its horizontal coordinate at any value of thickness is in the ratio of 1·155 to that of line OH. The point of intersection of line OJ with the experimental curve locates C which has a vertical coordinate of 90% of the amount of primary consolidation settlement. From the figure OD = 0·75, therefore OA = 0·75 × 10/9 = 0·833 and since there is no zero correction this is the amount of primary consolidation.

Also $\quad$ AB $= 2·27 = \sqrt{t_1}$ $\quad$ and $\quad$ $t_1 = 5·15$ min

c_v, the coefficient of consolidation, is then given by the expression

$$c_v = \frac{\pi d^2}{4 t_1}$$

239

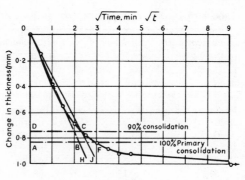

Fig. 8.16

where d = the drainage path length,

            = $\frac{1}{2}$ × mean thickness of oedometer specimen,

            = $\frac{1}{2}$ × 18·663 = 9·331 mm

Thus

$$c_v = \frac{\pi \times (9\cdot331)^2}{4 \times 5\cdot15 \times 60} = 0\cdot221 \ \text{mm}^2/\text{s}$$

8.17 *Using the data given in Problem 8.16, repeat the calculation for the coefficient of consolidation, but correct for secondary consolidation using the method attributed to Casagrande. Show how the coefficient of permeability can be calculated from the results of a consolidation test.*

In this approach the time-settlement curve is plotted using a semi-logarithmic plot as shown in Fig. 8.17. The procedure is then as follows.

The graph consists of a curve followed by two nearly straight portions which are connected by a curve. The first straight line represents the primary consolidation and the second straight line the secondary. The intersection of these two lines represents 100% primary consolidation. To correct the zero point the assumption is made as in Problem 8.16 that the first part of the graph is of parabolic form. Point A is chosen at some convenient time ordinate, t, which lies at less than 50% consolidation, and the

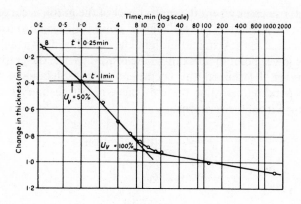

Fig. 8.17

thickness at a time of $t/4$ is determined. The difference between the thickness at time t and the thickness at time $t/4$ is then set off above $t/4$ to give the line of zero compression. In the example, point A gives $t = 1·0$ min and a thickness change of 0·381 mm. At $t/4 = 0·25$ min (point B) the thickness change is 0·127 mm. The difference is 0·254 mm, and this is set off above B giving the zero reading of $-0·127$ mm.

Now:

$$U_v = 0 \qquad \text{gives thickness change of } -0·127 \text{ mm}$$
$$U_v = 100\% \text{ gives thickness change of } +0·915 \text{ mm}$$

therefore

$$U_v = 50\% \quad \text{gives thickness change of } +0·394 \text{ mm.}$$

Hence at $U_v = 50\%$ thickness of specimen is 18·808 mm
Drainage path length is half this and equals 9·404 mm
The corresponding time t is 1·05 min.
At $U_v = 50\%$,

$$T_v = 0·197 \text{ (from theory; see Table 8.19A)}$$

Now $T_v = c_v t/d^2$. Thus

$$c_v = \frac{T_v d^2}{t} = \frac{0·197 \times (9·404)^2}{1·05}$$
$$= 16·59 \text{ mm}^2/\text{min} = 0·277 \text{ mm}^2/\text{s.}$$

241

In those cases where the central part of the graph is curved and not straight, the 100% consolidation point is determined from the intersection of the terminal straight line and a line drawn tangential to the lower point of inflexion of the central part of the graph.

Having determined the coefficient of consolidation and the corresponding m_v value the coefficient of permeability k can be obtained from the relationship

$$c_v = \frac{k}{\gamma_w m_v} \text{ (by definition)}$$

Hence $k = c_v \gamma_w m_v.$

8.18 *A raft foundation rests upon a sand layer which is underlain by a homogeneous bed of clay. The clay is underlain by a pervious stratum. An estimate of final settlement is required for the centre point of the foundation together with an estimate of the settlement at 10 years.*

Foundation size	*27 m × 18 m*
Contact pressure	*215 kN/m²*
Dry density of sand	*1830 kg/m³*
Specific gravity of sand particles	*2·65*
Water content of sand above water-table	*8%*
Bulk density of clay	*1920 kg/m³*
Specific gravity of clay particles	*2·70*
Ground surface level	*54 m O.D.*
Top of clay layer	*45 m O.D.*
Top of rock	*37·5 m O.D.*
Underside of foundation	*51 m O.D.*
Water-table level	*48 m O.D.*

The average consolidation properties of the clay are summarised in Table 8.18 A.

An average coefficient of consolidation of 0·027 mm²/s is applicable for the pressure ranges involved.

In Problem 8.15 we saw that the coefficient m_v was equal to $1/h \times \delta h/\delta p$ from which $\delta h = m_v h \delta p$.

The reduction in thickness of a layer of initial thickness h subjected to an effective pressure increase dp can thus be

Table 8·18A

Effective pressure (kN/m^2)	Coefficient of compressibility (m^2/kN)
(a)	(b)
12	0·000423
24	0·000426
57	0·000433
112	0·000285
224	0·000239
448	0·000144
896	0·000049

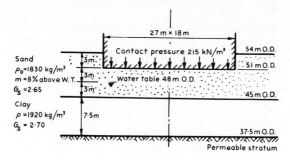

Fig. 8.18A

determined if m_v is known. This latter quantity is a function of p (see Fig. 8.18B) and thus a knowledge of p is required as well as the change in effective pressure.

To solve the problem we therefore require to know

(*i*) the initial distribution of effective pressure throughout the depth of the compressible stratum,

(*ii*) the final distribution of effective pressure,

(*iii*) the relationship between p and m_v.

The latter is given and we therefore have to determine the first two items as an essential starting point to the calculation.

Since the clay is of significant thickness there will be a variation of pressure throughout its depth. For a precise calculation the settlement would be computed by performing the integration

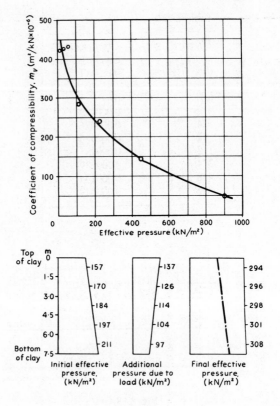

Fig. 8.18B

$$s = \int_0^h ds = \int_0^h m_v \, dh \delta p$$

in which ds replaces δh, and dh replaces h in the former equation. In this equation δp is a function of h, and m_v is a function of p and hence of h. The easiest way to solve for s is by a summation method considering the total thickness h as being divided up into discrete layers of thickness δh, an average m_v being evaluated for each layer. Thus

$$s = \Sigma m_v \delta h . \delta p$$

The clay stratum is therefore divided into a convenient number of

244

Table 8.18B

Layer	Depth of layer below top of clay (m)	Depth to centre of layer z (m)	Thickness of layer δh (m)	Initial effective pressure p (kN/m²)	Increase in pressure due to load δp (kN/m²)	Final effective pressure $p + \delta p$ (kN/m²)	Mean effective pressure $p + \delta p/2$ (kN/m²)	Coefficient of compressibility m_v (m²/kN)	$\delta h \delta p$ (kN/m)	Settlement $\delta s = m_v \delta h \delta p$ (m)
(a)	(b)	(c)	(d)	(e)	(f)	(g)	(h)	(i)	(j)	(k)
1	0 – 1·5	0·75	1·5	157	137	294	226	0·000235	206	0·0484
2	1·5 – 3·0	2·25	1·5	170	126	296	233	0·000229	189	0·0433
3	3·0 – 4·5	3·75	1·5	184	114	298	241	0·000225	171	0·0385
4	4·5 – 6·0	5·25	1·5	197	104	301	249	0·000220	156	0·0343
5	6·0 – 7·5	6·75	1·5	211	97	308	260	0·000215	146	0·0314

Total settlement $\Sigma m_v \delta h \delta p = 0.1959\ m$
$= 196\ mm$

245

layers (5 in this example) and the settlement of each computed as shown in Table 8.18B.

The initial effective pressure at mid-height of each layer is calculated thus.

Above the water table the bulk density of the sand is

$$1830 \times \frac{108}{100} = 1976 \text{ kg/m}^3$$

Below the water table it will be fully saturated with a bulk density of

$$\rho = \frac{G_s + e}{1 + e} \rho_w = \frac{2 \cdot 65 + e}{1 + e} \times 1000 \text{ kg/m}^3$$

The dry density of the sand is 1830 kg/m^3

Thus
$$1830 = \frac{G_s \rho_w}{1 + e} = \frac{2 \cdot 65 \times 1000}{1 + e}$$

whence $1 + e = 1 \cdot 45$

and $e = 0 \cdot 45$

Hence
$$\rho = \frac{3 \cdot 10}{1 \cdot 45} \times 1000 = 2138 \text{ kg/m}^3$$

For the clay the bulk density = 1920 kg/m^3.

At depth z m below the top of the clay layer the initial total pressure is

$$\{(6 \times 1976) + (3 \times 2138) + 1920\,z\} \times 9 \cdot 81 \text{ N/m}^2$$
$$= (179 + 18 \cdot 8\,z) \text{ kN/m}^2$$

The pore-water pressure due to the static water table is

$$(3 + z)1000 \times 9 \cdot 81 \text{ N/m}^2 = (29 + 9 \cdot 8\,z) \text{ kN/m}^2$$

Therefore the initial effective pressure is

$$(150 + 9 \cdot 0\,z) \text{ kN/m}^2 \quad (z \text{ being in metres})$$

The values appear in Col. (e).

The pressure due to the load can be determined in a number of ways as shown earlier in this chapter. It is important to remember, however, that it is the nett pressure at foundation level that should be used in finding the additional pressure. For example, if the weight of structure and superimposed loads was just sufficient to create a contact pressure equal to the former overburden pressure at the foundation level the nett pressure would be zero and increased pressures would not be exerted on the underlying strata. Settlements would therefore theoretically be zero.

For the purpose of this calculation it will be assumed that the nett foundation loading gives a uniform contact pressure distribution.

Nett pressure intensity at foundation level is

$$215 - \frac{3 \times 1976 \times 9\cdot81}{1000} = 157 \text{ kN/m}^2$$

The vertical stresses due to this foundation pressure, as calculated by the methods of this chapter are given in Col. (f). These have only been evaluated for points below the centre of the foundation since because of the symmetry of the problem the maximum settlement will occur there.

The values of m_v corresponding to the mean effective pressures in Col. (h) are taken from the curve in Fig. 8.18B and appear in Col. (i). The final two columns are completed as shown in the table, and the summation of the values δs gives the total settlement. It will be seen in this example that the m_v values are close to one another and no great error would have been obtained by using the arithmetic mean value or a value based on the average mean effective pressure. This is not always the case.

The additional or nett effective pressure producing consolidation is seen to vary almost linearly from nearly 150 kN/m² at the top of the clay to about 90 kN/m² at the bottom.

Settlement at 10 years:

The time factor $T_v = \dfrac{c_v t}{d^2}$

$$= \frac{0\cdot027 \times 10 \times 365 \times 24 \times 60^2}{[(7\cdot5/2) \times 10^3]^2}$$

$$= 0\cdot605$$

the drainage path length being taken as 3·75 m since the clay is underlain by a pervious stratum.

For this value of T_v the value of U_v is 0·81 (Table 8.19A).

The settlement at 10 years will therefore be
0·81 × 196 = 159 mm.

8.19 *A layer of clay beneath a building has consolidated and caused a settlement of 30 mm in 300 days since the building load became operative. According to the results of laboratory consolidation tests this corresponds to 25% consolidation of the layer. The likely time-settlement curve for a 10-year period is required. Drainage of the layer can take place in both directions.*

$$U_v = 0.25 \text{ at } t = 300 \text{ days}$$

$$s_t = 30 \text{ mm}$$

therefore, expected total settlement

$$s = \frac{30}{0.25} = 120 \text{ mm}$$

Table 8.19A *Relation between Degree of Consolidation and Time Factor*

	Types of pressure distribution (one-way flow)		
Top (permeable) Bottom (impermeable)	(1)	(2)	(3)
	Time factor T_v		
Degree of consolidation	Condition (1)	Condition (2)	Condition (3)
0·1	0·008	0·047	0·003
0·2	0·031	0·100	0·009
0·3	0·071	0·158	0·024
0·4	0·126	0·221	0·048
0·5	0·197	0·294	0·092
0·6	0·287	0·383	0·160
0·7	0·403	0·500	0·271
0·8	0·567	0·665	0·440
0·9	0·848	0·940	0·720

Note. For two-way drainage condition (1) is used for all linear distributions of pressure, and *d* is taken as half the thickness of the layer.

$$\text{For } U_v < 0.50 \qquad U_v = \frac{2}{\sqrt{\pi}} \sqrt{\left(\frac{c_v t}{d^2} \right)} = \frac{2}{\sqrt{\pi}} \sqrt{(T_v)}$$
$$= 1.13 \sqrt{T_v} \quad \text{for double drainage}$$

Hence, substituting known values

$$0.25 = 1.13 \sqrt{\left[\frac{c_v}{d^2} (300) \right]}$$

and

$$\sqrt{\left(\frac{c_v}{d^2} \right)} = \frac{0.25}{1.13 \sqrt{300}}$$

Thus, for U_v up to 0.50

$$U_v = \frac{1.13 \times 0.25}{1.13 \times \sqrt{300}} \sqrt{t} = \frac{0.25}{\sqrt{300}} \sqrt{t}$$

and $t = 4800 \, U_v^2$ days.

Substituting different values of U_v between 0 and 0.50, the corresponding times (in days) can be obtained. For the double drainage condition and values of $U_v > 0.50$, the corresponding values of T_v can be obtained from the approximate expression

$$U_v = 1 - \frac{8}{\pi^2} e^{-\pi^2 (T_v/4)} \text{ due to Fox;}$$

Table 8.19B

Degree of consolidation U_v	Time factor T_v	Time $t = \frac{d^2}{c_v} T_v$		Settlement s_t
		days	years	(mm)
(a)	(b)	(c)	(d)	(e)
0	—	0	0	0
0.20	—	192	0.53	24
0.25	—	300	0.82	30
0.40	—	768	2.10	48
0.50	—	1200	3.29	60
0.60	0.287	1759	4.82	72
0.70	0.403	2470	6.77	84
0.80	0.567	3475	9.52	96
0.90	0.848	5197	14.24	108

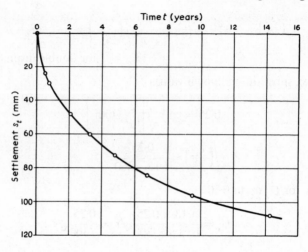

Fig. 8.19

from

$$T_v = 1{\cdot}781 - 0{\cdot}933 \log_{10} (100 - U\%) \text{ due to Terzaghi};$$

or from published tables (Table 8.19A). Thus Table 8.19B can be completed and the time-settlement curve drawn in Fig. 8.19.

8.20 *The loading period for a new building extended from May 1955 to May 1957. In May 1960 the average measured settlement was found to be 114 mm. It is known that the ultimate settlement will be about 356 mm. Estimate the settlement in May 1965. Assume double drainage to occur.*

For the majority of practical cases in which loading is applied over a period, acceptable accuracy is obtained when calculating time–settlement relationships by assuming the time datum to be midway through the loading or construction period.

In this problem therefore

$$s_t = 114 \text{ mm when } t = 4 \text{ years}$$

$$\text{and } s = 356 \text{ mm}$$

The settlement is required for $t = 9$ years, i.e. 1965. Assume as a starting point that at $t = 9$ years U_v will be ≤ 0.50.

Under these conditions

$$U_v = 1.13\sqrt{T_v}$$

If $\qquad\qquad s_{t1} = $ settlement at time t_1

and $\qquad\qquad s_{t2} = $ settlement at time t_2

$$\frac{s_{t1}}{s_{t2}} = \frac{U_{v1}}{U_{v2}}; \quad \frac{U_{v1}}{U_{v2}} = \sqrt{\frac{T_{v1}}{T_{v2}}}$$

Hence $\qquad\qquad \dfrac{s_{t1}}{s_{t2}} = \sqrt{\dfrac{T_{v1}}{T_{v2}}} = \sqrt{\dfrac{t_1}{t_2}}$

since c_v/d^2 is constant. Therefore

$$\frac{114}{s_{t2}} = \frac{\sqrt{4}}{\sqrt{9}}$$

and $\qquad\qquad s_{t2} = 171 \text{ mm}$

Therefore at $t = 9$ years, $U_v = \dfrac{171}{356} = 0.48$

Since this is less than 0.50 the relationships used are valid. Therefore the required estimate of settlement is 171 mm.

In the event of the degree of consolidation exceeding 0.50, the equations used would not be valid and recourse would have to be made to published values of U_v and T_v. For example, if for the conditions given earlier a settlement of 152 mm had occurred by May 1960 instead of the former value of 114 mm, then the calculation would proceed as follows.

$$s_t = 152 \text{ mm} \quad \text{at } t = 4 \text{ years}$$

$$s = 356 \text{ mm}$$

Thus for $U_v = \dfrac{152}{356} = 0.427$, $t = 4$ years.

For double-drainage this value of U_v yields

$$T_v = 0.15 \quad \text{(by interpolation from Table 8.19A)}$$

Then $\qquad\qquad \dfrac{c_v t}{d^2} = 0.15$

and since $t = 4$ years

$$\frac{c_v}{d^2} = \frac{0 \cdot 15}{4} = 0 \cdot 0375$$

For $t = 9$ years

$$T_v = 0 \cdot 0375 \times 9 = 0 \cdot 3375$$

and Table 8.19A gives the corresponding $U_v = 0 \cdot 65$.
Hence the settlement in May 1965 $= 0 \cdot 65 \times 356 = 231$ mm.

8.21 *An embankment is to be constructed over an area which is underlain by a compressible layer of clay overlying rock. The embankment is to be 7·35 m high and this will result in an increase in the mean effective vertical stress in the clay after consolidation, from a value of 86 kN/m^2 to 204 kN/m^2. The coefficient of consolidation for the clay in horizontal and vertical directions is 0·0699 mm^2/s and its coefficient of compressibility, m_v, is 0·00023 m^2/kN. The layer is 7·6 m thick. The embankment, which is to carry a road, will be constructed in 4 months and it is intended to place the surfacing one year after commencement of construction. A settlement of only 25 mm can be accepted after surfacing the road. Show how this can be achieved.*

In the problems dealt with so far, we have been concerned with applications of Terzaghi's theory of one-dimensional consolidation in which settlements occur due to the expulsion of water in a vertical direction only under pressure gradients created by the applied loading. The less permeable the soil and the greater the thickness involved the longer is the time required for the major part of the settlement to occur. In some cases long-term settlements are not acceptable and means must be sought to overcome this problem. One such method consists of the drilling of a series of holes up to 0·5 metre or more in diameter at regular spacings which traverse, partially or completely, the compressible layer. These holes are then filled with a suitably-graded filter medium of high permeability. The pore-water under excess pressure can then drain away horizontally to the drains as well as vertically and since the horizontal drainage paths can be made appreciably

252

shorter than the vertical one the rate of consolidation is accelerated. Such an installation is known by the name of sand drains.

In addition to speeding up the rate of settlement sand drains produce a more rapid increase in the associated shear strength and thus make possible the imposition of heavier loads on the soil at earlier stages of construction. A typical sand-drain layout is shown in Fig. 8.21A.

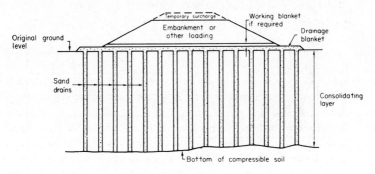

Fig. 8.21A

Calculation of ultimate settlement
The ultimate settlement due to consolidation of the compressible soil layer is calculated using the normal procedures described earlier. Thus settlement $= \int_0^h m_v \delta p \, \mathrm{d}h$, the presence of the sand drains being assumed to have no influence.

Calculation of rate of settlement
This is based on an extension of Terzaghi's theory to cater for radial horizontal drainage. For a particular arrangement of sand drains the procedure is to calculate the degrees of consolidation due to vertical and radial drainage separately and then combine them as described below.

The degree of consolidation from vertical drainage only, at time t after application of the load, is given by

$$U_v = f_1(T_v)$$

where U_v = average degree of consolidation from vertical drainage only,

T_v = time factor for consolidation due to vertical drainage
= $c_v t/d^2$,

c_v = coefficient of consolidation in the vertical direction, and

d = length of vertical drainage path (the value depends upon whether drainage is two-way or one-way).

This is the equation used earlier, the function $f_1(T_v)$ being given in Table 8.19A and Fig. 8.21B.

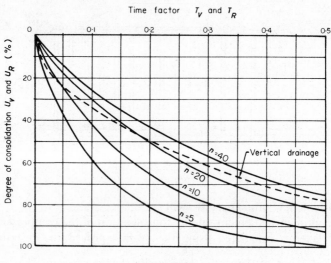

Fig. 8.21B

The degree of consolidation due to radial drainage is given by

$$U_R = f_2(T_R)$$

where U_R = average degree of consolidation from radial drainage only,

T_R = time factor for consolidation due to radial flow
= $c_h t/4R^2$

c_h = coefficient of consolidation in the horizontal direction,

R = effective radius of operation of each vertical drain.

Values of R in terms of spacing a for different layouts are as follows:

$R = 0.564a$ for square arrangement.

$R = 0.525a$ for triangular arrangement.

The solution of the equation for U_R involves a further quantity, n, which is the ratio of the effective radius R to the radius of the drain r, i.e. $n = R/r$.

Curves giving the relationship between U_R and T_R for a range of values of n are given in Fig. 8.21 B.

The resultant degree of consolidation, U, due to the combination of vertical and radial drainage is given by

$$100 - U = \frac{1}{100}(100 - U_v)(100 - U_R)$$

the values of U, U_v and U_R being expressed as percentages.

The settlement at time t is then obtained from the equation.

$$s_t = s\frac{U}{100}$$

For the problem posed the ultimate settlement is

$$\int_0^r m_v \delta p \, dh = 0.00023(204 - 86)7.6$$
$$= 0.206 \text{ m}$$
$$= 206 \text{ mm}$$

because m_v and δp are assumed independent of h and

$$\int_0^h dh = h = 7.6.$$

Taking the zero of the time scale at the middle of the construction period, the installation is required to produce

$$206 - 25 = 181 \text{ mm settlement in 10 months}$$

Thus when $t = 305$ days, $U \geq 88\%$

$$T_v = \frac{c_v t}{d^2} = \frac{0.0699 \times 305 \times 24 \times 60^2}{(7600)^2} = 0.0319$$

From graph (Fig. 8.21B), $U_v = 18\%$.

Try 380 mm diameter drains at 2·14 m centres placed in a square pattern

$$R = 0.564 \times 2140 = 1207 \text{ mm}$$

$$r = 190 \text{ mm}$$

255

Therefore, $n = \dfrac{1207}{190} = 6\cdot35$

$$T_R = \frac{c_h t}{4R^2} = \frac{0\cdot0699 \times 305 \times 24 \times 60^2}{4 \times (1207)^2} = 0\cdot3161$$

From graph (Fig. 8.21B)

$$U_R = 90\%$$

$$100 - U = \frac{1}{100}(100 - 18)(100 - 90)$$

$$= 8\cdot2$$

and $U = 91\cdot8\%$

This is greater than the desired minimum value and hence the layout is satisfactory from the point of view of performance. Increasing the spacing to 2·29 m would reduce U to 86·9%, which is slightly below the desired value. In practice, a number of possible layouts would be investigated with different diameters, spacings and plan arrangements, and the solution adopted would be based on economic as well as technical grounds.

8.22 *As an alternative to the exclusive use of sand drains to accelerate consolidation a temporary surcharge is sometimes used in addition. This permits a reduction in the number of sand drains required. In the situation described in Problem 8.21 a temporary additional height of embankment is constructed which increases the effective vertical stress to 236 kN/m². It is required to find what modification can be made to the drain installation.*

Assume that the pressure increase due to the temporary surcharge is not sufficient to alter the design values of the coefficients of consolidation and compressibility.

The ultimate settlement will be

$$0\cdot00023(236 - 86)7\cdot6 = 0\cdot262 \text{ m} = 262 \text{ mm}$$

The surcharge will be removed at a settlement of 181 mm, which is to occur as in the previous case at 10 months. The installation must therefore produce

$$U = \frac{181}{262} = 69\% \text{ in 305 days}$$

Following through the former procedure, a drain spacing of 2·90 m on a square pattern (380 mm drains) would produce a value for U of 71·3% and therefore a satisfactory solution. Problem 8.21 required drains at 2·14 m centres (square pattern grid). The saving in drains would therefore be equal to

$$1 - \frac{(2·14)^2}{(2·90)^2} = 46\%$$

8.23 *Using the data of Problem 8.21, recalculate the drainage requirements if the compressible soil is found to have a horizontal consolidation coefficient four times that in the vertical direction, i.e. 0·280 mm²/s.*

This non-homogeneity is a common occurrence in nature and can have significant results, as this problem shows.

The ultimate settlement will be 206 mm.

$$U_v = 18\% \text{ (see Problem 8.21)}$$

Try 380 mm diameter sand drains at 3·66 m centres placed in a square pattern.

$$R = 0·564 \times 3660 = 2064 \text{ mm}$$

$$r = 190 \text{ mm}$$

$$n = \frac{2064}{190} = 10·9$$

$$T_R = \frac{0·280 \times 305 \times 24 \times 60^2}{4 \times (2064)^2} = 0·433$$

From Fig. 8.21B

$$U_R = 87·7\%$$

$$100 - U = \frac{1}{100}(100 - 18)(100 - 88)$$

$$= 9·8$$

and

$$U = 90{\cdot}2\%,$$

which complies with the requirement $U \geq 88\%$.

The effect of the anisotropy is therefore to reduce the drains required by

$$1 - \frac{(2{\cdot}14)^2}{(3{\cdot}66)^2} = 66\%$$

In practice, disturbance of the soil during installation of the drains may lead to a modification of the drainage properties of the 'smeared zone'. It is not proposed to deal with this type of problem here, but it can be allowed for by a reduction in the diameter of the drain when performing the calculation.

8.24 *A circular tank 36 m in diameter rests on a normally-consolidated clay stratum of 30 m thickness. What is the range of error that is likely in a determination of consolidation settlement on the basis of the one-dimensional consolidation theory?*

In Problem 8.18 the settlement calculation was based on the results of a laboratory consolidation test. In addition it was assumed that the pore-water pressure rise at each horizon on application of loading was equal to the increase in vertical pressure at that level, and that this eventually dissipated completely to give a final effective pressure increase equal to the applied pressure at that level. At this stage the 100% consolidation would be reached. This is in fact what occurs in the oedometer test, if one neglects secondary consolidation effects and assumes that no load is carried by friction between the specimens and ring holder.

In field problems the analogy between the oedometer test results and the field results is valid if the conditions are such to give:

(a) A relatively thin layer of clay lying between incompressible layers;
(b) A large loaded area of which the horizontal extent is great compared with the thickness of the underlying clay.

Under these conditions lateral strains will be of little significance except towards the edge of the loaded area.

Despite these limitations the majority of settlement calculations are still made on the basis of a straightforward application of the Terzaghi one-dimensional consolidation theory.

Alternative approaches have been suggested and the method put forward by Skempton and Bjerrum represents an easily applied one. The application of this method follows, but it is advisable before solving the problem to indicate the basis of solution.

The application of principal stress changes $\Delta\sigma_1$ and $\Delta\sigma_3$ leads to an increase of excess pore pressure u given by the expression:

$$\Delta u = B[\Delta\sigma_3 + A(\Delta\sigma_1 - \Delta\sigma_3)]$$

where A and B are the pore pressure coefficients. For saturated clays $B = 1$. The value of A can be determined from pore pressure measurements in undrained triaxial tests. Generally it depends on the values of the applied stresses and is therefore strictly speaking not a constant for any given clay.

A typical range of values is given in Table 8.24A

Table 8.24A

Type of clay	A
Very sensitive soft clays	> 1
Normally-consolidated clays	$0.50 - 1$
Overconsolidated clays	$0.25 - 0.50$
Heavily overconsolidated sandy clays	$0 \quad - 0.25$

From the above equation when $A = 1$ and $B = 1$

$$\Delta u = \Delta\sigma_1$$

which is the conventional assumption. When $A \neq 1$ the pore pressure which is to be dissipated is a function of $\Delta\sigma_3$ as well as of $\Delta\sigma_1$. From the earlier part of this chapter it has been seen how $\Delta\sigma_1$ can be calculated for various shapes and sizes of loaded area. Values of $\Delta\sigma_3$ can be obtained similarly.

The settlement equation should therefore be more correctly written as

$$s = \int_0^h m_v[\Delta\sigma_3 + A(\Delta\sigma_1 - \Delta\sigma_3)]\,dh$$

259

or

$$s = \int_0^h m_v \Delta\sigma_1 \left[A + \frac{\Delta\sigma_3}{\Delta\sigma_1}(1 - A) \right] dh$$

For the oedometer case

$$s_{\text{oed}} = \int_0^h m_v \Delta\sigma_1 \, dh$$

For calculation purposes it is easier to deal with the expression

$$s = \mu \, s_{\text{oed}}$$

in which $\mu = A + \alpha(1 - A)$

and α is a function of the geometry of the problem. Values of α are given in Table 8.24B in terms of the z/b ratio, where z is the thickness of clay beneath a footing of breadth b.

These are plotted in Fig. 8.24.

For the kind of clay in this problem the value of A is likely to be in the range $0.50 - 1$ (Table 8.24A).

The z/b ratio is $30/36 = 0.83$.

From Table 8.24B or Fig. 8.24

$$\alpha = 0.41 \text{ (by interpolation)}$$

For $A = 0.50$ $\mu = 0.50 + 0.41(1 - 0.5)$

$$= 0.70$$

Table 8.24B

z/b	Circular footing α	Strip footing α
(a)	(b)	(c)
0	1.00	1.00
0.25	0.67	0.74
0.50	0.50	0.53
1.0	0.38	0.37
2.0	0.30	0.26
4.0	0.28	0.20
10.0	0.26	0.14
∞	0.25	0

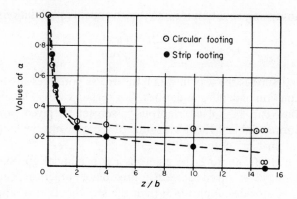

Fig. 8.24

For $A = 1.00$ $\mu = 1.0 + 0.41(1 - 1)$
                   $= 1.0$

The consolidation settlement may therefore be overestimated by up to $0.30/0.70 = 43\%$.

If the soil concerned was a heavily overconsolidated sandy clay, then the overestimation could be of even greater significance.

In this case A would vary between 0 and 0.25.

For $A = 0.25$ $\mu = 0.25 + 0.41(1 - 0.25)$
                   $= 0.56$
For $A = 0$ $\mu = 0.41$

The overestimation would therefore be in the range of 79–144%.

8.25 *A horizontal clay stratum of thickness h m is subjected to a loading which produces a presssure distribution varying linearly from a maximum of p kN/m² at its top surface to 0·5p kN/m² at its lower boundary. The layer is overlain by permeable strata and rests on a permeable layer. Determine the relationship between the time factor T_v and the degree of consolidation U_v for this stratum. Plot the distribution of excess pore pressures for time factors up to 0·20.*

The governing equation for one-dimensional consolidation is

$$c_v \frac{\partial^2 u}{\partial z^2} = \frac{\partial u}{\partial t}$$

which describes the way in which the excess pore pressure u varies as a function of depth z and time t. For certain cases of loading this equation can be solved rigorously, subject to given boundary conditions. Table 8.19A gives some of these results, including the kind of problem posed here.

Instead of adopting the rigorous mathematical approach the problem will be solved using an approximate numerical procedure, which is of wider application than the strictly classical approach since it can cater for many forms of pore pressure distribution.

The governing equation is replaced by its finite difference approximation which gives

$$u_0 + \Delta u_0 = \frac{c_v \Delta t}{(\Delta z)^2}(u_2 + u_4 - 2u_0) + u_0$$

In this equation u_0, u_2 and u_4 denote the excess pore pressures at time t at points 0, 2 and 4 in the clay, separated vertically by distances Δz; Δt denotes a small time increment and Δu_0 is the increment of excess pore pressure at point 0 (Fig. 8.25A).

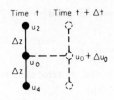

Fig. 8.25A

Putting $\beta = c_v \Delta t/(\Delta z)^2$ the equation becomes

$$u_0 + \Delta u_0 = \beta(u_2 + u_4 - 2u_0) + u_0$$

β can be assigned a convenient value (which should be less than 0·5) and having subdivided the compressible layer into a number of convenient layers such that $h = m\Delta z$ then Δt is of fixed value for any c_v value. Repeated application of this equation enables evaluation of u at various depths and times.

In this problem the total thickness h will be divided into 10 layers. Thus $m = 10$ and $\Delta z = 0 \cdot 1h$. Take $\beta = 0 \cdot 25$.

By definition

$$T_v = \frac{c_v t}{d^2}$$

putting $\qquad t = n\Delta t$

where $\qquad n = 1, 2, 3 \ldots$ in succession,

and $\qquad h = m\Delta z$

$$T_v = \frac{c_v n\Delta t}{\left(\dfrac{m\Delta z}{2}\right)^2}$$

since $d = h/2$ (drainage both ways).

Hence $\qquad T_v = \dfrac{4c_v n \,\Delta t}{m^2 (\Delta z)^2}$ or $T_v = \dfrac{4\beta n}{m^2}$

In the example, $\beta = 0 \cdot 25; m = 10$. Thus

$$T_v = 0 \cdot 01\, n$$

In Fig. 8.25B the initial excess pore-pressure values are written on the left-hand vertical axis at the various levels in the clay stratum. For calculation purposes the upper value is taken at 100 units $(= p)$ and the value at the lower surface is 50 units $(= 0 \cdot 5p)$. The remaining values are interpolated linearly. These are the excess pore pressures generated by the loading system at time $t = 0$, and they will eventually be completely dissipated at $t = \infty$, the loading then becoming wholly effective on the soil structure.

Because drainage is taking place at the upper and lower boundaries the excess pore pressures at these points will immediately fall to zero values. These values are written in at the top and bottom of the next vertical grid line which represents the distribution at a time factor of $0 \cdot 01$ (or alternatively at time $t = \Delta t$).

By applying the equation

$$u_0 + \Delta u_0 = 0 \cdot 25(u_2 + u_4 - 2u_0) + u_0$$

the new value at the point X will be equal to

$$0 \cdot 25(95 + 85 - 2 \times 90) + 90 = 90$$

Depth \ $\frac{T_v}{\Delta_v}$	0	1	2	3	4	5	6	7	8	9	10	11	12	13	14	15	16	17	18	19	20
0	100	0	0	0	0	0	0	0	0	0	0	0	0	0	0	0	0	0	0	0	0
	95	95	70	57·5	50	44·5	40	37·5	35	33	31	29	27·5	26·5	25·5	24·5	23·5	22·5	21·5	20·5	20
0·2h	90	90 (X)	90	84	77·5	72	70	64·5	61	58	55	52·5	50	48	46	44·5	43	41·5	40	39	37·5
	85	85	85	85	83·5	81	78·5	76·5	74	71·5	69	66·5	64·5	62·5	60·5	58·5	56·5	55	53·5	52	50·5
0·4h	80	80	80	80	80	79·5	79	78	76·5	75	73·5	72	70·5	69	67	65·5	64	62	60·5	59·5	58
	75	75	75	75	75	75	75	74·5	74	73	72	71	70	68·5	67·5	66	64·5	63·5	62·5	61	59·5
0·6h	70	70	70	70	70	70	69·5	69	68	67	66	65	64	63	62	61	60	59	58	57	55·5
	65	65	65	65	64	63	62	60·5	59	58	56·5	55·5	54·5	53·5	52·5	51·5	50·5	49·5	48·5	47·5	46·5
0·8h	60	60	60	57	54	51	48·5	46·5	45	43·5	42	41	40	39	38	37	36	35·5	34·5	34	33
	55	55	42·5	36	32	29·5	27·5	26	24·5	23·5	22·5	21·5	21	20·5	20	19·5	19	18·5	18	17·5	17·5
1·0h	50	0	0	0	0	0	0	0	0	0	0	0	0	0	0	0	0	0	0	0	0

Fig. 8.25B Values of excess pore pressure, u

This value is written in and the remainder of the values at $T_v = 0·01$ are evaluated in a similar fashion.

One then proceeds to the next time interval giving $T_v = 0·02$ and the procedure repeated, making use of the values calculated at $T_v = 0·01$. The whole of the remaining values are obtained in the same way, up to $T_v = 0·20$. Fig. 8.25C shows the distributions of pressure at various n values ($T_v = 0·01n$).

To determine the degree of consolidation U_v, proceed as follows.

The compression or settlement varies directly with the effective stress change and equals

$$\int_0^h m_v \delta p \, dh$$

Now δp at any level and at time $t = u_{t=0} - u_t$. Therefore

$$\text{settlement} = \int_0^h m_v (u_{t=0} - u_t) \, dh$$

The values $u_{t=0}$ appear as the starting values of u in Fig. 8.25B, and the values of u_t are obtained from the same figure for the various values of t. The calculation is performed by numerical summation, replacing the differential equation by its equivalent:

$$\text{settlement} = m_v \Sigma (u_{t=0} - u_t) \Delta z$$

The final settlement will be $m_v \Sigma (u_{t=0}) \Delta z$, since the final u value is zero throughout the depth.

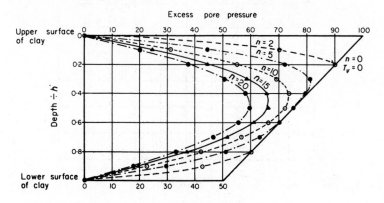

Fig. 8.25C

Table 8.25A

Depth in terms of h	Excess pore pressure u	Average excess pore pressure over range Δz
(a)	(b)	(c)
0	0	
		10·0
0·1	20·0	
		28·8
0·2	37·5	
		44·0
0·3	50·5	
		54·2
0·4	58·0	
		58·8
0·5	59·5	
		57·5
0·6	55·5	
		51·0
0·7	46·5	
		39·8
0·8	33·0	
		25·2
0·9	17·5	
		8·8
1·0	0	
		$\Sigma378·1$

Table 8.25B

T_v	U_v
(a)	(b)
0	0
0·01	0·10
0·03	0·19
0·06	0·27
0·10	0·35
0·15	0·43
0·20	0·50

The degree of consolidation therefore equals

$$U_v = \frac{m_v \Sigma(u_{t=0} - u_t)\Delta z}{m_v \Sigma(u_{t=0})\Delta z}$$

This may be written

$$U_v = 1 - \frac{\Sigma u_t \Delta z}{\Sigma u_{t=0} \Delta z}$$

The numerator in the expression is the area of the excess pore-pressure diagram at time t, and the denominator is the area of the initial excess pore-pressure diagram. Both can be easily determined by planimeter or the application of Simpson's rule or other approximation. For example, consider $T_v = 0 \cdot 20$. The pore-pressure values are given in Fig. 8.25B and are shown in Col. (b) Table 8.25A.

$$\text{Area of } u_t \text{ diagram} \quad = 378 \cdot 1 \ \Delta z$$

$$\text{Area of } u_{t=0} \text{ diagram} = \left(\frac{100 + 50}{2}\right)10\Delta z$$

$$= 750 \ \Delta z$$

Hence
$$U_v = 1 - \frac{378}{750} = 0 \cdot 50 \text{ at } T_v = 0 \cdot 20$$

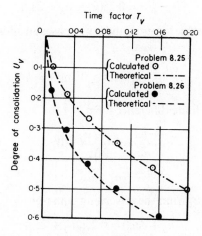

Fig. 8.25D

From Fig. 8.25B other values of U_v have been obtained, and these are given in Table 8.25B.

The values are plotted on Figure 8.25D, together with the curve given by Table 8.19A, from which the excellent agreement will be noted.

8.26 *Repeat the previous calculation (Problem 8.25) for the case of a layer subjected to a triangular distribution of initial excess pore pressure with the maximum value at the top surface of the clay and drainage on the top surface only.*

The layer will be divided into 5 strips, i.e. $m = 5$, with $\beta = 0.25$.

$$T_v = \frac{c_v t}{d^2}$$

$$h = m\Delta z \text{ and } t = n\Delta t$$

$$T_v = \frac{c_v n\Delta t}{(m\Delta z)^2} = \beta \frac{n}{m^2} = 0.01\, n$$

since $h = d$ (drainage one way only).

As in the previous problem:

$$(u_0 + \Delta u_0) = \beta(u_2 + u_4 - 2u_0) + u_0$$
$$= 0.25(u_2 + u_4 + 2u_0).$$

The impermeable lower boundary imposes an additional requirement, i.e.

$$\frac{\partial u}{\partial z} = 0 \text{ when } t \geq 0 \text{ and } z = h$$

Putting this in finite difference form

$$\frac{\partial u}{\partial z} \doteq \frac{u_4 - u_2}{2\Delta z} = 0$$

Hence $u_4 = u_2$

Eliminating u_4 from the governing equation

$$(u_0 + \Delta u_0) = 0.25(2u_2 + 2u_0)$$
$$= 0.5(u_2 + u_0)$$

Fig. 8.26A Values of excess pore pressure, u

Depth \ $\frac{T_v}{\Delta t_v}=$	0	1	2	3	4	5	6	7	8	9	10	11	12	13	14	15	16
0	100	0	0	0	0	0	0	0	0	0	0	0	0	0	0	0	0
0·2h	80	80	55	42·5	34·5	29·5	25·5	22·5	20	18	16·5	15	14	13	12·5	12	11·5
0·4h	60	60	60	54	48	42·5	38·5	35	32	29·5	27·5	26	24·5	23·5	22·5	21·5	20·5
0·6h	40	40	40	40·5	40	39	37·5	36	34·5	33·5	32	31	30	29	28	27	26·5
0·8h	20	20	22·5	25	27	29	30·5	31·5	32	32	32	32	31·5	31	30·5	30	29·5
1·0h	0	10	15	18·5	22	24·5	26·5	28·5	30	31	31·5	31·5	31·5	31·5	31	31	30·5

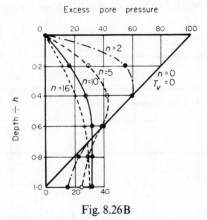

Fig. 8.26B

This equation replaces the former one for points on the lower boundary only.

With this exception the calculation proceeds along the same lines as those used in Problem 8.25. Figs. 8.26A and B give the results of the pressure calculation and Fig. 8.25D shows the $U_v - T_v$ relationship thus derived compared with the theoretical one.

8.27 *A foundation 3 m square rests on a uniform deposit of clay of great depth. If it is loaded to one-third of its ultimate bearing capacity and the axial strain at one-third of the failure stress in a triaxial test on the clay is 0.7%, estimate the immediate settlement of the foundation.*

The immediate settlement occurs on loading and before consolidation settlements occur and is due to elastic deformation of the soil structure. The solution is based on the method proposed by Skempton. The total settlement is the sum of the immediate settlement and the consolidation settlement.

The mean immediate settlement of an elastic medium under a loaded area of width B is given by the expression:

$$\rho_i = I_s q \frac{B(1 - v^2)}{E}$$

where I_s is an influence factor depending upon the shape of the loaded area and the distribution of contact pressure. Values of I_s

are given in Table 8.27. For saturated clays v may be taken as 0·5.

For any shape of foundation therefore

$$\frac{\rho_i}{B} = \frac{I_s q}{E} \times \frac{3}{4}$$

Now $cN_c = q$ at failure $= q_D$.

We can write

$$\frac{\rho_i}{B} = \frac{3}{4} I_s \frac{q}{q_D} \frac{q_D}{c} \frac{c}{E}$$

Thus substituting cN_c for q_D

$$\frac{\rho_i}{B} = \frac{3}{4} I_s \frac{q}{q_D} N_c \frac{c}{E}$$

In the triaxial test the deviator stress $\sigma_1 - \sigma_3$ produces an axial strain

$$\varepsilon = \frac{\sigma_1 - \sigma_3}{E} = \frac{\sigma_1 - \sigma_3}{(\sigma_1 - \sigma_3)_f} \frac{(\sigma_1 - \sigma_3)_f}{c} \frac{c}{E}$$

where $(\sigma_1 - \sigma_3)_f$ is the deviator stress at failure and equals $2c$ for a clay with no moisture content change.

Hence

$$\varepsilon = \frac{\sigma_1 - \sigma_3}{(\sigma_1 - \sigma_3)_f} \frac{2c}{E}$$

If the same factor of safety is involved

$$\frac{\sigma_1 - \sigma_3}{(\sigma_1 - \sigma_3)_f} = \frac{q}{q_D}$$

Table 8.27

L/B	I_s	N_c	$\frac{3}{8} I_s N_c$
(a)	(b)	(c)	(d)
1:1 rectangle	0·82	6·2	1·9
2:1	1·00	5·7	2·1
5:1	1·22	5·4	2·4
10:1	1·26	5·3	2·5
Circle	0·73	6·2	1·7

271

and therefore
$$\frac{\rho_i}{B} = \frac{3}{4} I_s N_c \frac{\varepsilon}{2} = \frac{3}{8} I_s \, \varepsilon N_c$$

Values of $\frac{3}{8} I_s N_c$ are also given in Table 8.27.

For the problem posed

$$\frac{\rho_i}{B} = 1 \cdot 9 \varepsilon = 1 \cdot 9 \times 0 \cdot 007$$

Hence
$$\rho_i = 3 \times 1000 \times 1 \cdot 9 \times 0 \cdot 007$$
$$= 40 \text{ mm.}$$

8.28 *A saturated clay has a modulus E of 24 MN/m^2, obtained from site loading tests. What immediate settlements would occur under (a) a corner, (b) the centre, and (c) a point 1 m from each of two adjacent sides, of a surface foundation, of size 5 m × 3 m, carrying a total load of 3 MN? The foundation may be considered flexible and to deliver its load uniformly to the soil.*

The corner settlement of a rectangular, uniformly loaded, flexible surface foundation is given by:

$$\rho_i = q \, B \frac{(1 - v^2)}{E} I_s$$

where I_s is an influence coefficient, a function of the length/breadth ratio (L/B) of the foundation, and the other symbols have the same meanings as in Problem 8.27. The expression for I_s is:

$$I_s = \frac{1}{\pi} \left\{ \left(\frac{L}{B} \right) \log_e \left(\frac{1 + \sqrt{[(L/B)^2 + 1]}}{L/B} \right) \right.$$
$$\left. + \log_e \left[\left(\frac{L}{B} \right) + \sqrt{[(L/B)^2 + 1]} \right] \right\}$$

Some values for I_s are given in Table 8.28.

Table 8.28

L/B ratio	1·0	1·5	2·0	2·5	3·0	3·5	4·0	5·0	7·5	10·0
I_s	0·561	0·679	0·766	0·835	0·892	0·940	0·982	1·052	1·181	1·272

(*a*) *Corner settlement*

$$L/B = 5/3 = 1{\cdot}67$$

Hence $I_s = 0{\cdot}710$ (by calculation using the formula).

For a saturated clay, loaded without drainage, there is no volume change and thus $v = 0{\cdot}5$.

$$q = 3/(5 \times 3) = 0{\cdot}2 \text{ MN/m}^2 = 200 \text{ kN/m}^2$$

Substituting in the equation for settlement

$$\rho_i = 200 \times 3 \frac{(1 - 0{\cdot}5^2)}{24 \times 1000} \times 0{\cdot}710 = 0{\cdot}0133 \text{ m} = 13 \text{ mm}$$

(*b*) *Centre settlement*

The foundation can be considered to consist of four separate foundations with a common corner and the resultant settlement obtained by summation (the principle of superposition is applicable because of the linear elasticity assumptions made in deriving the equation for settlement).

For each subfoundation

$$L/B = \frac{5/2}{3/2} = 1{\cdot}67$$

Hence $I_s = 0{\cdot}710$.

For the centre point

$$\rho_i = 4 \times 200 \times 1{\cdot}5 \frac{(1 - 0{\cdot}5^2)}{24 \times 1000} \times 0{\cdot}710 = 2 \times \text{ corner settlement}$$

$$= 27 \text{ mm} \quad \text{(difference due to rounding)}$$

(*c*) *Internal point*

Subdivide the foundation into four parts of dimensions given below and obtain the respective I_s values from Table 8.28:

(i)   1 m × 1 m; $L/B = 1{\cdot}0$; $I_s = 0{\cdot}561$
(ii) 2 m × 1 m; $L/B = 2{\cdot}0$; $I_s = 0{\cdot}766$
(iii) 4 m × 1 m; $L/B = 4{\cdot}0$; $I_s = 0{\cdot}982$
(iv) 4 m × 2 m; $L/B = 2{\cdot}0$; $I_s = 0{\cdot}766$

Then

$$\rho_i = \frac{200 \times 0.75}{24 \times 1000} \sum BI_s$$

$$= \frac{0.75}{120} \left[(1 \times 0.561) + (1 \times 0.766) + (1 \times 0.982) + (2 \times 0.766) \right]$$

$$= 0.024 \text{ m} = 24 \text{ mm}$$

8.29 *For the conditions of Problem 8.28, calculate the mean settlement of the foundation if it is placed at a depth of 1·5 m below ground surface.*

Use will be made of the relationships developed by Fox and shown in Fig. 8.29.

First calculate the mean settlement of the foundation when placed at the surface. To a close approximation this may be taken to be 85% of the maximum (centre) settlement, i.e.

$$0.85 \times 27 = 23 \text{ mm}$$

To use Fig. 8.29, calculate

$$L/B = 5/3 = 1.67$$

and

$$\frac{D}{\sqrt{(BL)}} = \frac{1.5}{\sqrt{(5 \times 3)}} = 0.39$$

From the Figure

$$\rho_m / \rho_{ms} = 0.89$$

and the mean settlement of the foundation at depth 1·5 m is

$$0.89 \times 23 = 20 \text{ mm}$$

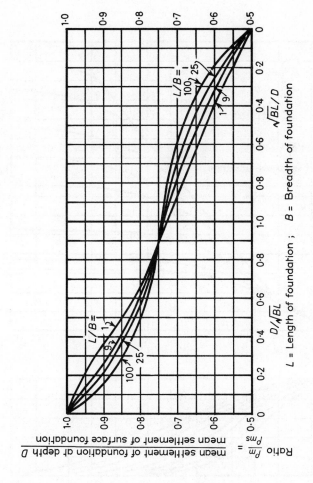

Fig. 8.29

L = Length of foundation ;   B = Breadth of foundation

Ratio $\dfrac{\rho_m}{\rho_{ms}} = \dfrac{\text{mean settlement of foundation at depth } D}{\text{mean settlement of surface foundation}}$

275

8.30 *Calculate the immediate mean settlement of a rectangular (flexible) foundation 7 m × 3·5 m, founded at a depth of 3·5 m in a saturated clay which overlies a rock stratum at a depth of 14 m. The gross uniform bearing pressure is 320 kN/m²; E for the clay is 22 MN/m²; unit weight of the clay is 20 kN/m³.*

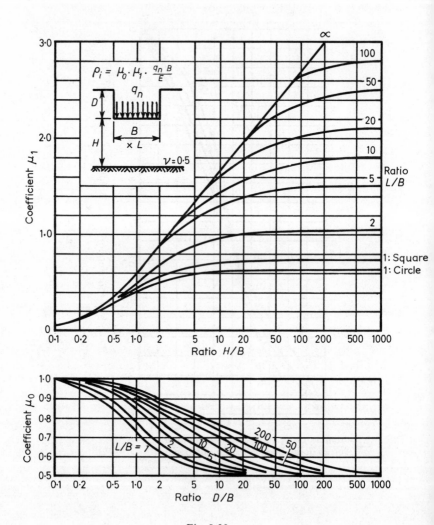

Fig. 8.30

The immediate settlement is caused by the increase in loading at foundation level, i.e. the nett bearing pressure q_n, where

$$q_n = 320 - 20 \times 3.5 = 250 \text{ kN/m}^2$$

This problem will be solved using the graphs by Janbu, Bjerrum and Kjaernsli (Fig. 8.30), which allow for the presence of a strong stratum at a limited depth below the compressible stratum.

In the problem:

$$\frac{\text{Foundation depth}}{\text{Breadth}} = \frac{D}{B} = \frac{3.5}{3.5} = 1.0$$

$$\frac{\text{Length}}{\text{Breadth}} = \frac{L}{B} = \frac{7.0}{3.5} = 2.0$$

$$\frac{\text{Depth of strong stratum below foundation}}{\text{Breadth}} = \frac{H}{B} = \frac{(14 - 3.5)}{3.5} = 3.0$$

From Fig. 8.30

$$\mu_1 = 0.78 \qquad \mu_0 = 0.79$$

Hence

$$\text{Mean settlement} = \mu_0 \mu_1 q_n \frac{B}{E} = \frac{0.78 \times 0.79 \times 250 \times 3.5 \times 1000}{22 \times 1000}$$

$$= 25 \text{ mm}$$

8.31 *For the conditions of Problem 8.30, repeat the calculation for the immediate settlement, if the undrained modulus E varies linearly with depth from a minimum of 12 MN/m² at ground surface to 28 MN/m² at rock head.*

This problem will be solved by subdividing the clay stratum below the foundation level, into several layers of assumed constant, but different, E values. Three equal layers will be used here.

Each layer will be $(14 - 3.5)/3 = 3.5$ m deep. First determine the E values E_A, E_B, E_C at the mid-height of each layer. Hence E at depth z from the surface is

$$12 + \frac{28 - 12}{14} \times z = \left(12 + \frac{8}{7}z\right) \text{MN/m}^2$$

where z is in metres, and

$$E_A = 12 + \tfrac{8}{7}(3 \cdot 5 + 1 \cdot 75) = 18 \cdot 0 \text{ MN/m}^2$$
$$E_B = 12 + \tfrac{8}{7}(8 \cdot 75) \qquad = 22 \cdot 0 \text{ MN/m}^2$$
$$E_C = 12 + \tfrac{8}{7}(12 \cdot 25) \qquad = 26 \cdot 0 \text{ MN/m}^2$$

Referring to Fig. 8.30, if $E_A = E_B = E_C = 26$ MN/m^2 the settlement would be, for

$$D/B = 3 \cdot 5/3 \cdot 5 = 1 \cdot 0; \quad L/B = 7 \cdot 0/3 \cdot 5 = 2 \cdot 0;$$
$$H/B = 10 \cdot 5/3 \cdot 5 = 3 \cdot 0 \quad \mu_1 = 0 \cdot 78; \quad \mu_0 = 0 \cdot 79$$

$$\rho_{ABC(26)} = 0 \cdot 78 \times 0 \cdot 79 \times \frac{250 \times 3 \cdot 5 \times 1000}{26 \times 1000} = 20 \cdot 7 \text{ mm}$$

If $E_A = E_B = 26$ MN/m^2, underlain by a rigid layer

$$D/B = 1 \cdot 0; \quad L/B = 2 \cdot 0; \quad H/B = 7 \cdot 0/3 \cdot 5 = 2 \cdot 0$$
$$\mu_1 = 0 \cdot 69; \quad \mu_0 = 0 \cdot 79$$

$$\rho_{AB(26)} = 0 \cdot 69 \times 0 \cdot 79 \times \frac{250 \times 3 \cdot 5}{26} = 18 \cdot 3 \text{ mm}$$

The contribution of layer C to the settlement is thus

$$20 \cdot 7 - 18 \cdot 3 = 2 \cdot 4 \text{ mm}$$

Similarly if $E_A = E_B = 22 \cdot 0$ MN/m^2, underlain by a rigid layer

$$D/B = 1 \cdot 0; \quad L/B = 2 \cdot 0; \quad H/B = 7 \cdot 0/3 \cdot 5 = 2 \cdot 0$$
$$\mu_1 = 0 \cdot 69; \quad \mu_0 = 0 \cdot 79$$
$$\rho_{AB(22)} = 0 \cdot 69 \times 0 \cdot 79 \times \frac{250 \times 3 \cdot 5}{22} = 21 \cdot 7 \text{ mm}$$

and for $E_A = 22 \cdot 0$ MN/m^2, underlain by a rigid layer

$$D/B = 1 \cdot 0; \quad L/B = 2 \cdot 0; \quad H/B = 3 \cdot 5/3 \cdot 5 = 1 \cdot 0$$
$$\mu_1 = 0 \cdot 51; \quad \mu_0 = 0 \cdot 79$$
$$\rho_{A(22)} = 0 \cdot 51 \times 0 \cdot 79 \times \frac{250 \times 3 \cdot 5}{22} = 16 \cdot 0 \text{ mm}$$

The contribution of layer B to the settlement is thus

$$21 \cdot 7 - 16 \cdot 0 = 5 \cdot 7 \text{ mm}$$

Finally for $E_A = 18 \cdot 0$ MN/m^2, underlain by a rigid layer

$$D/B = 1\cdot0; \quad L/B = 2\cdot0; \quad H/B = 3\cdot5/3\cdot5 = 1\cdot0$$

$$\mu_1 = 0\cdot51; \quad \mu_0 = 0\cdot79$$

$$\rho_{A(18)} = 0\cdot51 \times 0\cdot79 \times \frac{250 \times 3\cdot5}{18} = 19\cdot6 \text{ mm}$$

which is the contribution of layer A to the settlement.

Hence the total immediate settlement is

$$19\cdot6 + 5\cdot7 + 2\cdot4 = 27\cdot7 \quad \text{say 28 mm}$$

8.32 *A 0·3 m square bearing test plate settled 10 mm under a pressure of 210 kN/m² when loading a sand layer of great depth. What settlement might be expected for a foundation 2·5 m square loaded to the same pressure on the same stratum?*

If the deposit is assumed to be uniform, an estimate may be based on the equation:

$$\frac{\rho_f}{\rho_p} = \left(\frac{2B}{B + 0\cdot3} \right)^2 \quad \text{(Terzaghi and Peck)}$$

in which ρ_f is the foundation settlement, ρ_p is the plate settlement (0·3 m plate), and B is the breadth of the foundation.

Hence

$$\rho_f = 10 \times \left(\frac{2 \times 2\cdot5}{2\cdot5 + 0\cdot3} \right)^2 = 32 \text{ mm}$$

Experience shows that this may be a conservative value, the true value being two or more times this, depending on the size of the foundation and the nature and relative density of the soil.

8.33 *A site exploration produces a design standard penetration test value of $N' = 30$, after correction for depth of overburden and pore water pressure. If the sand involved is to carry a footing centrally loaded to 850 kN/m at a depth of 1·3 m, what width should it have to limit the settlement to 38 mm? It is estimated that the ground water conditions will not change adversely.*

There are several methods of making such an assessment, most of which are based on design curves produced by Terzaghi and

Table 8.33

D	B assumed	q_n $(= 850/B)$	$\left(\dfrac{B}{B+0\cdot33}\right)^2$	K_D $(= 1+0\cdot33D/B)$ $\ngtr 1\cdot33$	$\left(= 1.41\dfrac{q_n}{N'} \times Col(e)\right)$ $\overset{\rho}{}$	$\left(= 2\cdot12\dfrac{q_n}{N'} \times Col(d)\,Col(e)\right)$ $\overset{\rho}{}$
(m)	(m)	(kN/m^2)			(mm)	(mm)
(a)	(b)	(c)	(d)	(e)	(f)	(g)
1·3	1·00	850	0·565	1·429 (1·330)	53	—
	1·22	697	0·620	1·352 (1·330)	44	—
	1·30	654	0·636	1·330	—	39
	1·40	607	0·655	1·306	—	37
	1·50	567	0·672	1·286	—	35

280

Peck. The latter are currently regarded as excessively conservative for conventional applications. We will use adaptations of the equations proposed by Meyerhof:

$$\rho = \begin{cases} 1 \cdot 41 \dfrac{q_{\mathrm{n}}}{N'} K_{\mathrm{D}} & \text{for } B \le 1 \cdot 22 \text{ m} \\[2ex] 2 \cdot 12 \dfrac{q_{\mathrm{n}}}{N'} \left(\dfrac{B}{B + 0 \cdot 33} \right)^2 K_{\mathrm{D}} & \text{for } B > 1 \cdot 22 \text{ m} \\[2ex] 2 \cdot 12 \dfrac{q_{\mathrm{n}}}{N'} K_{\mathrm{D}} & \text{for large rafts} \end{cases}$$

in which

$\rho =$ the settlement (mm),

$q_{\mathrm{n}} =$ the nett bearing pressure (kN/m^2),

$N' =$ the corrected penetration value (SPT),

$B =$ the foundation breadth (m),

$K_{\mathrm{D}} =$ a coefficient given by

$$K_{\mathrm{D}} = 1 + 0 \cdot 33 \left(\frac{D}{B} \right) \quad \text{and} \le 1 \cdot 33.$$

For the problem assume a range of values for B and perform the calculations shown by the column headings (Table 8.33), making use of the first two equations in turn according to the value of B.

By interpolation from the table, the required width of foundation is 1·35 m.

Check calculation:

$$\rho = 2 \cdot 12 \times \frac{850}{1 \cdot 35 \times 30} \left(\frac{1 \cdot 35}{1 \cdot 35 + 0 \cdot 33} \right)^2 \left(1 + 0 \cdot 33 \times \frac{1 \cdot 3}{1 \cdot 35} \right)$$

$$= 37 \cdot 86 \text{ mm} = 38 \text{ mm}.$$

In practice a foundation width of 1·5 m would possibly be used.

Index

References are made by Problem number

Index

Index

Index